Lecture Notes in Computer Science   13563

More information about this series at https://link.springer.com/bookseries/558

Carole H. Sudre · Christian F. Baumgartner ·
Adrian Dalca · Chen Qin · Ryutaro Tanno ·
Koen Van Leemput · William M. Wells III (Eds.)

Uncertainty for Safe Utilization of Machine Learning in Medical Imaging

4th International Workshop, UNSURE 2022
Held in Conjunction with MICCAI 2022
Singapore, September 18, 2022
Proceedings

Editors

Carole H. Sudre 🔟
University College London
London, UK

King's College London
London, UK

Adrian Dalca 🔟
Massachusetts General Hospital
Charlestown, MA, USA

Massachusetts Institute of Technology
Cambridge, USA

Ryutaro Tanno 🔟
Google DeepMind
London, UK

William M. Wells III
Harvard Medical School
Boston, MA, USA

Massachusetts Institute of Technology
Cambridge, USA

Christian F. Baumgartner 🔟
University of Tübingen
Tübingen, Germany

Chen Qin 🔟
Imperial College London
London, UK

Koen Van Leemput 🔟
Technical University of Denmark
Kongens Lyngby, Denmark

Harvard Medical School
Boston, USA

ISSN 0302-9743   ISSN 1611-3349 (electronic)
Lecture Notes in Computer Science
ISBN 978-3-031-16748-5   ISBN 978-3-031-16749-2 (eBook)
https://doi.org/10.1007/978-3-031-16749-2

This Springer imprint is published by the registered company Springer Nature Switzerland AG
The registered company address is: Gewerbestrasse 11, 6330 Cham, Switzerland

Preface

The Fourth Workshop on UNcertainty for Safe Utilization of machine lEarning in mEdical imaging (UNSURE 2022) was prepared as a satellite event of the 25th International Conference on Medical Image Computing and Computer Assisted Intervention (MICCAI 2022). With an ever-increasing diversity in machine learning techniques for medical imaging applications, the need to quantify and acknowledge the limitations of such techniques has been a growing topic of interest for the MICCAI community over the last few years. Since its inception, the purpose of this workshop has been to develop awareness and encourage research in the field of uncertainty modeling to enable safe implementation of machine learning tools in the clinical world. The proceedings of UNSURE 2022 include 13 high-quality papers that have been selected among 22 submissions following a double-blind review process. Each submission was reviewed by three members of the Program Committee, formed by 25 experts in the field of deep learning, Bayesian theory, and uncertainty modeling. The accepted papers cover the fields of uncertainty quantification and modeling, as well as uncertainty calibration, annotation uncertainty, and uncertainty when dealing with out-of-distribution samples. The proposed methods apply to a large variety of imaging acquisition techniques (CT, MR, OCT...) and were developed for a wide range of clinical contexts from histopathology to radiotherapy planning. Two keynote presentations, from experts Ben Glocker, Imperial College London, UK and Sergios Gatidis, University of Tübingen, Germany, further contributed to place this workshop at the interface between methodological advances and practical considerations. We hope this workshop highlighted both new theoretical advances and reflections on practical challenges in quantifying and communicating uncertainties, and will foster new research to improve safety in the application of machine learning tools and assist in the translation of such tools to clinical practice. We would like to thank all the authors for submitting their manuscripts to UNSURE, as well as the Program Committee members for the quality of their feedback and dedication to the review process.

August 2022

Carole H. Sudre
Christian F. Baumgartner
Adrian Dalca
Chen Qin
Ryutaro Tanno
Koen Van Leemput
William M. Wells III

Organization

Program Committee Chairs

Christian F. Baumgartner	University of Tübingen, Germany
Adrian Dalca	Harvard Medical School and Massachusetts Institute of Technology, USA
Chen Qin	Imperial College London, UK
Carole H. Sudre	University College London and King's College London, UK
Ryutaro Tanno	Google Deep Mind, UK
Koen van Leemput	Harvard Medical School, USA, and Technical University of Denmark, Denmark
William M. Wells III	Harvard Medical School, USA

Program Committee

Tim Adler	DKFZ, Germany
Tewodros Arega	University of Burgundy, France
Riccardo Barbano	University College London, UK
Melanie Bernhardt	Imperial College London, UK
Pedro Borges	King's College London, UK
Robin Camarasa	Erasmus Medical Centre, The Netherlands
Liane Canas	King's College London, UK
M. Jorge Cardoso	King's College London, UK
Adrian Galdran	Universitat Pompeu Fabra, Spain
Tristan Glatard	Concordia University, USA
Mark Graham	King's College London, UK
Alejandro Granados	King's College London, UK
Irina Grigorescu	King's College London, UK
Leo Joskowicz	HUJI, Israel
Max-Heinrich Laves	Leibniz University Hannover, Germany
Hongwei Li	Technical University Munich, Germany
Hongxiang Lin	Zheijiang Lab, China
Stephen J. McKenna	University of Dundee, UK
Raghav Mehta	McGill University, Canada
Tanya Nair	McGill University, Canada
Di Qiu	The Chinese University of Hong Kong, China
Fons van der Sommen	Eindhoven University of Technology, The Netherlands

Evan Yu   Cornell University, USA
Jinwei Zhang   Cornell University, USA

Contents

Uncertainty Modelling

MOrphologically-Aware Jaccard-Based ITerative Optimization (MOJITO)
for Consensus Segmentation 3
    Dimitri Hamzaoui, Sarah Montagne, Raphaële Renard-Penna,
    Nicholas Ayache, and Hervé Delingette

Quantification of Predictive Uncertainty via Inference-Time Sampling 14
    Katarína Tóthová, Ľubor Ladický, Daniel Thul, Marc Pollefeys,
    and Ender Konukoglu

Uncertainty Categories in Medical Image Segmentation: A Study
of Source-Related Diversity 26
    Luke Whitbread and Mark Jenkinson

On the Pitfalls of Entropy-Based Uncertainty for Multi-class
Semi-supervised Segmentation 36
    Martin Van Waerebeke, Gregory Lodygensky, and Jose Dolz

What Do Untargeted Adversarial Examples Reveal in Medical Image
Segmentation? 47
    Gangin Park, Chunsan Hong, Bohyung Kim, and Won Hwa Kim

Uncertainty Calibration

Improved Post-hoc Probability Calibration for Out-of-Domain MRI
Segmentation 59
    Cheng Ouyang, Shuo Wang, Chen Chen, Zeju Li, Wenjia Bai,
    Bernhard Kainz, and Daniel Rueckert

Improving Error Detection in Deep Learning Based Radiotherapy
Autocontouring Using Bayesian Uncertainty 70
    Prerak Mody, Nicolas F. Chaves-de-Plaza, Klaus Hildebrandt,
    and Marius Staring

Stochastic Weight Perturbations Along the Hessian: A Plug-and-Play
Method to Compute Uncertainty 80
    Hariharan Ravishankar, Rohan Patil, Deepa Anand, Vanika Singhal,
    Utkarsh Agrawal, Rahul Venkataramani, and Prasad Sudhakar

Calibration of Deep Medical Image Classifiers: An Empirical Comparison
Using Dermatology and Histopathology Datasets   89
   Jacob Carse, Andres Alvarez Olmo, and Stephen McKenna

Annotation Uncertainty and Out of Distribution Management

nnOOD: A Framework for Benchmarking Self-supervised Anomaly
Localisation Methods   103
   *Matthew Baugh, Jeremy Tan, Athanasios Vlontzos, Johanna P. Müller,
and Bernhard Kainz*

Generalized Probabilistic U-Net for Medical Image Segementation   113
   Ishaan Bhat, Josien P. W. Pluim, and Hugo J. Kuijf

Joint Paraspinal Muscle Segmentation and Inter-rater Labeling Variability
Prediction with Multi-task TransUNet   125
   *Parinaz Roshanzamir, Hassan Rivaz, Joshua Ahn, Hamza Mirza,
Neda Naghdi, Meagan Anstruther, Michele C. Battié, Maryse Fortin,
and Yiming Xiao*

Information Gain Sampling for Active Learning in Medical Image
Classification   135
   Raghav Mehta, Changjian Shui, Brennan Nichyporuk, and Tal Arbel

Author Index   147

Uncertainty Modelling

MOrphologically-Aware Jaccard-Based ITerative Optimization (MOJITO) for Consensus Segmentation

Dimitri Hamzaoui[1(✉)], Sarah Montagne[2], Raphaële Renard-Penna[2], Nicholas Ayache[1], and Hervé Delingette[1]

[1] Université Côte d'Azur, Inria, Epione Project-Team, Sophia Antipolis, France
dimitri.hamzaoui@inria.fr
[2] Radiology Department, CHU La Pitié Salpétrière/Tenon, Sorbonne Université, Paris, France

Abstract. The extraction of consensus segmentations from several binary or probabilistic masks is important to solve various tasks such as the analysis of inter-rater variability or the fusion of several neural network outputs. One of the most widely used method to obtain such a consensus segmentation is the STAPLE algorithm. In this paper, we first demonstrate that the output of that algorithm is heavily impacted by the background size of images and the choice of the prior. We then propose a new method to construct a binary or a probabilistic consensus segmentation based on the Fréchet means of Jaccard distances which make it totally independent of the image background size. We provide a heuristic approach to optimize this criteria such that a voxel's class is fully determined by its morphological distance, the connected component it belongs to and the group of raters who segmented it. We compared extensively our method on three datasets with the STAPLE method and the naive segmentation averaging method, showing that it leads to consensus masks of intermediate size between Majority Voting and STAPLE and to different posterior probabilities than those methods. Codes are available at https://gitlab.inria.fr/dhamzaou/jaccardmap.

Keywords: Image segmentation · Consensus · Distance

1 Introduction

The fusion of several segmentations into a single consensus segmentation is a classical problem in the field of medical image analysis related to the need to merge multiple segmentations provided by several clinicians into a single "consensus" segmentation. This problem has been recently revived by the development of deep learning and the multiplication of ensemble methods based on neural networks [10].

Supplementary Information The online version contains supplementary material available at https://doi.org/10.1007/978-3-031-16749-2_1.

One of the most well-known methods to obtain a consensus segmentation is the STAPLE algorithm [22], where an Expectation-Maximization algorithm is used to jointly construct a consensus segmentation and to estimate the raters' performances posed in terms of sensitivities and specificities. The seminal STAPLE method [22] creating a probabilistic consensus from a set of binary segmentations was followed by several follow-up works. For instance, Asman *et al.* [2] replaced global indices of performance by spatially dependent performance fields and Commowick *et al.* [6] combined STAPLE with a sliding window approach, in order to allow spatial variations of rater performances. Another improvement consisted in introducing the original image intensity information [3]. Many other fusion methods were proposed based on generative models [4,21], label fusion with intensity images [17], neural networks [24] or simple majority voting (MV) [1,16]. The STAPLE method is based on simple probabilistic models, is widely applicable [8,22] but it suffers from several limitations, some of them already addressed in the literature [2,3,6] and some, to the best of our knowledge, never raised before.

In this article, we first analytically characterize the dependence of the STAPLE algorithm on the size of the background image and the choice of prior consensus probability. We then introduce an alternative consensus segmentation method, coined MOJITO, which is based on the minimization of the squared distance between each binary segmentation and the consensus. By adopting the Jaccard distance between binary or probabilistic shapes, the consensus is thus posed as the estimation of a Fréchet mean which is independent from the size of the background image. We show that the adoption of specific heuristics based on morphological distances during the optimization allows to provide a novel binary or probabilistic globally consistent consensus method which creates masks of intermediate size between Majority Voting and the STAPLE methods.

2   STAPLE Dependence on Background Size and Prior

2.1   Principle of STAPLE

The STAPLE algorithm [22] takes as input a set of K binary segmentations $\mathcal{S} = \{S^1, ..., S^K\}$ of size N and produces for each voxel a single probabilistic consensus $T_n \in [0,1]$, $1 \le n \le N$. The consensus prior probability $P(T_n) = w_n$ is an important parameter of the algorithm giving the prior probability that voxel n belongs to the consensus. Rater k's performance is characterized by a sensitivity (p_k) and a specificity (q_k) parameter, estimated throughout the algorithm. From Bayes law, the consensus posterior probability $u_n = P(T_n|\mathcal{S})$ is:

$$u_n = \frac{w_n \prod_k p_k^{S_n^k}(1-p_k)^{1-S_n^k}}{w_n \prod_k p_k^{S_n^k}(1-p_k)^{1-S_n^k} + (1-w_n)\prod_k q_k^{1-S_n^k}(1-q_k)^{S_n^k}} \quad (1)$$

where the parameters p_k and q_k are updated as follows:

$$p_k = \frac{\sum_{n,S_n^k=1} u_n}{\sum_n u_n} = \frac{TP_k}{FN_k+TP_k} \quad q_k = \frac{\sum_{n,S_n^k=0}(1-u_n)}{\sum_n(1-u_n)} = \frac{TN_k}{TN_k+FP_k} \quad (2)$$

with TP_k, TN_k, FP_k, FN_k respectively the continuous extension of the number of true positive, true negative, false positive and false negative voxels from rater k. Then, we use those updated values of p_k and q_k to compute the updated version of u_n, until convergence.

We can see that by definition u_n is impacted by the value of w_n and, through TN_k, by the background size $BS = |\{n|\forall k, S_n^k = 0\}|$ (i.e. the number of voxels that no rater segmented). In the following subsections we will characterize the dependence of the produced consensus to those parameters.

2.2 STAPLE Dependence to Background Size at Fixed Foreground

It is easy to show that $\mathrm{logit}(u_n) = \ln\left(\frac{u_n}{1-u_n}\right)$ can be expressed as

$$\mathrm{logit}(u_n) = \mathrm{logit}(w_n) + \sum_{k, S_n^k=1} \left(\ln(p_k) - \ln(1 - q_k)\right) + \sum_{k, S_n^k=0} \left(\ln(1 - p_k) - \ln(q_k)\right).$$

By definition, when the background size increases TN_k also increases whereas TP_k, FP_k and FN_k remain constants. So, $q_k \to 1$ when $BS \to \infty$ and we can write $\mathrm{logit}(u_n) \sim \mathrm{logit}(w_n) + \sum_{k,S_n^k=1}(\ln(N - B_k) + \ln(\frac{p_k}{FP_k})) + \sum_{k,S_n^k=0} \ln(1 - p_k)$ with $B_k = TP_k + FN_k$.

2.3 Impact of the Consensus Prior w_n on the Limit

In [22], Warfield et $al.$ proposed to set w_n as a spatially uniform value $w_n = w$ where w is either a constant (typically $w = 0.5$) or defined as the average occurrence ratio ($w = \frac{1}{NK} \sum_{n,k} S_n^k$). We further consider more general priors of the form $w = \frac{A}{N^\alpha}$, with A a constant independent of the image size BS, thus having $\mathrm{logit}(w_n) = -\ln\left(\frac{N^\alpha - A}{A}\right)$. We show in the supplementary material that, for large values of the background size,

$$\mathrm{logit}(u_n) \sim \left(\sum_k S_n^k - \alpha\right) \ln(N) + \ln(A) + \sum_{k, S_n^k=1} \ln\left(\frac{p_k}{FP_k}\right) + \sum_{k, S_n^k=0} \ln(1 - p_k).$$

Therefore, when the background size increases, the consensus obtained by STAPLE converges towards a limit which is characterized by the consensus prior. More precisely, the asymptotic value of u_n when $BS \to \infty$ depends only on the sign of $\sum_k S_n^k - \alpha$ if non-null: if strictly positive, then $u_n \to 1$ whereas if strictly negative, $u_n \to 0$. If $\sum_k S_n^k = \alpha$, this limit value depends on A, p_k and FP_k. An example of the impact of the background image size on the STAPLE algorithm is provided in Fig. 1, and another example of the impact of α is available on supplementary material. This dependence of the STAPLE consensus can be explained by the fact that it is a generative model that should explain both the foreground and the background voxels.

The use of local sliding windows in STAPLE as in [6] can somewhat mitigate the background size effect, but smallest structures in images can still be impacted and the window size remains a hyperparameter which is difficult to set.

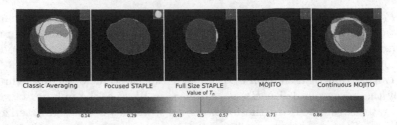

Fig. 1. Impact of the background size on STAPLE results between 7 segmentations (with an empty one) with $w = (\sum_{n,k} S_n^k)/NK$, computed with sizes of 67×61 (focused STAPLE) and 640×640 (full size STAPLE); and comparisons with other methods. The relative size of the structure used for computation can be seen at the top right corner. Contours after 0.5 thresholding are in grey.

3   MOJITO Algorithm

We propose an alternative framework to the STAPLE algorithm that is solely based on the distance between foreground masks which makes the estimation of the consensus independent from the background image size. Furthermore, unlike the MV consensus, it takes into account the shape of each binary connected component surrounding each voxel to decide whether or not a voxel should be in the consensus, instead of just looking at the voxel value.

More formally, we propose to set the probability of generating a rater mask S^k from a consensus T to be of the form: $p(S^k|T) \propto \exp(-\lambda d(T, S^k)^2)$ where $d(T, S^k)$ is a distance or a metric between the two masks S^k and T. With this formulation, finding the consensus as the maximum likelihood is equivalent to minimizing the Fréchet variance $\mu_d = \operatorname{argmin}_M \sum_k d(M, S^k)^2$. It is easy to show that when setting the distance as the square root of the symmetric difference between the 2 masks, $d(T, S^k) = \sqrt{|T \Delta S^k|} = \sqrt{|(T \cup S^k) \setminus (T \cap S^k)|}$, the Fréchet mean becomes the majority voting (MV) consensus (see the supplementary material). Yet, in the MV consensus, each voxel is processed independently of its neighbors which may lead to isolated voxels and non symmetric binary results.

3.1   MOJITO Binary Algorithm

Jaccard Distance. Instead of the square root symmetric distance, we propose to use the Jaccard distance between binary masks A and $B \in \{0, 1\}^N$ defined as the complementary to the Jaccard index: $\mathrm{d}_J(A, B) = \frac{|A \Delta B|}{|A \cup B|} = 1 - \frac{|A \cap B|}{|A \cup B|}$. One can show [11] that this is a distance following the triangular inequality unlike the complementary to the Dice coefficient. By construction, the Jaccard consensus only depends on the foreground binary masks and is independent of the background size. Therefore, its computation can be restricted to the union of all rater masks: $\mathcal{E}_\mathcal{S} = \{n| \sum_{k=1}^K S_n^k > 0\}$. In addition, we consider that to decide if a voxel belongs to the consensus, one should only take into account the context associated with the connected components surrounding that voxel, since far away components are considered irrelevant. Therefore, we choose to minimize separately the Jaccard distance for each connected component St of the masks union $\mathcal{E}_S$ (i.e. each structure). This is equivalent to minimize the local mean squared Jaccard distance: $\mathrm{lMSJD}(S, M) = \sum_{St} \mathrm{d}_J(S_{\|St}, M_{\|St})$. To lighten notations, we consider in the remainder only a single structure in $\mathcal{E}_S$.

Heuristic Computation Based on Morphological Distance and Crowns. The minimization of the Fréchet variance is a combinatorial problem with a complexity of $2^{|\mathcal{E}_S|}$ for the naive approach. Furthermore, it may lead to several global minima when the number of raters K is small. This is why we propose instead to seek a local minimum of the Fréchet variance by introducing some heuristics in the optimization. The resulting local minimum has a lower complexity to compute and is by construction maximally connected to avoid isolated voxels. More precisely, we take into account the global morphological relationships between each rater mask by decomposing the set $\mathcal{E}_S$ into a set of *sub-crowns*. The algorithm then proceeds in a greedy fashion by iteratively removing or adding sub-crown to the current estimate of the consensus in order to minimize the mean square Jaccard distance. More precisely, we define $Dm_{\mathcal{N}}(S)$ as the distance map to the binary mask S on $\mathcal{E}_S$ according to the considered neighborhood $\mathcal{N}$, which can be either the 4 or 8 (resp. 6 or 26) connexity in 2D (resp. 3D). The distance is null for voxels inside each structure. The global morphological distance map is the sum of those maps $D_{\mathcal{S}}^{\mathcal{N}} = \sum_{S^k \in \mathcal{S}} Dm_{\mathcal{N}}(S^k)$ on $\mathcal{E}_S$. A crown $C_d^{\mathcal{N}}$ is then defined as the set of voxels at a distance d in the global map $D_{\mathcal{S}}^{\mathcal{N}}$. It can be shown that crowns realize a partition of $\mathcal{E}_S$ ($\mathcal{E}_S = \coprod_d C_d^{\mathcal{N}}$), and that the 0-crown corresponds to the intersection of all masks in $\mathcal{S}$. We propose to further partition each crown as a set of sub-crowns:

$$C_d^{\mathcal{N}} = \coprod_{g \in \mathcal{P}(\llbracket 1, K \rrbracket)} (C_d^{\mathcal{N}})^g, \text{with}(C_d^{\mathcal{N}})^g = \{n | n \in C_d^{\mathcal{N}} \ \& \ \forall k \ S_n^k = (k \in g)\} \quad (3)$$

where $\mathcal{P}(\llbracket 1, K \rrbracket)$ is the power set (i.e. the set of all subsets) of the first K integers. In other words, a sub-crown corresponds to a group of voxels located at the same morphological distance from the intersection (or union) of all rater masks and which have been segmented by exactly the same group of raters, as seen in Fig. 2a. Thus, our method leads to a consistent grouping since all voxels belonging to the same connected component, having the same morphological distance, and being generated by the same group of raters will end up in the same class.

MOJITO Algorithm. We proceed in a greedy approach by adding or removing sub-crowns until the lMSJD criteria stops decreasing. We use two concurrent strategies: either we start from the union of all masks (as seen in Fig. 2a) and then remove sub-crowns with decreasing distances or we start with the crown with the minimum distance and then add sub-crowns of increasing distances. Both growing and shrinking strategies are applied in order to mitigate the risk of falling

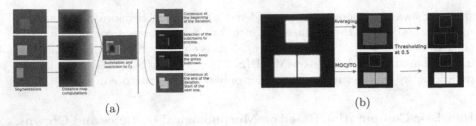

(a)   (b)

Fig. 2. (a) Left: Preprocessing step of the MOJITO algorithm, with the construction of the crowns. Right: An iteration of the shrinking approach with selection of sub-crowns and the evaluation of their contribution to the lMSJD. (b) Application of averaging and MOCJITO on a toy example with three segmentations (red, green and blue contours). After thresholding, averaging gives an empty segmentation whereas the MOCJITO method is more inclusive and outputs one connected component (Color figure online).

into a local minimum and the consensus associated with the minimum lMSJD of either strategy is kept. Because it proceeds by adding or removing sub-crowns of increasing or decreasing distance, this algorithm enforces the compactness of the consensus with a low risk of having isolated voxels. Furthermore, adding or removing entire crowns would lead to suboptimal results because they can be fairly large. Therefore, we found this MOrphologically-aware Jaccard-based ITerative Optimization (MOJITO) approach to be a good compromise in terms of compactness, consistency and efficiency as seen in Fig. 1, with a number of iterations exponentially depending on K but lower than the naive $2^{|\mathcal{E}_\mathcal{S}|}$.

3.2 Continuous Algorithm

Instead of seeking a binary consensus $T_n \in \{0,1\}$ between K raters, we may be interested to get a soft consensus like a probability map $T_n \in [0,1]$ as in the STAPLE algorithm. The trivial consensus solution is the mean $T_n = \frac{1}{K}S_n^k$ which corresponds to choosing $d_{\mathrm{Mean}}(x,y) = \|x - y\|$. As for the MV, the mean consensus considers each voxel independent from its neighbors. Below, we introduce a continuous extension of the MOJITO approach called MOCJITO.

Extension of Jaccard Distance. Several extensions of the Jaccard distance to the continuous case have been proposed. Among them, the Soergel metric [9, 18] $d_{\mathrm{Soergel}}(x,y) = \frac{\sum_i \max(x_i,y_i) - \min(x_i,y_i)}{\sum_i \max(x_i,y_i)}$ has the advantage of following the triangle inequality but is not differentiable. Instead, we consider the widely-used Tanimoto distance [9,13,23] $d_{\mathrm{Tan}}(x,y) = 1 - \frac{\sum_i x_i y_i}{\sum_i x_i^2 + y_i^2 - x_i y_i} = \frac{\|x-y\|^2}{\|x-y\|^2 + <x,y>}$.

Continuous MOJITO Algorithm. The brute force optimization of the sum of squared Tanimoto distances leads to optimize a sum of K rational polynomials over a set of $|\mathcal{E}_\mathcal{S}|$ scalars. So, we proceed in a greedy manner, separately on each connected component, by starting with the mean consensus and optimizing successively sub-crowns of increasing distances. All sub-crowns of increasing distances are iteratively considered until $\text{lMSJD}(T, \mathcal{S})$, similarly extended on the continuous domain with the Tanimoto distance, stops decreasing. For each sub-crown $r = (C_d^N)^g$, we optimize its scalar value $n_r \in [0, 1]$ such that it minimizes

$$n_r = \underset{x \in [0,1]}{\text{argmin}}(\text{d}_{\text{Tan}}(T^{r,x}, \mathcal{S})), \text{ with } T^{r,x} = \begin{cases} T_n^{r,x} = x \text{ if } n \in r \\ T_n^{r,x} = T_n \text{ otherwise} \end{cases}$$

For the optimization process we used the SLSQP algorithm [12] implemented in Scipy v1.7.3 [20]. Outputs of this method can be seen in Figs. 1 and 4, and the difference of behaviour with the classic averaging can be seen in Fig. 2b.

4   Results

4.1   Datasets and Metrics

We applied our method on 2 datasets: a private database of transition zones of prostate MR images and the publicly available MICCAI MSSEG 2016 dataset of Multiple Sclerosis lesions segmentations [7]. The two datasets include 5 (resp. 7) raters' binary delineations for 40 (resp. 15) subjects. Images from the private dataset (resp. MSSEG dataset) have a size of $[80–288] \times [320–640] \times [320–640]$ voxels (resp. $[144–261] \times [224–512] \times [224–512]$ voxels). It was possible to extract from the private dataset bounding boxes of size $[58–227] \times [53–184] \times [62–180]$ voxels. From the 3D private dataset, we created a 2D subset by extracting a single slice for each patient located at the basis of the prostate since this region is subject to a high inter-rater variability [5,15].

We compared our algorithm to the STAPLE method implemented in SimpleITK v2.0.2 [14] and the naive segmentation averaging using the lMSJD (minimized by our method) and the mean squared error (MSE, minimized by the classic averaging). The statistical significance was evaluated with the Wilcoxon signed-rank test corrected with the Bonferroni-Holm method implemented in Pingouin v0.5.0 [19]. We used in all cases the neighborhood linked to the 8 or 26-connexity. We also compared those methods on the MSSEG dataset with mean lesion-wise precision, recall and F1-score across all subjects and raters, considering binarized consensus as the ground truth.

4.2   Evaluation of the Different Methods

We show in Fig. 1 comparison of our methods to the STAPLE method applied on the whole image and on a cropped image centered on the segmentation and to the MV. In Fig. 3 are represented the results for all considered methods on the three datasets, exact numerical results being available in supplementary material. Largest differences have been observed on the MSSEG dataset - an example being shown in Fig. 4. On the 3D private dataset, applying STAPLE on the whole image took 9.5 ± 6.8 s by image, against 14.7 ± 15.9 s for MOJITO and 30.7 ± 33.2 s for MOCJITO. On the MSSEG dataset the processing time

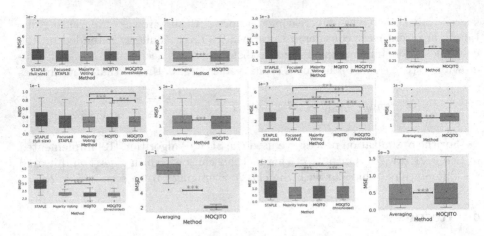

Fig. 3. Results on the private 3D (top) and 2D (middle) datasets and on the MSSEG dataset (bottom) with regards to the lMSJD (first two columns) and to the MSE (last two columns). Crosses indicate means and lines medians. ***: p-val $\leq$ .001; *: p-val $\leq$ .05. All statistically significant differences are indicated except for full size STAPLE which always differ from other methods with a p-value $\leq$ .001, so we did not represent its differences for clarity reasons.

was 45.5 ± 56.6 s for the binary version and 75.5 ± 82.0 s for the continuous one, against 20.5 ± 20.4 s for STAPLE. At the lesion level, if MV is slightly better than our method for recall (0.967 for MV vs 0.931 for MOJITO) and F1-score (0.892 vs 0.887), MOJITO has a higher precision (0.887 vs 0.914). Both methods have a smaller precision than STAPLE (0.941) but a largely better recall (0.809) and F1-score (0.836).

Discussion. In all datasets, we see the significant impact of the background size on the STAPLE result with a p-value $<$ .001 between the full size STAPLE, which produces very large consensuses, and other methods. MOJITO algorithms

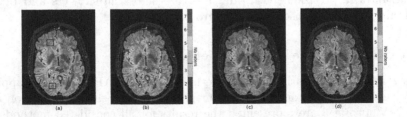

Fig. 4. Two consecutive slices of a MSSEG sample on which we applied STAPLE (pink), Majority Voting (purple) and our method (green contour) (a, c), and for each voxel of those slices the number of raters who segmented them (b, d). Differences between MV and MOCJITO are highlighted by brown squares (Color figure online).

also output consensuses that are significantly different from the ones produced by averaging especially on datasets where the inter-rater variability is higher. The MOJITO consensuses often include voxels segmented by less than half of the raters (as seen in Fig. 4), which may explain the results at the lesion level. More rarely they exclude voxels segmented by a majority of raters (as seen in the supplementary material). In general, our method appears to produce consensus segmentations of larger size than MV but smaller than those produced by full size STAPLE. This is particularly true on cases with a high inter-rater variability, as in the MSSEG dataset with 14 out of 15 cases with a MOJITO consensus strictly larger than the MV one (as shown in the supplementary material). Besides, posterior probabilities for a voxel to belong to the MOCJITO consensus differ from the ones obtained by averaging, as seen in Fig. 1. This is why significant statistical differences can be observed between averaging and MOCJITO in Fig. 3.

5   Conclusion

We have shown that the STAPLE method is impacted by the image background size and the choice of prior law. This dependence was also verified experimentally on two datasets. We have also introduced a new background-size independent method to generate a consensus based on the Jaccard distance. Our approach generalizes the Majority Voting and mean consensus, by taking into account local morphological configurations between rater masks and the proposed MOJITO and MOCJITO algorithms lead to consistent masks. Therefore, we believe that the MOJITO (resp. MOCJITO) algorithm is a good alternative to MV (resp. STAPLE) method to define consensus segmentation.

Acknowledgements. We thank Julien Castelneau, software Engineer Inria, for his help in the development of MedInria Software (MedInria - Medical image visualization and processing software by Inria https://med.inria.fr/ - RRID:SCR_001462). The authors are grateful to the OPAL infrastructure from Université Côte d'Azur for providing resources and support. We also thank Alexandre Allera, Malek Ezziane, Anna Luzurier, Raphaelle Quint and Mehdi Kalai for providing prostate segmentations, Yann Fraboni and Etrit Haxholli for insightful discussions, and Federica Cruciani and Lucia Innocenti for feedback. This work has been supported by the French government, through the 3IA Côte d'Azur Investments and UCA DS4H Investments in the Future project managed by the National Research Agency (ANR) with the reference numbers ANR-19-P3IA-0002 and ANR-17-EURE-0004 and by the Health Data Center of the AP-HP (Assistance Publique-Hôpitaux de Paris). Private data was extracted from the Clinical Data Warehouse of the Greater Paris University Hospitals (Assistance Publique-Hôpitaux de Paris).

12   D. Hamzaoui et al.

References

1. Aljabar, P., Heckemann, R., Hammers, A., Hajnal, J., Rueckert, D.: Multi-atlas based segmentation of brain images: Atlas selection and its effect on accuracy. Neuroimage **46**(3), 726–738 (2009). https://doi.org/10.1016/j.neuroimage.2009.02.018
2. Asman, A., Landman, B.: Formulating spatially varying performance in the statistical fusion framework. IEEE Trans. Med. Imaging **31**, 1326–1336 (2012). https://doi.org/10.1109/TMI.2012.2190992
3. Asman, A.J., Landman, B.A.: Non-local statistical label fusion for multi-atlas segmentation. Med. Image Anal. **17**(2), 194–208 (2013). https://doi.org/10.1016/j.media.2012.10.002
4. Audelan, B., Hamzaoui, D., Montagne, S., Renard-Penna, R., Delingette, H.: Robust fusion of probability maps. In: Martel, A.L., et al. (eds.) MICCAI 2020. LNCS, vol. 12264, pp. 259–268. Springer, Cham (2020). https://doi.org/10.1007/978-3-030-59719-1_26
5. Becker, A.S., et al.: Variability of manual segmentation of the prostate in axial T2-weighted MRI: a multi-reader study. Eur. J. Radiol. **121**, 108716 (2019). https://doi.org/10.1016/j.ejrad.2019.108716
6. Commowick, O., Akhondi-Asl, A., Warfield, S.K.: Estimating a reference standard segmentation with spatially varying performance parameters: local MAP STAPLE. IEEE Trans. Med. Imaging **31**(8), 1593–1606 (2012). https://doi.org/10.1109/TMI.2012.2197406
7. Commowick, O., et al.: Objective evaluation of multiple sclerosis lesion segmentation using a data management and processing infrastructure. Sci. Rep. **8**(1), 13650 (2018). https://doi.org/10.1038/s41598-018-31911-7
8. Dewalle-Vignion, A.S., Betrouni, N., Baillet, C., Vermandel, M.: Is STAPLE algorithm confident to assess segmentation methods in PET imaging? Phys. Med. Biol. **60**, 9473 (2015). https://doi.org/10.1088/0031-9155/60/24/9473
9. Deza, M.M., Deza, E.: Distances and similarities in data analysis. In: Encyclopedia of Distances, pp. 327–345. Springer, Heidelberg (2016). https://doi.org/10.1007/978-3-662-52844-0_17
10. Isensee, F., Jaeger, P.F., Kohl, S.A.A., Petersen, J., Maier-Hein, K.H.: nnU-Net: a self-configuring method for deep learning-based biomedical image segmentation. Nat. Meth. **18**, 203–211 (2021). https://doi.org/10.1038/s41592-020-01008-z
11. Kosub, S.: A note on the triangle inequality for the Jaccard distance. Pattern Recogn. Lett. **120**, 36–38 (2019)
12. Kraft, D.: A software package for sequential quadratic programming. Technical report, DFVLR-FB 88-28, DLR German Aerospace Center - Institute for Flight Mechanics, Koln, Germany (1988)
13. Leach, A.R., Gillet, V.J.: Similarity methods. In: An Introduction To Chemoinformatics, pp. 99–117. Springer, Dordrecht (2007). https://doi.org/10.1007/978-1-4020-6291-9_5
14. Lowekamp, B., Chen, D., Ibanez, L., Blezek, D.: The design of SimpleITK. Front. Neuroinf. **7**, 1–14 (2013). https://doi.org/10.3389/fninf.2013.00045
15. Montagne, S., et al.: Challenge of prostate MRI segmentation on T2-weighted images: inter-observer variability and impact of prostate morphology. Insights Imaging **12**(1), 71 (2021). https://doi.org/10.1186/s13244-021-01010-9
16. Rohlfing, T., Maurer, C.R.: Shape-based averaging. IEEE Trans. Image Process. **16**(1), 153–161 (2007). https://doi.org/10.1109/TIP.2006.884936

17. Sabuncu, M.R., Yeo, B.T.T., Van Leemput, K., Fischl, B., Golland, P.: A generative model for image segmentation based on label fusion. IEEE Trans. Med. Imaging **29**(10), 1714–1729 (2010). https://doi.org/10.1109/TMI.2010.2050897
18. Späth, H.: The minisum location problem for the Jaccard metric. Oper. Res. Spektrum **3**, 91–94 (1981)
19. Vallat, R.: Pingouin: statistics in Python. J. Open Source Softw. **3**(31), 1026 (2018). https://doi.org/10.21105/joss.01026
20. Virtanen, P., et al.: SciPy 1.0: fundamental algorithms for scientific computing in Python. Nat. Meth. **17**, 261–272 (2020). https://doi.org/10.1038/s41592-019-0686-2
21. Wang, Z., et al.: Bayesian logistic shape model inference: application to cochlear image segmentation. Med. Image Anal. **75**, 102268 (2022). https://doi.org/10.1016/j.media.2021.102268
22. Warfield, S., Zou, K., Wells, W.: Simultaneous truth and performance level estimation (STAPLE): an algorithm for the validation of image segmentation. IEEE Trans. Med. Imaging **23**(7), 903–921 (2004). https://doi.org/10.1109/TMI.2004.828354
23. Willett, P., Barnard, J.M., Downs, G.M.: Chemical similarity searching. J. Chem. Inf. Comput. Sci. **38**(6), 983–996 (1998). https://doi.org/10.1021/ci9800211
24. Zhang, L., et al.: Disentangling human error from ground truth in segmentation of medical images. In: Larochelle, H., Ranzato, M., Hadsell, R., Balcan, M., Lin, H. (eds.) Advances in Neural Information Processing Systems, vol. 33, pp. 15750–15762. Curran Associates, Inc. (2020)

Quantification of Predictive Uncertainty via Inference-Time Sampling

Katarína Tóthová[1]([✉])(iD), Ľubor Ladický[1,2], Daniel Thul[1], Marc Pollefeys[1,3], and Ender Konukoglu[1]

[1] ETH Zurich, Zurich, Switzerland
katarina.tothova@inf.ethz.ch, ender.konukoglu@vision.ee.ethz.ch
[2] Apagom AG, Zurich, Switzerland
[3] Microsoft Mixed Reality and AI lab, Zurich, Switzerland

Abstract. Predictive variability due to data ambiguities has typically been addressed via construction dedicated models with built-in probabilistic capabilities that are trained to predict uncertainty estimates as variables of interest. These approaches require distinct architectural components and training mechanisms, may include restrictive assumptions and exhibit overconfidence, i.e., high confidence in imprecise predictions. In this work, we propose a post-hoc sampling strategy for estimating predictive uncertainty accounting for data ambiguity. The method can generate different plausible outputs for a given input and does not assume parametric forms of predictive distributions. It is architecture agnostic and can be applied to any feed-forward deterministic network without changes to the architecture nor training procedure. Experiments on regression tasks on imaging and non-imaging input data show the method's ability to generate diverse and multi-modal predictive distributions and how estimated uncertainty correlates with prediction error.

Keywords: Uncertainty quantification · Deep learning · Metropolis-Hastings MCMC

1 Introduction

Estimating uncertainty in deep learning (DL) models' predictions, i.e., predictive uncertainty, is of critical importance in a wide range of applications from diagnosis to treatment planning, e.g., [3]. One generic formulation for predictive uncertainty, i.e., $p(y|x)$, using DL is through the following probabilistic model

$$p(y|x) \triangleq \int_{\mathcal{M}} \int_{\mathcal{D}} \int_{\theta} p(y|x, \theta, \mathcal{D}, \mathcal{M}) dp(\theta|\mathcal{D}, \mathcal{M}) dp(\mathcal{D}) dp(\mathcal{M}), \qquad (1)$$

where $x, y, \theta, \mathcal{M}$ and $\mathcal{D}$ represent input, output, model parameters, model specification, and training set, respectively. The joint distribution $p(y, \mathcal{D}, \mathcal{M}, \theta|x)$ is modeled with the factorization $p(y|x, \theta, \mathcal{D}, \mathcal{M})p(\theta|\mathcal{D}, \mathcal{M})p(\mathcal{D})p(\mathcal{M})$ and $p(y|x)$ is defined through marginalization of $\theta, \mathcal{D}$ and $\mathcal{M}$.

© The Author(s), under exclusive license to Springer Nature Switzerland AG 2022
C. H. Sudre et al. (Eds.): UNSURE 2022, LNCS 13563, pp. 14–25, 2022.
https://doi.org/10.1007/978-3-031-16749-2_2

Different components contribute to $p(y|x)$ in the marginalization and represent different sources of uncertainty. Borrowing terminology from [36], $p(y|x, \theta, \mathcal{D}, \mathcal{M})$ is often considered as the *aleatoric* component that models input-output ambiguities, i.e., when the input may not uniquely identify an output [39]. $p(\theta|\mathcal{D}, \mathcal{M})$ on the other hand is considered as the *epistemic* component stemming from parameter uncertainty or model bias [8], which can be alleviated by training on more data or using a more appropriate model. Modeling $p(\theta) \triangleq \int_{\mathcal{M}} \int_{\mathcal{D}} p(\theta|\mathcal{M}, \mathcal{D}) dp(\mathcal{D}) dp(\mathcal{M})$ as the epistemic component is also possible, however, this is prohibitively costly in DL models, and therefore mostly not done. Here, we focus on the aleatoric component $p(y|x, \theta, \mathcal{D}, \mathcal{M})$ and propose a model agnostic method.

The common approach to model $p(y|x, \theta, \mathcal{D}, \mathcal{M})$ in the recent DL literature is to build models that predict probability distributions instead of point-wise predictions. Pioneering this effort, Tanno et al. [35,36] and Kendall and Gal [20] simultaneously proposed models that output pixel-wise factorized distributions for pixel-wise prediction problems, such as segmentation. Going beyond this simplified factorization, more recent models predict distributions modeling dependencies between multiple outputs, notably for pixel-wise prediction models, such as [2,23,37,38]. These later models are more apt for real world applications as they also could produce realistic samples from the modelled $p(y|x, \theta, \mathcal{D}, \mathcal{M})$. On the downside, (i) these models require special structures in their architectures, and therefore the principles cannot be easily applied to any top performing architecture without modification, and (ii) they rely on the assumption that input-output ambiguities present in a test sample will be similarly present in the training set, so that models can be trained to predict posterior distributions.

In this work, we propose a novel model for $p(y|x, \theta, \mathcal{D}, \mathcal{M})$ and the corresponding Metropolis-Hasting (MH) [16] scheme for sampling of network outputs for a given input, which can be used during inference. We restrict ourselves to problems where a prior model for the outputs, i.e., $p(y)$, can be estimated. While this may seem limiting, on the contrary this restriction is often *exploited* in medical image analysis to improve model robustness and generalization, e.g., [19,26,29,37]. Inspired by the ideas of network inversion via gradient descent [22] and neural style transfer [12], our main contribution is a new definition of a *likelihood* function that can be used to evaluate the MH acceptance criterion. The new likelihood function uses *input backpropagation* and distances in the input space, which (i) makes it architecture agnostic, (ii) does not require access to training or ground truth data, (iii) avoids explicit formulation of analytically described energy functionals, or (iv) implementation of dedicated neural networks (NNs) and training procedures.

We present experiments with two regression problems and compare our method with state-of-the-art methods [11,30,38], as well as MC Dropout [11] for completeness, even though it is a method for quantifying epistemic uncertainty. Our experimental evaluation focuses on regression problems, however, the proposed technique can be easily applied to classification problems as well.

2   Related Work

Post-hoc uncertainty quantification of trained networks has been previously addressed by Qiu et al. [30]. In their work (RIO), the authors augment a pre-trained deterministic network with a Gaussian process (GP) with a kernel built around the network's inputs and outputs. The GP can be used for a post-hoc improvement of the network's outputs and to assess the predictive uncertainty. This model can be applied to any standard NN without modifications. While mathematically elegant and computationally inexpensive, this approach requires access to training data and impose that the posteriors be normally distributed.

One of the dedicated DL models addressing aleatoric uncertainty prediction with an assumption that a prior over outputs $p(y)$ is available is probPCA [37, 38]. Developed for parametric surface reconstruction from images using a principal component analysis (PCA) to define $p(y)$, the method predicts multivariate Gaussian distributions over output mesh vertices, by first predicting posterior distributions over PC representation for a given sample. While the model takes into account covariance structure between vertices, it also requires specific architecture and makes a Gaussian assumption for the posterior.

Sampling techniques built on Monte Carlo integration [15] provide a powerful alternative. Traditional Markov Chain Monte Carlo (MCMC) techniques [27] can construct chains of proposed samples y' with strong theoretical guarantees on their convergence to posterior distribution [13]. In MH [16], this is ensured by evaluation of acceptance probabilities. This involves calculation of a prior $p(y')$ and a likelihood $L(y'; x) = p(x|y', \theta, \mathcal{D}, \mathcal{M})$. At its most explicit form, the evaluation of $L(y'; x)$ would translate to the generation of plausible inputs for every given y' and then calculation of the relative density at the input x.

In some applications, the likelihood function can be defined analytically with energy functionals [17, 21, 25]. General DL models, however, do not have convenient closed form formulations that allow analytical likelihood definitions. Defining a tractable likelihood with invertible neural networks [34] or reversible transition kernels [24, 33] is possible, but these approaches require specialized architectures and training procedures. To the best of our knowledge, a solution that can be applied to any pre-trained network has not yet been proposed. Sampling methods without likelihood evaluation, i.e., Approximate Bayesian Computation (ABC) methods [31], can step up to the task, however, they rely on sampling from a likelihood, hence the definition of an appropriate likelihood remains open.

3   Method

We let $f(x|\theta)$ be a deep neural network that is trained on a training set of (x, y) pairs and θ representing its parameters. The network is trained to predict targets from inputs, i.e., $y \approx f(x|\theta)$. We would like to asses the aleatoric uncertainty $p(y|x, \theta, \mathcal{D}, \mathcal{M})$ associated with $f(x|\theta)$. Note that while $f(x|\theta)$ is a deterministic mapping, if there is an input-output ambiguity around an x, then a trained model will likely show high sensitivity around that x, i.e., predictions will greatly vary with small changes in x. We exploit this sensitivity to model $p(y|x, \theta, \mathcal{D}, \mathcal{M})$ using $f(x|\theta)$. Such modeling goes beyond a simple sensitivity analysis [32] by allowing drawing realistic samples of y from the modeled distribution.

3.1 Metropolis-Hastings for Target Sampling

Our motivation comes from the well established MH MCMC methods for sampling from a posterior distribution [16]. For a given input x and an initial state y^0, the MH algorithm generates Markov chains (MC) of states $\{y^t, t = 1, 2, \ldots, n\}$. At each step t a new proposal is generated $y' \sim g(y'|y^t)$ according to a symmetric proposal distribution g. The sample is then accepted with the probability

$$A(y', y^t|x) = \min \left(1, \underbrace{\frac{g(y^t|y', x)}{g(y'|y^t, x)}}_{\text{transitions}} \underbrace{\frac{p(x|y', \theta, \mathcal{D}, \mathcal{M})}{p(x|y^t, \theta, \mathcal{D}, \mathcal{M})}}_{\text{likelihoods}} \underbrace{\frac{p(y')}{p(y^t)}}_{\text{priors}} \right) \tag{2}$$

and the next state is set as $y^{t+1} = y'$ if the proposal is accepted, and $y^{t+1} = y^t$ otherwise. The sufficient condition for asymptotic convergence of the MH MC to the posterior $p(y|x, \theta, \mathcal{D}, \mathcal{M})$ is satisfied thanks to the reversibility of transitions $y^t \rightarrow y^{t+1}$ [5]. The asymptotic convergence also means that for arbitrary initialization, the initial samples are not guaranteed to come from $p(y|x)$, hence a burn-in period, where initial chain samples are removed, is often implemented [5]. The goal of the acceptance criterion is to reject the unfeasible target proposals y' according to prior and likelihood probabilities. The critical part here is that for every target proposal y', the prior probability $p(y')$ and the likelihood $p(x|y')$ needs to be evaluated. While the former is feasible for the problems we focus on, the latter is not trivial to evaluate.

3.2 Likelihood Evaluation

In order to model $p(y|x, \theta, \mathcal{D}, \mathcal{M})$, unlike prior work that used a dedicated network architecture, we define a likelihood function $p(x|y, \theta, \mathcal{D}, \mathcal{M})$ that can be used with any pre-trained network. Given f and a proposed target y', like [6,7,10,28], we define likelihood with an energy function as

$$p(x|y', f(\cdot, \theta)) \propto \exp(-\beta E(x, y')) \tag{3}$$

where β is a "temperature" parameter and $E(x, y')$ is evaluated through a process we call gradient descent *input backpropagation* inspired by neural network inversion approximation in [22] and neural style transfer work [12].

To evaluate $E(x, y')$, we generate an input sample $x'_{y'}$ that is as close as possible to x and lead to the proposed shape $y' = f(x'_{y'}|\theta)$. This action can be formulated as an optimisation problem

$$x'_{y'} = \underset{x'}{\arg\min} \; \lambda \underbrace{\rho(x', x)}_{\text{input loss}} + \underbrace{\mu(f(x'), y')}_{\text{target loss}}, \tag{4}$$

where $\rho : \mathcal{X} \times \mathcal{X} \to \mathbb{R}^+$, $\mu : \mathcal{Y} \times \mathcal{Y} \to \mathbb{R}^+$ are distances and $\lambda \in \mathbb{R}$ is a scaling constant ensuring proper optimisation of both loss elements. μ can be defined as the original distance used for training $f(x|\theta)$. We then define

$$E(x,y'):=\rho(x'_{y'},x). \tag{5}$$

We set $\rho(\cdot,x)$ as the squared L_2 distance in this work, i.e., $\rho(x'_{y'},x) = \|x'_{y'} - x\|_2^2$, but other options are possible, as long as (5) combined with (3) define a proper probability distribution over x. Note that the L_2 distance corresponds to a Gaussian distribution centered around $x'_{y'}$ as $p(x|y',\theta,\mathcal{D},\mathcal{M})$. Even though $p(x|y',\theta,\mathcal{D},\mathcal{M})$ is a Gaussian, it is crucial to note that this does not correspond to $p(y|x,\theta,\mathcal{D},\mathcal{M})$ being a Gaussian due to the non-linearity the optimization in Eq. 4 introduces. Different y''s can lead to very different $x'_{y'}$, and aggregating the samples through the MH MC process can lead to complex and multi-modal as confirmed by the experiments in Sect. 4.

Within the MCMC context, the minimisation formulation ensures that we only generate $x'_{y'}$ close to test image x that also lead to the proposed y' as prediction. Provided the two terms in (4) are balanced correctly, a low likelihood value assigned to a proposal y' indicates y' either lies outside the range of f (the trained network is incapable of producing y' for any input), or outside of the image (understood as a subset of codomain of f) of the inputs similar to x under f. A high likelihood value on the other hand, means an $x'_{y'}$ very close to x can produce y', therefore around x the model is sensitive and y' can be considered as a sample from $p(y|x,\theta,\mathcal{D},\mathcal{M})$ if it also attains.

The choice of β parameter in (3) is important as it affects the acceptance rate in MH sampling. Correctly setting β ensures the acceptance ratio is not dominated by either $p(y)$ or $p(x|y,\theta,\mathcal{D},\mathcal{M})$. The optimisation problem (4) needs to be solved for every MCMC proposal y'. We will refer to the full proposed MH MCMC sampling scheme as **Deep MH**.

3.3   Shape Sampling Using Lower Dimensional Representations

As mentioned, we focus on applications where $p(y)$ can be estimated. For low dimensional targets, this can be achieved by parametric or non-parametric models, e.g., KDEs [18]. For high dimensional targets, one can use lower dimensional representations. Here, we illustrate our approach on shape sampling and, as in [38], use a probabilistic PCA prior for $p(y)$

$$y = US^{\frac{1}{2}}z + \mu + s, \tag{6}$$

where U is the matrix of principal vectors, S the diagonal principal component matrix and μ the data mean. All three were precomputed using surfaces in the training set of f. PCA coefficients z and global shift s then modulate and localise the shape in space, respectively. The posterior $p(y|x,\theta,\mathcal{D},\mathcal{M})$ is then approximated by deploying the MH sampling process to estimate the joint posterior of the parameterisation $p(z, s|x, \theta, \mathcal{D}, \mathcal{M})$. Proposal shapes y' are constructed at every step of the MCMC from proposals z' and s' for the purposes of likelihood computation as defined by (3) and (5). PCA coefficients and shifts are assumed to be independently distributed. We set $p(z) = \mathcal{N}(z; 0, I)$ as in [4] and $p(s) = \mathcal{U}([0, D]^2)$ for an input image $x \in \mathbb{R}^{D \times D}$. In practice, we restrict the prior on shift to a smaller area within the image to prevent the accepted shapes from crossing the image boundaries. Assuming both proposals are symmetrical Gaussian, the MH acceptance criterion (2) then becomes

$$A((z', s'), (z^t, s^t)|x) = \min\left(1, \frac{p(x|z', s', f(\cdot; \theta))}{p(x|z^t, s^t, f(\cdot; \theta))} \frac{p(z')}{p(z^t)} \frac{p(s')}{p(s^t)}\right).$$

4 Results

The method was compared against three uncertainty quantification baselines: (1) **Post-hoc uncertainty estimation method** RIO [30], using the code provided by the authors; and **Dedicated probabilistic forward systems:** (2) probPCA [37] and (3) MC Dropout [11]. We compare with MC dropout to provide a complete picture even though it is quantifying epistemic uncertainty.

We evaluate the uncertainty estimates on two regression problems on imaging and non-imaging data. The first is left ventricle myocardium surface delineation in cardiac MR images from the UK BioBank data set [1] where network $f :$ $\mathbb{R}^D \times \mathbb{R}^D \to \mathbb{R}^{50 \times 2}$ predicts coordinates of 50 vertices on the surface in small field of view (SFOV) and large FOV (LFOV) images for $D = 60, 200$, respectively. The data sets are imbalanced when it comes to location and orientation of the images with propensity towards the myocardium being in the central area of the image (90% of the examples). We tested the method on a 10-layer CNN trained to predict a lower dimensional PCA representation from images, as described in Sect. 3.3 and proposed in [26], which is a deterministic version of probPCA. The CNN predicts 20 PCA components which are then transformed into a surface with 50 vertices. The second is a 1D problem of computed tomography (CT) slice localisation within the body given the input features describing the tissue content via histograms in polar space [9, 14] and $f : \mathbb{R}^{384} \to [0, 100]$. We use the same data set and training setup as in the original RIO paper [30] and tested the method on a fully connected network with 2 hidden layers.

The same base architectures were used across baselines, with method pertinent modifications where needed, following closely the original articles [11, 38]. No data augmentation was used for forward training. Hyperparameter search for Deep MH was done on the validation set by hand tuning or grid search to get a good balance between proper optimisation of (4), good convergence times and optimal acceptance rates (average of ~20% for high and ~40% for the one-dimensional tasks). This lead to $\beta = 10000$ (SFOV), 30000 (LFOV), 60000 (CT) and Gaussian proposal distributions: $z' \sim \mathcal{N}(z^t, \sigma_z^2 I)$ and $s' \sim \mathcal{N}(s^t, \sigma_s^2 I)$, with $(\sigma_z, \sigma_s) = (0.1, 2)$ in SFOV, and $(0.2, 8)$ in LFOV; in CT $y' \sim \mathcal{N}(y^t, I)$. Choice of priors for the delineation task followed Sect. 3.3. In CT, we used an uninformative prior $\mathcal{U}([0, 100])$ to reflect that the testing slice can lie anywhere in the body. Parameters of the input backpropagation were set to $\lambda = 1$ and

$\sigma_n = 0.1$. We employed independent chain parallelization to speed up sampling and reduce auto-correlation within the sample sets. Chains were initialised randomly and run for a fixed number of steps with initial burn in period removed based on convergence of trace plots of the sampled target variables. The final posteriors were then approximated by aggregation of the samples across the chains. For comparisons, we quantify uncertainty in the system via dispersion of $p(y|x, \theta, \mathcal{D}, \mathcal{M})$: standard deviation $\sigma_{y|x}$ in 1D problems; trace of the covariance matrix $\Sigma_{y|x}$ in multi-dimensional tasks (sample covariance matrix for Deep MH and MC Dropout, and predictive covariance for probPCA).

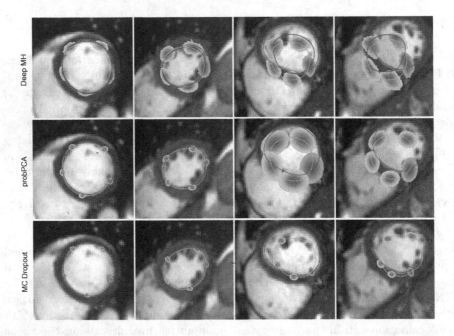

Fig. 1. Comparison of estimated $p(y|x, \theta, \mathcal{D}, \mathcal{M})$ for selected test subjects: GT shape (red), forward prediction $f(x_i|\theta)$ (blue), sample/predicted mean (yellow). Kernel density estimates were used for visualization. Only 5 vertices were visualised for clarity. Test subjects are ordered column-wise according to growing fixed network prediction error (RMSE($f(x), y_{GT}$) = 0.48; 2.72; 5.25; 6.31; test set average RMSE = 1.46). Outlier test subjects (column 3–4) are associated with higher uncertainty and lower accuracy for all methods.

Predictive Posteriors: Figure 1 shows qualitative comparison of target distributions produced by Deep MH, MC Dropout and probPCA in the SFOV surface reconstruction task. We include two images representative of the majority of the data set (well centered) and two from the 10% outlier group (images with large translation and/or reflection compared to rest of the data set). The posteriors obtained by Deep MH exhibited greater variability, including multimodality,

Table 1. Correlation between uncertainty and accuracy (RMSE).

	Spearman [r;p]	Pearson [r;p]	Spearman [r;p]	Pearson [r;p]
Method	*Shape delineation SFOV: full*		*Shape delineation SFOV: homogeneous*	
Deep MH	$0.30; 3 \times 10^{-3}$	$0.62; 1 \times 10^{-11}$	$0.26; 2 \times 10^{-2}$	$0.38; 3 \times 10^{-4}$
probPCA	$0.35; 5 \times 10^{-4}$	$0.57; 8 \times 10^{-10}$	$0.19; 8 \times 10^{2}$	$0.40; 9 \times 10^{-5}$
MC Dropout	$0.34; 5 \times 10^{-4}$	$0.61; 3 \times 10^{-11}$	$0.21; 5 \times 10^{2}$	$0.29; 7 \times 10^{-3}$
Method	*Shape delineation LFOV: full*		*Shape delineation LFOV: homogeneous*	
Deep MH	$0.33; 3 \times 10^{-3}$	$0.38; 7 \times 10^{-4}$	$0.20; 9 \times 10^{-2}$	$0.26; 3 \times 10^{-2}$
probPCA	$0.17; 1 \times 10^{-2}$	$0.33; 3 \times 10^{-3}$	$0.04; 7 \times 10^{-1}$	$0.03; 8 \times 10^{-1}$
MC Dropout	$0.52; 9 \times 10^{-7}$	$0.55; 2 \times 10^{-7}$	$0.42; 2 \times 10^{-4}$	$0.42; 2 \times 10^{-4}$
Method	*CT slice localisation*			
Deep MH	$0.55; 1 \times 10^{-7}$	$0.64; 2 \times 10^{-9}$		
RIO	$0.07; 6 \times 10^{-1}$	$0.13; 3 \times 10^{-1}$		
MC Dropout	$0.53; 2 \times 10^{-6}$	$0.51; 7 \times 10^{-6}$		

than the baseline methods even for the test images with lower forward prediction RMSE. In contrast, probPCA produced unimodal Gaussians, expectedly. MC Dropout, at $p = 0.5$, produced tight distributions around the sample mean.

Deep MH posteriors also showed a larger dispersion of vertex locations along the surface as can be seen in the first two columns. This uncertainty reflects the ambiguity in the target generation process. Boundaries seen in the images can identify the placement of a vertex in the orthogonal direction to the boundary, but placement along the boundary is much less obvious and variable. Deep MH posteriors captured this ambiguity well while others were not able to do so. Irrespective of the method, the high probability regions of the predicted $p(y|x, \theta, \mathcal{D}, \mathcal{M})$ might not cover the GT shapes when the prediction fails, as can be seen in the last two columns of Fig. 1.

Correlation with Accuracy: We investigated the relationship between accuracy of the network and the predictive uncertainty. An good model should yield a non-decreasing relationship between uncertainty and prediction accuracy, and not show overconfidence, i.e., assign high confidence to imprecise predictions.

Table 1 presents the correlation coefficients between quantified uncertainties and the accuracy (RMSE) of either the forward prediction of the pre-trained network in the case of Deep MH, or predictive mean for the baselines. We include results for shape delineation task analysed in two settings: on the full imbalanced test sets, and on the homogeneous subsets of the test sets with two outliers, detected manually, removed. Deep MH yielded higher Spearman and Pearson's correlation for most cases than probPCA and RIO. Correlation of epistemic uncertainty, as quantified by MC Dropout, with prediction error was higher in some cases than that of aleatoric uncertainty quantified by Deep MH.

5 Conclusion

In this work we proposed a novel method—Deep MH—for uncertainty estimation of trained deterministic networks using MH MCMC sampling. The method is architecture agnostic and does not require training of any dedicated NNs or access to training or GT data. Experiments on regression tasks showed the better quality of the Deep MH uncertainty estimates not only in comparison to a post-hoc baseline [30], but dedicated probabilistic forward models as well [37,38].

The main limitation of Deep MH is its computational complexity. Some of it is because this is a sampling technique. The rest stems from the proposed evaluation of likelihood. A possible alternative to the proposed likelihood computation via optimisation is the simulation of an inversion process via a generative adversarial network (GAN). Deep MH can be applied to problems where it is possible to define or estimate a prior distribution $p(y)$. While this is easy for problems with low effective dimensions, applications to problems with higher dimensional targets is an open research question.

Acknowledgements. This research has been conducted using the UK Biobank Resource under Application Number 17806.

References

1. UK Biobank homepage. https://www.ukbiobank.ac.uk/about-biobank-uk. Accessed 24 May 2021
2. Baumgartner, C.F., et al.: PHiSeg: capturing uncertainty in medical image segmentation. In: Shen, D., et al. (eds.) MICCAI 2019. LNCS, vol. 11765, pp. 119–127. Springer, Cham (2019). https://doi.org/10.1007/978-3-030-32245-8_14
3. Begoli, E., Bhattacharya, T., Kusnezov, D.: The need for uncertainty quantification in machine-assisted medical decision making. Nat. Mach. Intell. **1**(1), 20–23 (2019). https://doi.org/10.1038/s42256-018-0004-1
4. Bishop, C.M.: Pattern Recognition and Machine Learning. Information Science and Statistics, Springer, New York (2006)
5. Brooks, S., Gelman, A., Jones, G., Meng, X.L.: Handbook of Markov Chain Monte Carlo. CRC Press (2011)
6. Chang, J., Fisher, J.W.I.: Efficient MCMC sampling with implicit shape representations. In: CVPR, pp. 2081–2088. IEEE Computer Society (2011). http://dblp.uni-trier.de/db/conf/cvpr/cvpr2011.html#ChangF11
7. Chen, S., Radke, R.J.: Markov chain Monte Carlo shape sampling using level sets. In: 2009 IEEE 12th International Conference on Computer Vision Workshops, ICCV Workshops, pp. 296–303 (2009). https://doi.org/10.1109/ICCVW.2009.5457687
8. Draper, D.: Assessment and propagation of model uncertainty. J. R. Stat. Soci. Ser. B (Methodol.) **57**(1), 45–97 (1995). http://www.jstor.org/stable/2346087
9. Dua, D., Graff, C.: UCI machine learning repository (2017). http://archive.ics.uci.edu/ml

10. Erdil, E., Yildirim, S., Çetin, M., Tasdizen, T.: MCMC shape sampling for image segmentation with nonparametric shape priors. In: 2016 IEEE Conference on Computer Vision and Pattern Recognition (CVPR), pp. 411–419 (2016). https://doi.org/10.1109/CVPR.2016.51
11. Gal, Y., Ghahramani, Z.: Dropout as a Bayesian approximation: representing model uncertainty in deep learning. In: Balcan, M.F., Weinberger, K.Q. (eds.) Proceedings of The 33rd International Conference on Machine Learning. Proceedings of Machine Learning Research, vol. 48, pp. 1050–1059. PMLR, New York, 20–22 June 2016. http://proceedings.mlr.press/v48/gal16.html
12. Gatys, L.A., Ecker, A.S., Bethge, M.: Image style transfer using convolutional neural networks. In: Proceedings of the IEEE Conference on Computer Vision and Pattern Recognition (CVPR), June 2016
13. Gelman, A., Carlin, J.B., Stern, H.S., Rubin, D.B.: Bayesian Data Analysis, 2nd edn. Chapman and Hall/CRC (2004)
14. Graf, F., Kriegel, H.-P., Schubert, M., Pölsterl, S., Cavallaro, A.: 2D image registration in CT images using radial image descriptors. In: Fichtinger, G., Martel, A., Peters, T. (eds.) MICCAI 2011. LNCS, vol. 6892, pp. 607–614. Springer, Heidelberg (2011). https://doi.org/10.1007/978-3-642-23629-7_74
15. Hammersley, J.M., Handscomb, D.C.: Monte Carlo Methods. Springer, Dordrecht (1964). https://doi.org/10.1007/978-94-009-5819-7
16. Hastings, W.K.: Monte Carlo sampling methods using Markov chains and their applications. Biometrika 57(1), 97–109 (1970). http://www.jstor.org/stable/2334940
17. Houhou, N., Thiran, J.P., Bresson, X.: Fast texture segmentation model based on the shape operator and active contour. In: 2008 IEEE Conference on Computer Vision and Pattern Recognition, pp. 1–8 (2008). https://doi.org/10.1109/CVPR.2008.4587449
18. Izenman, A.J.: Modern Multivariate Statistical Techniques. Regression, Classification and Manifold Learning. Springer, New York (2008). https://doi.org/10.1007/978-0-387-78189-1
19. Karani, N., Erdil, E., Chaitanya, K., Konukoglu, E.: Test-time adaptable neural networks for robust medical image segmentation. Med. Image Anal. 68, 101907 (2021). https://doi.org/10.1016/j.media.2020.101907, https://www.sciencedirect.com/science/article/pii/S1361841520302711
20. Kendall, A., Gal, Y.: What uncertainties do we need in Bayesian deep learning for computer vision? In: Guyon, I., von Luxburg, U., et al. (eds.) Advances in Neural Information Processing Systems 30: Annual Conference on Neural Information Processing Systems 2017, 4–9 December 2017, Long Beach, CA, USA, pp. 5574–5584 (2017)
21. Kim, J., Fisher, J.W., III., Yezzi, A., Çetin, M., Willsky, A.S.: A nonparametric statistical method for image segmentation using information theory and curve evolution. IEEE Trans. Image Process. 14(10), 1486–1502 (2005)
22. Kindermann, J., Linden, A.: Inversion of neural networks by gradient descent. Parallel Comput. 14(3), 277–286 (1990). https://doi.org/10.1016/0167-8191(90)90081-J
23. Kohl, S., et al.: A probabilistic u-net for segmentation of ambiguous images. In: Bengio, S., Wallach, H., Larochelle, H., Grauman, K., Cesa-Bianchi, N., Garnett, R. (eds.) Advances in Neural Information Processing Systems, vol. 31. Curran Associates, Inc. (2018). https://proceedings.neurips.cc/paper/2018/file/473447ac58e1cd7e96172575f48dca3b-Paper.pdf

24. Levy, D., Sohl-dickstein, J., Hoffman, M.: Generalizing Hamiltonian Monte Carlo with neural networks. In: ICLR 2018 (2018). https://openreview.net/pdf?id=B1n8LexRZ

25. Michailovich, O., Rathi, Y., Tannenbaum, A.: Image segmentation using active contours driven by the Bhattacharyya gradient flow. IEEE Trans. Image Process. **16**(11), 2787–2801 (2007). https://doi.org/10.1109/TIP.2007.908073

26. Milletari, F., Rothberg, A., Jia, J., Sofka, M.: Integrating statistical prior knowledge into convolutional neural networks. In: Descoteaux, M., Maier-Hein, L., Franz, A., Jannin, P., Collins, D.L., Duchesne, S. (eds.) MICCAI 2017. LNCS, vol. 10433, pp. 161–168. Springer, Cham (2017). https://doi.org/10.1007/978-3-319-66182-7_19

27. Neal, R.M.: Probabilistic inference using Markov chain Monte Carlo methods. Technical report, CRG-TR-93-1, Department of Computer Science, University of Toronto (1993)

28. Neal, R.M.: Bayesian Learning for Neural Networks. Lecture Notes in Statistics, vol. 118. Springer, New York (1996). https://doi.org/10.1007/978-1-4612-0745-0

29. Oktay, O., et al.: Anatomically constrained neural networks (ACNNs): application to cardiac image enhancement and segmentation. IEEE Trans. Med. Imaging **37**(2), 384–395 (2018). https://doi.org/10.1109/TMI.2017.2743464

30. Qiu, X., Meyerson, E., Miikkulainen, R.: Quantifying point-prediction uncertainty in neural networks via residual estimation with an I/O kernel. In: 8th International Conference on Learning Representations, ICLR 2020, Addis Ababa, Ethiopia, 26–30 April 2020. OpenReview.net (2020). https://openreview.net/forum?id=rkxNh1Stvr

31. Rubin, D.B.: Bayesianly justifiable and relevant frequency calculations for the applied statistician. Ann. Stat. **12**(4), 1151–1172 (1984). https://doi.org/10.1214/aos/1176346785

32. Saltelli, A., Tarantola, S., Campolongo, F., Ratto, M., et al.: Sensitivity Analysis in Practice: A Guide to Assessing Scientific Models. Wiley, Chichester (2004)

33. Song, J., Zhao, S., Ermon, S.: A-NICE-MC: adversarial training for MCMC. In: Guyon, I., et al. (eds.) Advances in Neural Information Processing Systems, vol. 30. Curran Associates, Inc. (2017). https://proceedings.neurips.cc/paper/2017/file/2417dc8af8570f274e6775d4d60496da-Paper.pdf

34. Song, Y., Meng, C., Ermon, S.: MintNet: building invertible neural networks with masked convolutions. In: Wallach, H., Larochelle, H., Beygelzimer, A., d'Alché-Buc, F., Fox, E., Garnett, R. (eds.) Advances in Neural Information Processing Systems, vol. 32. Curran Associates, Inc. (2019). https://proceedings.neurips.cc/paper/2019/file/70a32110fff0f26d301e58ebbca9cb9f-Paper.pdf

35. Tanno, R., et al.: Bayesian image quality transfer with CNNs: exploring uncertainty in dMRI super-resolution. In: Descoteaux, M., Maier-Hein, L., Franz, A., Jannin, P., Collins, D.L., Duchesne, S. (eds.) MICCAI 2017. LNCS, vol. 10433, pp. 611–619. Springer, Cham (2017). https://doi.org/10.1007/978-3-319-66182-7_70

36. Tanno, R., et al.: Uncertainty modelling in deep learning for safer neuroimage enhancement: demonstration in diffusion MRI. NeuroImage **225**, 117366 (2021). https://doi.org/10.1016/j.neuroimage.2020.117366, https://www.sciencedirect.com/science/article/pii/S1053811920308521

37. Tóthová, K., et al.: Probabilistic 3D surface reconstruction from sparse MRI information. In: MICCAI 2020. LNCS, vol. 12261, pp. 813–823. Springer, Cham (2020). https://doi.org/10.1007/978-3-030-59710-8_79

38. Tóthová, K., et al.: Uncertainty quantification in CNN-based surface prediction using shape priors. In: Reuter, M., Wachinger, C., Lombaert, H., Paniagua, B., Lüthi, M., Egger, B. (eds.) ShapeMI 2018. LNCS, vol. 11167, pp. 300–310. Springer, Cham (2018). https://doi.org/10.1007/978-3-030-04747-4_28
39. Wang, H., Levi, D.M., Klein, S.A.: Intrinsic uncertainty and integration efficiency in bisection acuity. Vis. Res. **36**(5), 717–739 (1996). https://doi.org/10.1016/0042-6989(95)00143-3

Uncertainty Categories in Medical Image Segmentation: A Study of Source-Related Diversity

Luke Whitbread[1]([✉])[iD] and Mark Jenkinson[1,2][iD]

[1] School of Computer Science, The University of Adelaide, Adelaide, Australia
{luke.whitbread,mark.jenkinson}@adelaide.edu.au
[2] Wellcome Centre for Integrative Neuroimaging, University of Oxford, Oxford, UK

Abstract. Measuring uncertainties in the output of a deep learning method is useful in several ways, such as in assisting with interpretation of the outputs, helping build confidence with end users, and for improving the training and performance of the networks. Several different methods have been proposed to estimate uncertainties, including those from epistemic (relating to the model used) and aleatoric (relating to the data) sources using test-time dropout and augmentation, respectively. Not only are these uncertainty sources different, but they are governed by parameter settings (e.g., dropout rate or type and level of augmentation) that establish even more distinct uncertainty categories. This work investigates how different the uncertainties are from these categories, for magnitude and spatial pattern, to empirically address the question of whether they provide usefully distinct information that should be captured whenever uncertainties are used. We take the well characterised BraTS challenge dataset to demonstrate that there are substantial differences in both magnitude and spatial pattern of uncertainties from the different categories, and discuss the implications of these in various use cases.

Keywords: Uncertainties · Stability · Diversity · Reliability

1 Introduction

Anatomical segmentations of magnetic resonance imaging (**MRI**) scans are commonly used to support a number of clinical and research tasks using either manual or automated methods. While optimising overall measures of success (e.g., Dice/F1 scores) is important for any segmentation task, the uncertainties associated with image segmentations have become a salient field of enquiry for researchers; to (i) improve the quality and interpretability of structural delineations, and (ii) improve trust when applying automated techniques to clinical practice [1]. Whilst it is not uncommon in the literature to implicitly consider a single uncertainty distribution, different sources for uncertainties exist (e.g., epistemic and aleatoric). Therefore, a thorough treatment of uncertainties arising from different sources is needed to understand their usefulness, distinctiveness and stability.

2   Related Work

Researchers have investigated uncertainties for some time but, more recently, specific epistemic and aleatoric sources of uncertainty have been addressed for deep convolutional networks. Here, two complementary estimation paradigms have emerged; namely, test-time dropout (**TTD**) for model or epistemic uncertainty and test-time augmentation (**TTA**) for data or aleatoric uncertainty. The proposed use of Monte Carlo dropout at test-time by Gal and Ghahramani [2] overcomes the computational problems of traditional Bayesian approaches, although other approximate models of uncertainty, including Monte Carlo batch normalisation [3] and Markov Chain Monte Carlo methods [4] have also been proposed. The use of TTD, however, has become more widespread amongst researchers than these other methods. To measure aleatoric uncertainties, Ayhan and Berens proposed the use of TTA [5], with Wang and colleagues proposing a systematic approach to assess aleatoric uncertainties in medical imaging [6]. Building upon these paradigms, much research attention has now turned to the incorporation of uncertainties to improve model performance [7–10].

As the use of uncertainties in imaging pipelines is becoming increasingly common, it is important to perform explorations around which sources of uncertainty are the most beneficial, the most stable and reliable, and the most interpretable. A key question related to this is whether a single uncertainty source and distribution is sufficient for a general use case, or whether multiple sources and distributions should be used. Jungo and colleagues [11,12] have addressed issues around reliability and model confidence of epistemic uncertainties for some TTD model architecture strategies and learned aleatoric uncertainty (σ^2); where σ^2 is determined using a method proposed by Kendall and Gal [13]. While these and other works (e.g., [14,15]) address uncertainty reliability and model calibration generally, they do not consider different levels of TTD parameters or how aleatoric uncertainties from different underlying sources manifest in observations. Additionally, further important work on modelling uncertainty related to annotator variation has emerged. This utilises latent space encoding techniques derived from the Variational Autoencoder framework [16] to directly model segmentation distributions using a Bayesian approach [17,18]. These methods provide a mathematically rigorous model for capturing complex voxel dependencies, and though they are currently designed to produce one distribution, they could be modified to capture a number of distinct uncertainty sources, in order to report the most appropriate information for each individual use case.

3   Methods

We assess the range and stability of uncertainty measures for epistemic and aleatoric categories by considering various TTD and TTA parameter settings. The parameter space for assessing epistemic uncertainty with TTD is typically less complex than that for aleatoric categories using TTA. While there are different approaches for how dropout is applied structurally to a model, once this is determined, the key variables are the probabilities of the applied dropout. In contrast, TTA has both a number of augmentation types that can be applied (some particularly relevant to MRI), and a number of parameter settings for each type of augmentation. In addition, as is done in model calibration analyses (e.g., [14, 15]), we have estimated a prediction error likelihood for the underlying segmentation model, to test how similar it is to other uncertainty types.

3.1   Epistemic Uncertainties with TTD

We used the common approach of dropping network filters with a constant global probability. Although researchers sometimes use higher probability parameters at the encoder-decoder junction of a U-net based network, we took the approach of a single probability setting, which still tends to drop more filters at the encoder-decoder junction, given the increasing number of filters with depth.

We have selected 6 TTD probabilities to evaluate the range and stability of epistemic uncertainties: 0.03, 0.06, 0.09, 0.12, 0.15, and 0.40. The first 5 cases represent a range of typical network-wide dropout settings; while the final setting is intended to test what happens when this is set substantially higher.

3.2   Aleatoric Uncertainties Using TTA

To evaluate the stability of aleatoric uncertainties, we have used 8 TTA cases across three categories common for MRI data: affine transformations (reflecting varying subject orientation), image ghosting and bias-field transforms (both common MRI artefacts). For each category, low and high range parameters have been selected, where the final two cases are transforms composed of all three low or all three high cases. The low settings represent cases that are very likely in practice, whilst the high range settings represent uncommon but plausible cases. These settings are:

Affine transformation cases:

- Scaling range: Low $\sim \mathcal{U}(0.98, 1.02)$; High $\sim \mathcal{U}(0.80, 1.20)$.
- Rotation (degrees): Low $\sim \mathcal{U}(-5, 5)$; High $\sim \mathcal{U}(-45, 45)$.
- Image translation (mm): $\sim \mathcal{U}(-5, 5)$ for both cases.

Ghosting artefacts (usually caused by subject motion in MRI):

- Intensity strength (max of k-space): Low $\sim \mathcal{U}(0.0, 0.15)$; High $\sim \mathcal{U}(0.25, 0.75)$.
- Number of ghosts: $\sim \mathcal{U}\{2, 6\}$ for both cases, applied on the 2nd image axis.

Bias-field artefacts (smooth intensity changes caused by RF inhomogeneities):

- Maximum polynomial coefficients: Low $= 0.2$; High $= 0.8$.
- Polynomial order: 3 for both cases.

3.3 Dataset

This work utilises the well characterised Multimodal Brain Tumor Segmentation (BraTS) 2020 data [19–21]. We split the 369 publicly available samples into a hold-out test-set of 78 subjects, a validation-set of 42 subjects, and a training-set of 249 subjects. All contain both high-grade and low-grade glioma cases.

3.4 Experiments and Uncertainty Measures

We have trained a 2.5-dimensional U-net to segment each tumor class (i.e., whole tumor, tumor core, and enhancing tumor) using: 6-block encoder-decoder pathway, 8 initial filters (doubling per level), Adamax optimiser ($\beta_1, \beta_2 = 0.9, 0.999$), learning rate schedule starting 0.001 reducing by 0.25 factor after patience/cooldown of 3/2 epochs, 50 training epochs, cross-entropy/soft-Dice loss weighted 0.3/0.7, and 2.5D input stacks with 2 adjacent axial slices each side per reference slice.

For each TTD and TTA case (as in Sects. 3.1 and 3.2), each test-set sample is evaluated to produce voxelwise probabilities (of belonging to each class). Each sample is processed 50 times with random dropout or data augmentation applied on each forward pass, creating separate distributions, in each voxel, for each uncertainty case. From each distribution, the mean, variance and entropy are calculated and stored as voxelwise maps for each uncertainty case.

To assess how consistent and repeatable these uncertainty values are, we calculated the median and interquartile range, in each voxel separately, as stable measures should have a small range of values. These robust measures would not be substantially affected by one or two unusual/outlier cases.

In addition, to assess whether there is a range of different spatial patterns generated by different settings we measure the spatial correlation, being independent of the global magnitude. This was done for each combination of TTD and TTA cases by calculating the correlation of uncertainty spatial maps, using a mask, within each subject, since the tumor shape and location varies with each subject and so we cannot mix spatial maps across subjects. The spatial mask consisted of all voxels with a non-zero median entropy value (across all cases), thereby excluding a large number of background voxels that otherwise would inflate correlation values. These values form a correlation matrix for each subject. Additionally, we also calculated the mean of these matrices across subjects, allowing us to assess: (i) if the relationships between spatial patterns from different uncertainty sources are consistent or not, and (ii) if more than a single map is needed to capture their diversity or not.

Finally, we assess the magnitude of the uncertainty values, independent of spatial patterns, by calculating the mean of non-zero uncertainty values for each case and subject, to capture the average uncertainty level. We also trained an auxiliary network to predict the error likelihood of the primary segmentation network ("predicted error network") for comparative purposes and as an analogue to the model calibration methods highlighted in Sect. 2; here, we use the primary network voxel-wise classification confidence levels to define a loss that is minimised when the predicted error network outputs equate to the distance between ground-truth labels and primary network confidence levels.

4   Results

For brevity, we report results only for tumor core tissue using voxelwise entropy values as our measure of uncertainty. These results generalise to using the variance as the uncertainty measure, as well as to other tumor tissue categories. The U-net performance (Dice = 0.74) is not the focus but is comparable with the mean of BraTS 2020 challenge submissions.

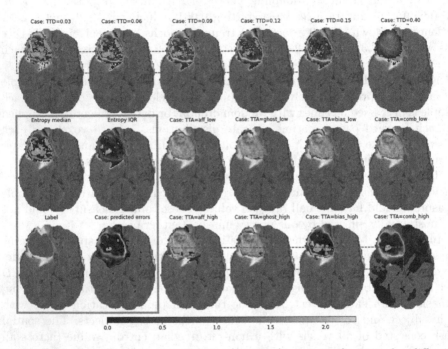

Fig. 1. Subject 197, axial slice 81/155: entropy (uncertainty) maps for different TTD/TTA cases (see Sects. 3.1 and 3.2); along with the median and interquartile range across all uncertainty cases, a predicted error map for the underlying network and the ground-truth label in the green highlight box. The maximum predicted error value (bright yellow) is 0.248 for this axial slice. The dashed red boxes highlight one example of the diversity of uncertainties derived from various sources—here, the affine, bias-field and combined aleatoric cases express considerably greater uncertainty in the small discontiguous tumor region (shown in the lower left part of the main label region for this axial slice) as compared to the TTD cases. (Color figure online)

4.1 Voxelwise Uncertainty with TTD/TTA Parameter Variations

Figure 1 provides examples of individual entropy maps for all uncertainty cases, as well as the median and interquartile range, in a randomly selected test subject (ID: 197). Across the TTD/TTA parameter settings, it is clear that median entropy levels are reasonably consistent, as we would want them to be. Perhaps more interesting is the interquartile range, where it is clear that even with moderate parameter settings, there is a substantial spread of values in many locations. Purely for comparative purposes, a predicted error likelihood map is also produced using the predicted error network and is displayed in Fig. 1 showing a similar, but also slightly different, spatial map.

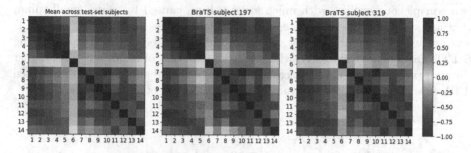

Fig. 2. Correlation matrices (of spatial correlations) for the entropy maps generated from the different TTD and TTA uncertainty cases. The first is the mean across all test subjects, while the others are individual subjects (IDs: 197 and 319). Rows and columns represent the different uncertainty cases in the following order: Cases 1–6 epistemic TTD probability = [0.03, 0.06, 0.09, 0.12, 0.15, 0.40] respectively; Cases 7–14 aleatoric TTA = [7: affine low, 8: ghosting low, 9: bias-field low, 10: combined (affine, ghosting, bias-field) low, 11: affine high, 12: ghosting high, 13: bias-field high, 14: combined (affine, ghosting, bias-field) high]. Section 3.2 provides TTA details.

4.2 Spatial Correlations

Matrices of spatial correlations between uncertainty cases are shown in Fig. 2. These quantify the similarity of spatial patterns, independent of the location and size of the tumors. Average correlation matrices, across subjects, show if the high and low uncertainty regions are consistently placed.

It can be seen from these results that there are clear similarities among the first 5 TTD cases, although the correlation values reduce as probability settings diverge. A striking result is the negative and near-zero correlation exhibited between case 6 (TTD probability of 0.40) and each of the other TTD and TTA cases. Case 6 provides significant disruption to the network such that non-zero uncertainty values are spread across the whole image (including non-brain regions). Correlations between TTA cases are more varied with a less discernible pattern. This is not unexpected given the variety of data manipulations that are possible using various techniques. Finally, correlations between TTD and TTA cases show a discernible, repeatable pattern, with correlation dropping as the TTD probability parameter is increased; signifying that while low probability TTD cases have similar patterns to aleatoric cases, as this probability increases the spatial pattern of high and low uncertainty regions for these estimates of epistemic and aleatoric uncertainty become increasingly different.

4.3 Mean Uncertainty Levels

Since the spatial correlations are invariant to the global magnitude of the uncertainties, we have also measured the mean of non-zero voxel entropy values for each subject, for each uncertainty case, to quantify global magnitude. These results can be seen in Fig. 3. Once again, the extreme TTD case (i.e., case 6) is a conspicuous outlier, with much lower values, caused by many small values that are spread across the image. This provides further confirmation that TTD settings with higher probability values are unlikely to be of use. The remaining 5 TTD cases behave similarly, with wider distribution of mean levels for higher dropout probabilities. For TTA cases, the high bias-field and high-level combined TTA case show lower distributions of means than the other TTA cases.

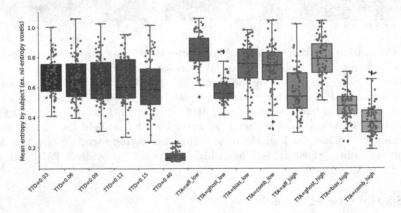

Fig. 3. Boxplots of the mean of non-zero voxelwise entropy values, for each subject, shown for epistemic (TTD) and aleatoric (TTA) uncertainty cases. For TTD case 6, the large network disruption led to many voxels with low, but non-zero, entropy values.

5 Discussion and Conclusion

It is clear from these results that uncertainty distributions for epistemic (TTD) and aleatoric (TTA) sources are distinctly different from each other and that the parameter types and values within them also have a substantial impact on the uncertainty distributions. This indicates that more than one category of uncertainty should be modeled and estimated for a variety of use cases, such as to

(i) aid interpretability, (ii) capture a diversity of uncertainty sources, (iii) indicate reliability, or (iv) incorporate into uncertainty-aware networks. Although reported results only used entropy, these conclusions also hold for variance and other tissue classes. We chose to show entropy values as they are better for distributions that are not unimodal, which were likely to be produced. In this early work we chose not to include all uncertainty sources (e.g., inter-rater variability) or compare to further techniques such as ensembles or Bayesian-based network architectures, but rather demonstrate the diversity of uncertainties generated by two common methods—especially accounting for MR artefacts with TTA.

In some instances, the interquartile range approached the full range of possible entropy values. This shows that the parameters used for TTD or TTA uncertainty estimation are important. For more extreme dropout rates the TTD uncertainty estimates are not useful for any purpose and so researchers should err on the side of using reduced dropout probability settings. Furthermore, the calculated uncertainties may gradually change from being useful to non-informative, based on the gradual changes in correlations found at lower dropout values, although further testing would be required to establish this generally.

Aleatoric uncertainties spanned a range of distinctly different maps, as shown by the correlation matrices, indicating that a number of different data augmentation types need to be included to capture aleatoric uncertainty. The augmentation parameters also clearly have an effect, and when pushed to higher values can sometimes result in widespread low-grade uncertainties across images. This could be used to establish a practical upper-bound for these parameter settings.

Careful consideration of different parameter settings is needed when using TTD and TTA estimation methods, and researchers should consider that there is no single uncertainty map, but rather a set of different distributions governed by the TTD and TTA hyper-parameter values and types. In order to have reliable, repeatable, interpretable measures of uncertainty it is important to specify the types of augmentation and all hyper-parameters. When using uncertainties with uncertainty-aware networks, we expect incorporating maps from multiple categories to be beneficial. Finally, while a predicted error map may share similarities with some uncertainty cases, they measure at most one aspect of uncertainty and possibly something different again, and are thus not a replacement for a *set* of maps from different uncertainty categories. Researchers should carefully consider parameter settings for each method, as Fig. 3 demonstrates how larger parameter settings can produce unhelpful, unrepresentative uncertainties, indicating that upper-bounds should be established in each case (e.g., TTA cases: bias-field and combined).

In this study one major limitation is the size and nature of the dataset. BraTS is a well studied and characterised dataset, which contains several different segmentation tasks, and thus allowed us to verify that the findings generalised to different tissue types and also different uncertainty measures. However, to establish these results more generally, further studies are required.

In conclusion, we have shown that there are multiple sources of uncertainties that generate distinctly different uncertainty maps (see Fig. 2), and that these should be incorporated into all uncertainty work. The epistemic and aleatoric uncertainty estimates, as obtained through TTD and TTA respectively, are sensitive to their hyper-parameter settings and to obtain repeatable maps it is important to specify the hyper-parameters involved. These settings need to be thought through carefully when building and running networks that produce uncertainty estimates. Furthermore, we found that there is a richness in the set of uncertainty estimations that is not captured by a single distribution, and this should be considered when feeding maps into uncertainty-aware networks, or when using them to aid interpretability or indicate reliability. Therefore, although a chosen distribution or summary may capture uncertainties to some degree, it is unlikely to provide comprehensive estimates across all regions where uncertainties could manifest; which could be vital to ensuring clinical efficacy in challenging situations.

References

1. Dinsdale, N., et al.: Challenges for machine learning in clinical translation of big data imaging studies. arXiv:2107.05630 (2021)
2. Gal, Y., Ghahramani, Z.: Dropout as a Bayesian approximation: representing model uncertainty in deep learning. In: Proceedings of the 33rd International Conference of Machine Learning, ICML 2016, vol. 48, pp. 1050–1059. JMLR.org (2016)
3. Taye, M., Azizpour, H., Smith, K.: Bayesian uncertainty estimation for batch normalized deep networks. In.: International Conference on Machine Learning, pp. 4907–4916. PMLR (2018)
4. Neal, R.M.: Bayesian Learning for Neural Networks, vol. 118. Springer (2012)
5. Ayhan, M.S., Berens, P.: Test-time augmentation for estimation of heteroscedastic aleatoric uncertainty in deep neural networks (2018)
6. Wang, G., et al.: Aleatoric uncertainty estimation with test-time augmentation for medical image segmentation with convolutional neural networks. Neurocomputing **338**, 34 (2019)
7. Ozdemir, O., et al.: Propogating uncertainty in multi-stage Bayesian convolutional neural networks with application to pulmonary nodule detection. arXiv:1712.00497 (2017)
8. Herzog, L., et al.: Integrating uncertainty in deep neural networks for MRI based stroke analysis. Med. Image Anal. **65**, 101790 (2020). https://doi.org/10.1016/j.media.2020.101790
9. Wang, G., et al.: Automatic brain tumor segmentation based on cascaded convolutional neural networks with uncertainty estimation. Front. Comput. Neurosci. **13**, 56 (2019). https://doi.org/10.3389/fncom.2019.00056
10. Arega, T.W., Bricq, S., Meriaudeau, F.: Leveraging uncertainty estimates to improve segmentation performance in cardiac MR. In: Sudre, C.H., et al. (eds.) UNSURE/PIPPI - 2021. LNCS, vol. 12959, pp. 24–33. Springer, Cham (2021). https://doi.org/10.1007/978-3-030-87735-4_3
11. Jungo, A., Reyes, M.: Assessing reliability and challenges of uncertainty estimations for medical image segmentation. In: Shen, D., et al. (eds.) MICCAI 2019. LNCS, vol. 11765, pp. 48–56. Springer, Cham (2019). https://doi.org/10.1007/978-3-030-32245-8_6

12. Jungo, A., et al.: Analyzing the quality and challenges of uncertainty estimations for brain tumor segmentation. Front. Neurosci. **14**, 282 (2020). https://doi.org/10.3389/fnins.2020.00282
13. Kendall, A., Gal, Y.: What uncertainties do we need in Bayesian deep learning for computer vision? In: Advances in Neural Information Processing Systems 30, pp. 5574–5584. Curran Associates, Inc. (2017)
14. Mehrtash, A., et al.: Confidence calibration and predictive uncertainty estimation for deep medical image segmentation. IEEE Trans. Med. Imaging **39**(12), 3868–3878 (2020). https://doi.org/10.1109/TMI.2020.3006437
15. Rousseau, A.-J., et al.: Post training uncertainty calibration of deep networks for medical image segmentation. In: 2021 IEEE 18th International Symposium on Biomedical Imaging (ISBI), pp. 1052–1056 (2021). https://doi.org/10.1109/ISBI48211.2021.9434131
16. Kingma, D., Welling, M.: Auto-encoding variational Bayes. arXiv:1312.6114 (2013)
17. Kohl, S., et al.: A probabilistic U-Net for segmentation of ambiguous images. arXiv:1806.05034 (2018)
18. Baumgartner, C., et al.: PHiSeg: capturing uncertainty in medical image segmentation. arXiv:1906.04045 (2019)
19. Menze, A., et al.: The multimodal brain tumor image·segmentation benchmark (BRATS). IEEE Trans. Med. Imaging **34**(10), 1993–2024 (2015). https://doi.org/10.1109/TMI.2014.2377694
20. Bakas, H., et al.: Advancing the Cancer Genome Atlas glioma MRI collections with expert segmentation labels and radiomic features. Nat. Sci. Data **4**, 170117 (2017). https://doi.org/10.1038/sdata.2017.117
21. Bakas, S., et al.: Identifying the best machine learning algorithms for brain tumor segmentation, progression assessment, and overall survival prediction in the BRATS challenge. arXiv:1811.02629 (2018)

On the Pitfalls of Entropy-Based Uncertainty for Multi-class Semi-supervised Segmentation

Martin Van Waerebeke[1(✉)], Gregory Lodygensky[2], and Jose Dolz[3,4]

[1] CentraleSupélec, Paris, France
martin.wrbk@gmail.com
[2] CHU Sainte-Justine, Montreal, Canada
[3] LIVIA, ETS Montreal, Montreal, Canada
[4] International Laboratory on Learning Systems (ILLS),
McGill - ETS - MILA - CNRS - Université Paris-Saclay - CentraleSupélec,
Calgary, Canada

Abstract. Estimating the prediction uncertainty of a deep segmentation network is very useful in multiple learning scenarios. For example, in the semi-supervised learning paradigm, the vast majority of recent methods rely on pseudo-label generation to leverage unlabeled data, whose training is guided by uncertainty estimates. While the commonly-used entropy-based uncertainty has shown to work well in a binary scenario, we demonstrate in this work that this common strategy leads to suboptimal results in a multi-class context, a more realistic and challenging setting. We argue, indeed, that these approaches underperform due to the erroneous uncertainty approximations in the presence of inter-class overlap. Furthermore, we propose an alternative solution to compute the uncertainty in a multi-class setting, based on divergence distances and which account for inter-class overlap. We evaluate the proposed solution on a challenging multi-class segmentation dataset and in two well-known uncertainty-based segmentation methods. The reported results demonstrate that by simply replacing the mechanism used to compute the uncertainty, our proposed solution brings consistent improvements.

Keywords: Segmentation · Semi-supervised learning · Uncertainty estimation

1 Introduction

To alleviate the need of large labeled datasets required to train fully supervised segmentation networks, several learning strategies have recently emerged as appealing alternatives. For example, weak supervision, which can come in the form of image-tags [15,20], scribbles [25] or bounding boxes [14], is paving the

Work done as part of a research internship at ETS Montreal and CHU Sainte-Justine.

way towards closing the gap with fully supervised models. Even though this setting reduces the burden of the labeling process, achieved performances are typically far from their fully supervised counterparts. In contrast, semi-supervised
learning (SSL), which learns from a limited amount of labeled data and a large
set of unlabeled data, offers an interesting balance between high-quality segmentation and a low regime of labeled data.

Despite the different nature of the many existing approaches, the preva-
lent principle of these techniques is to augment a standard supervised loss
over a reduced number of labeled images with an unsupervised regularization
term using unlabeled images. Adversarial learning based methods [7,36] typically leverage a discriminator network to encourage the segmentation model to
provide similar segmentation outputs for both labeled and unlabeled images.
Co-training [3] leverages the underlying idea that training examples can often
be described by two complementary sets of features, often referred to as views,
mining consensus information from multiple views [21,28,31,37]. More recently,
contrastive-learning [9] has also been adopted in the context of semi-supervised
medical image segmentation [5,22]. In particular, the model is pre-trained in an
unsupervised manner with a contrastive loss, improving its performance for a
subsequent downstream task, for which a few labeled samples are available.

Among these methods, consistency regularization is emerging as an appealing
alternative to existing approaches. The common idea behind these methods is to
have a dual-based architecture, similar to the teacher-student duple, and enforce
consistency between the predictions of the same image under a given set of perturbations, including affine transformations [16], intensity modifications [32] or
image permutations [17]. To account for noisy labels and errors produced in
the pseudo-segmentation masks, most recent papers resort to uncertainty-based
approaches, which weight the reliability of each pixel in the objective function.
By integrating this uncertainty-awareness scheme, the student model can gradually learn from reliable targets by exploiting the uncertainty information, ultimately resulting in better segmentation results. More concretely, the predictive entropy has been commonly preferred to approximate the uncertainty, as
originally proposed in [34]. In particular, authors employ Monte Carlo dropout
and random Gaussian noise to generate multiple segmentations from the same
image, even though other strategies, such as temporal ensembling [4], can also
be employed. This approach has been further improved by integrating additional
components [11,18,27,29,33,35]. For example, [29] explores a dual uncertainty
method which, in addition to the predictive uncertainty, includes the uncertainty
derived from the learned features. However, to the best of our knowledge, none
has questioned the validity of entropy-based uncertainty approaches.

In this work, we challenge the status-quo of SSL methods resorting to
entropy-based uncertainty and demonstrate that, under the multi-class scenario,
the results derived by these approaches are suboptimal. The proposed work
is based on the observation that the entropy-based metric, such as the ones
employed to compute the uncertainty in most SSL segmentation approaches,
fail to account for any overlap between the output distribution of several classes.

To illustrate this point, we provide a synthetic counterexample in Fig. 1 and a more theoretical explanation in Sect. 2.4. Furthermore, we experimentally evaluate the use of entropy as a measure of uncertainty for semi-supervised segmentation methods and demonstrate that it leads to suboptimal results in multi-class settings. In particular, we resort to two well-known methods that fall in this category, i.e., [34] and [29], which are evaluated on a public multi-class segmentation benchmark. We find that, surprisingly, *in the presence of multiple classes they bring none or marginal performance* compared to the baseline not integrating uncertainty. In contrast, by approximating the uncertainty with properly suited divergences, the problematic inter-class overlap is taken into account, ultimately resulting in better segmentation performances. We stress that we claim no novelty regarding a new SSL framework. Instead, we highlight the flaws of the current status-quo of existing entropy-based methods in the multi-class scenario and propose alternative metrics to address them.

2 Methodology

Notation. We denote the set of labeled training images as $\mathcal{D}_{\mathcal{L}} = \{(\mathbf{X}_n, \mathbf{Y}_n)\}_n$, where $\mathbf{X}_i \in \mathbb{R}^{\Omega_i}$ represents the ith image, Ω_i its spatial domain and $\mathbf{Y}_i \in \{0,1\}^{\Omega_i \times C}$ its corresponding ground-truth segmentation mask. Furthermore, the set of unlabeled images is denoted as $\mathcal{D}_{\mathcal{U}} = \{(\mathbf{X}_m)\}_m$, which contains only images and where $m >> n$. The goal of semi-supervised semantic segmentation is to learn a segmentation network $f(\cdot)$, by leveraging both the labeled and unlabeled datasets. Note that in dual-based architectures, there exist two different networks: the teacher, parameterized by θ_T and the student, represented by θ_S. In addition, for each image $\mathbf{X}_i$, we denote $\mathbf{P}_i \in [0,1]^{\Omega_i \times C}$ as the softmax probability output of the network, i.e., the matrix containing a simplex column vector $\mathbf{p}_i^v = \left(p_i^{v,1}, \ldots, p_i^{v,C}\right)^T \in [0,1]^C$ for each voxel $v \in \Omega_i$. Note that we omit the parameters of the network here to simplify notation.

2.1 Background

In this section, we revisit the standard setting for SSL segmentation based on uncertainty, which aim at minimizing the following combined objective:

$$\min_\theta \sum_{i=1}^{N} \mathcal{L}_s(f_{\theta_S}(\mathbf{X}_i), \mathbf{Y}_i) + \lambda \sum_{i=1}^{N+M} \mathcal{L}_c(f_{\theta_T}(\mathbf{X}_i; \xi^T), f_{\theta_S}(\mathbf{X}_i; \xi^S)) \quad (1)$$

where $\mathcal{L}_s$ can be any segmentation loss on the labeled images, and $\mathcal{L}_c$ is a consistency loss to enforce the similarity between teacher and student predictions for the same input $\mathbf{X}_i$ under different perturbations,[1] ξ^T and ξ^S. Furthermore, while the student parameters are updated via standard gradient descent, the teacher weights are updated as an exponential moving average (EMA) [23] of

---

[1] Adding noise to input images and dropout are standard perturbations in SSL.

the student parameters at different time steps. To account for unreliable and noisy predictions made by the teacher in low-data regimes, [34] introduced an uncertainty-aware consistency loss, which has been employed by many more recent works. In particular, for a given image $\mathbf{X}_i$, this loss can be defined as:

$$\mathcal{L}_c(\mathbf{P}_{\theta_T}, \mathbf{P}_{\theta_S}) = \frac{\sum_{v \in \Omega_i} \mathbb{I}(u_v < H) \|\mathbf{P}_{\theta_T, v} - \mathbf{P}_{\theta_S, v}\|^2}{\sum_{v \in \Omega_i} \mathbb{I}(u_v < H)} \tag{2}$$

where $\mathbb{I}$ is the indicator function, H is a threshold to select the most certain voxels and u_v is the estimated uncertainty at voxel v.

Uncertainty Estimation. Epistemic uncertainty is modeled using Monte Carlo DropOut (MCDO) [8,13]. More concretely, T stochastic forward passes are typically performed on the teacher model, each with random dropout and Gaussian noise, which results in a set of softmax probability predictions per volume, $\{\mathbf{P}^t\}_{t=1}^T$. In the current semi-supervised segmentation literature, the predictive entropy is preferred to approximate these uncertainty estimates. Thus, for each voxel v in the $i\text{-}th$ volume, we can compute the average softmax prediction for class c as $\mu_c = \frac{1}{T} \sum_t \mathbf{p}_t^c$. Finally, the voxel-wise uncertainty is computed as $u^v = -\sum_c \mu_c \log \mu_c$.

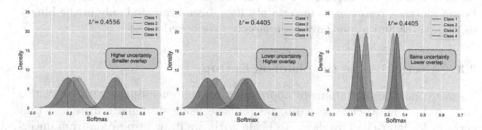

Fig. 1. Counterexample highlighting the weaknesses of entropy-based uncertainty (class prediction distributions and corresponding uncertainty values $\mathcal{U}$).

2.2 Empirical Limitations of Entropy-Based Uncertainty

Our hypothesis in this work is based on the observation that entropy-based metrics ignore the inter-class separability, overlooking potentially high overlapping between the distributions of softmax outputs over multiple perturbations for competing classes. We demonstrate this negative effect with a synthetic counterexample in Fig. 1. These plots show the class probability distributions of a given sample under different perturbations.[2] In particular, we depict three different scenarios, where class 4 is most likely to be predicted. For each setting,

---

[2] Note that in our setting, a sample represents a single voxel, which may result in different softmax predictions due to the Monte Carlo dropout step.

we show the predictive distributions across classes and their predicted entropy-based uncertainty. In the first case (*left*), we can observe that the distribution of the predictions results in almost no overlap between the distribution of the winner class (i.e., class 4) and the rest of the classes. In this case, one would safely argue that this sample indeed belongs to class 4. This contrasts with the estimated uncertainty, which flagged the prediction as more uncertain than its counterpart in the middle plot. On the other extreme, we can observe that predicted distributions for classes 3 and 4 highly overlap. Nevertheless, this strong overlap between the two classes is not taken into account to compute the uncertainty, whose obtained value is lower than in the left case. In other words, the entropy-based uncertainty has identified the middle example as having lower uncertainty, whereas one can clearly see that choosing between class 3 or 4 cannot be done confidently. Last, the third plot highlights another limitation of this type of uncertainty. Indeed, it fails to account for variance of the predictions, providing the same uncertainty value for the *middle* and *right* scenarios, whereas the standard deviation of the prediction distributions are wildly different. Even more, in the extreme case in which the variances were close to zero, but the means of the distributions remained unchanged, the predicted uncertainty values would stay the same. This counterexample demonstrates that, in a multi-class setting, the use of entropy-based metrics to approximate the uncertainty produce suboptimal results, as the inter-class relations are not considered in the estimation of the uncertainty. Furthermore, as the vast majority of semi-supervised segmentation methods resorting to uncertainty have been evaluated only in the binary setting, these limitations have been largely overlooked.

2.3   Alternatives to the Shannon Entropy

To overcome the limitations of approximating the uncertainty with predictive entropy in a multi-class scenario, we propose using divergence distances that account for inter-class overlaps. To begin with, we draw inspiration from uncertainty based approaches and perform T inferences per image, each of them with random dropout and Gaussian noise. Then, we compute the sample distributions for each class C at every voxel v, resulting in the following distributions $\mathbf{d}_1^v, ..., \mathbf{d}_C^v$, which are sorted in increasing order based on their means μ_c^v. To measure the overlapping between different distributions, we build a set of histograms, one per distribution, resulting in $\mathbf{h}_1^v, ..., \mathbf{h}_C^v$. We must now evaluate how much $\mathbf{h}_C^v$ stands out from the others.

Bhattacharyya. We first resort to the Bhattacharyya divergence [2], which has recently been proposed for class separability. More concretely, [19] proposed to quantify the transferability of deep models across domains by leveraging the class separability in the feature space via a Gaussian Bhattacharyya coefficient. In addition, [26] explored a Bhattacharyya coefficient to better approximate the inter-class confusion in uncertainty estimation compared to variance-based metrics. For two discrete distributions with K samples, $\mathbf{p} = (p_k)_{k=1}^K$ and $\mathbf{q} = (q_k)_{k=1}^K$, the Bhattacharyya divergence can be formally defined as:

$$\mathcal{D}_{BC}(\mathbf{p}, \mathbf{q}) = -\log \sum_{k=1}^{K} (p_k q_k)^{\frac{1}{2}} \tag{3}$$

Alpha-Divergences. We also investigate the Tsallis's formulation of α-divergence [1,6,10,24] which, by using the generalized logarithm [6]: $\log_\alpha(x) = \frac{1}{1-\alpha}(x^{1-\alpha} - 1)$ extends the Kullback-Leibler (KL) divergence. Note that with $\alpha = 0.5$ and $\alpha = 2.0$, it is equivalent to the Hellinger and Pearson Chi-square distances, respectively. The α-divergence is defined as:

$$\mathcal{D}_\alpha(\mathbf{p}\|\mathbf{q}) = -\sum_{k=1}^{K} p_k \log_\alpha \left(\frac{q_k}{p_k} \right) = \frac{1}{1-\alpha} \left(1 - \sum_{k=1}^{K} p_k^\alpha q_k^{1-\alpha} \right) \tag{4}$$

Then, the voxel-wise uncertainty map $\mathbf{U}$ can be derived from the pair-wise divergence distances as: $u_v = \max_{C>1} \mathcal{D}(\mathbf{h}_1^v, \mathbf{h}_C^v)$, where $\mathcal{D}$ denotes the divergence employed.

2.4   Theoretical Limitations of Entropy-Based Uncertainty

Uncertainty measures how likely the distribution with the highest mean probability is to be the 'right' one, and therefore assess how far this distribution is from its competitors, each corresponding to one class. Let us outline a few standard properties that any uncertainty measure $\mathcal{U}$ should verify:

1. The bounds of $\mathcal{U}(d_1, \ldots, d_C)$ should be reached when $d_i = d_j \; \forall i, j$ (upper bound) and when all the (d_i) are constant distributions with $d_C = 1$ and $d_i = 0 \; \forall i \neq C$ (lower bound).
2. The partial derivative of $\mathcal{U}$ w.r.t $|\mu_C - \mu_{C-1}|$ must be strictly negative (higher gap $\Rightarrow$ lower uncertainty).
3. $\forall i \neq C$, for a given measure O of the overlap between two distributions, the partial derivative of $\mathcal{U}$ w.r.t. $O(d_C, d_i)$ must be positive (higher overlap $\Rightarrow$ higher uncertainty).

Let us consider that we have normal distributions, which we think is a reasonable hypothesis according to the central limit theorem. While the entropy verifies property (1), it does not verify (2) nor (3) as demonstrated in Fig. 1 with a counterexample. Going from the left to the middle plot, we refute (2) since a lower gap caused a lower uncertainty. Furthermore, going from the middle to the right plot, we refute (3) since the substantial overlap decrease did not impact the uncertainty. In contrast, the Bhattacharyya divergence D_B verifies every one of these properties. Indeed, (1) is an easily demonstrable property. (2) holds true for many distributions but is easily demonstrated in the Gaussian case. Indeed, with normal distributions $N = N(\mu, \sigma)$ and $M = N(\rho, \tau)$, $-\partial D_B(N, M)/\partial|\mu - \rho| = -1/2 * |\mu - \rho|/(\sigma^2 + \tau^2) < 0$. (3) is verified by construction of D_B : D_B is itself a measure of overlap, because possible values that are common to several distributions are what increases D_B. Since $\partial D_B/\partial D_B = 1 > 0$, (3) is verified. Thus, we have now proven theoretically that

D_B verifies several standard properties that any uncertainty measure should have, whereas entropy does not. In this regard, we consider the Bhattacharyya divergence to be superior to the entropy to compute uncertainty. We might also add that these properties are also verified by the KL divergence, (1) being elementary, (2) is demonstrated in [30] and (3) is verified for the same reason that it is verified for D_B.

3 Experiments

Dataset: The empirical validation is performed on the public developing Human Connectome Project (dHCP) dataset [12], which contains multi-modal MR images (MRI) from infants born at term. In particular, we employ 440 MRI-T2 scans and their corresponding ground truth, which were generated using DrawEM. We divided the dataset into 3 labeled and 331 unlabeled images for training, 1 for validation and 105 for testing, which were cropped into $64 \times 64 \times 64$ patches. **Methods:** We conduct experiments on two well-known semi-supervised segmentation approaches: UA-MT [34] and DU-MT [29]. In addition to their popularity, another important factor is their simplicity, which facilitates the isolation of the entropy effect on the final performance. Furthermore, to have a better overview of the relative performance of these approaches, we include a *lower baseline* (trained without additional unlabeled data) and an *upper baseline* (trained on the whole labeled training set). **Evaluation:** we resort to the Dice coefficient, the 95% Hausdorff Distance (HD) and the average surface distance (ASD). **Implementation:** We employ 3D UNet as backbone for all the models, with cross-entropy and Dice loss as objective function. The networks parameters were optimized with SGD (momentum = 0.9) for a maximum of 200 epochs. The initial learning rate was set to 10^{-3} and divided by 2 every 15 epochs, and a batch size of 6. The EMA weighting factor was fixed at 0.99, and λ in Eq. (1) to 15 for all methods. Regarding H in Eq. 2, we set its value to 0.2. Furthermore, we do not employ any data-augmentation to isolate the impact of both entropy-based and proposed uncertainty estimations. To generate multiple inferences per image, we follow standard literature (MCDO and Gaussian noise) with the same number of inferences T across models, and use 10 bins to compute the histograms. Last, we empirically observed that exploiting the information from all the classes did not bring any significant improvement (DSC: 92.14 (all) vs 92.12 (top-2)), while it considerably increased time computation by 20 %. Thus, the final uncertainty map can be approximated as: $u_v = \mathcal{D}(\mathbf{h}_{C-1}^v, \mathbf{h}_C^v)$, where $\mathbf{h}_{C-1}^v$ and $\mathbf{h}_C^v$ are the histograms of the 2-top classes at voxel v.

Main Results: We first evaluate the effect of the entropy-based uncertainty on the segmentation performance of two well-known semi-supervised approaches (UA-MT and DU-MT). To this end, we report the per-class Dice scores obtained by the different baselines (Table 1). Furthermore, we replace the entropy as an approximator of the uncertainty by the Bhattacharyya divergence, denoted as *ours*. From these results, we can observe that by resorting to a divergence distance, e.g., Bhattacharyya, the performance is considerably improved for both analyzed approaches. Furthermore, the improvement is consistent across all the classes, suggesting that the inter-class relationship is indeed better modeled.

In addition, Table 2 reports the whole quantitative results across the different methods, which gives a better overview of their performance. We can see that the same trend is observed across the different metrics, with the proposed uncertainty approximation outperforming the original entropy-based methods. A surprising finding is that, compared to the lower-bound method, both original UA-MT and DU-MT *bring none or marginal performance*. We argue that this is due to the highlighted limitation of the entropy as an estimation of uncertainty in the multi-class setting. Indeed, at the beginning of the training, the softmax probabilities for the different classes are closer, resulting in higher overlapped regions which might lead to unreliable uncertainty values. Although our approach is intended for multi-class scenarios, we evaluated it in the *binary setting* of [34], obtaining 89.03 of DSC vs 88.88 [34] and 2.23 of ASD vs 2.26 [34].

Table 1. Per-class dice scores obtained across different methods. Our models are shadowed, and ∇ indicates the difference wrt the original entropy-based method.

	$\|\#N\|$	CSF	CGM	WM	O	V	Cr	DGM	BS	H-A	Mean	∇
Lower-bound	3	91.31	92.27	93.99	86.94	88.01	92.18	91.93	90.67	76.93	89.35	–
UA-MT [34]	3	90.84	91.91	93.66	85.93	88.60	93.57	92.43	92.23	78.35	89.72	–
UA-MT (ours)	3	93.25	94.17	95.93	88.61	91.44	96.09	94.77	94.62	80.18	92.12	+2.40
DU-MT [29]	3	90.74	91.74	93.46	85.89	88.16	91.37	90.88	90.23	73.73	88.47	–
DU-MT (ours)	3	92.31	93.34	95.71	88.51	87.43	94.25	93.82	93.03	75.44	90.44	+1.97
Upper-bound	334	96.42	97.51	98.37	92.85	95.92	98.09	97.91	97.98	94.20	96.58	

Table 2. Quantitative results (mean over the 9 classes) for different metrics.

	$\|\#N\|$	Dice	HD95	ASD
Lower-bound	3	89.35	3.39	1.65
UA-MT [34]	3	89.72	3.20	1.14
UA-MT (ours)	3	92.12	2.32	0.67
DU-MT [29]	3	88.47	4.10	1.33
DU-MT (ours)	3	90.44	2.87	1.04
Upper-bound	334	96.58	1.19	0.28

Table 3. Ablation study on divergence distances (mean over the 9 classes). Best results in bold, second best results underlined.

	Uncertainty	Dice	HD95	ASD
UA-MT [34]	Entropy	89.72	3.20	1.14
	Bhattacharyya	**92.12**	2.32	**0.67**
	α-div ($\alpha = 0.5$)	91.69	2.37	0.757
	α-div ($\alpha = 2.0$)	91.79	**2.09**	0.99
DU-MT [29]	Entropy	88.47	4.1	1.32
	Bhattacharyya	90.44	2.87	1.04
	α-div ($\alpha = 0.5$)	**90.99**	2.72	0.92
	α-div ($\alpha = 2.0$)	90.68	2.82	0.92

On the Divergence Distances. We now explore several divergence distances as alternative to the Bhattacharyya divergence. Results from this study, which are reported in Table 3 demonstrate that, regardless of the divergence employed, the entropy-based uncertainty leads to sub-optimal results in both UA-MT and DU-MT approaches. Note that the balancing term in Eq. 1 remained fixed across all the models. However, we believe that further exploration of gradient magnitudes during training should be investigated to obtain optimal weighting parameters, particularly for Bhattacharyya and α−divergences.

4   Discussion

In this work we have demonstrated an important limitation of entropy-based uncertainty for semi-supervised segmentation in the multi-class scenario. We have done this through an intuitive counterexample, which stressed the unreliable uncertainty predictions due to the erroneous estimations in the presence of several competing classes. We have further leveraged this finding to propose the use of several divergence distances as efficient alternatives for this task. The empirical validation on a challenging multi-class segmentation problem has supported our arguments related to the weaknesses of entropy-based methods, while confirming the superiority of divergence distances. Based on these findings, we advocate that the proposed solution should be preferred over common entropy-based uncertainty approaches in the multiclass scenario.

References

1. Amari, S.I.: α-divergence is unique, belonging to both f-divergence and Bregman divergence classes. IEEE Trans. Inf. Theory **55**(11), 4925–4931 (2009)
2. Bhattacharyya, A.: On some analogues of the amount of information and their use in statistical estimation. Sankhyā: Indian J. Stat., 1–14 (1946)
3. Blum, A., Mitchell, T.: Combining labeled and unlabeled data with co-training. In: Proceedings of the Eleventh Annual Conference on Computational Learning Theory, pp. 92–100 (1998)
4. Cao, X., Chen, H., Li, Y., Peng, Y., Wang, S., Cheng, L.: Uncertainty aware temporal-ensembling model for semi-supervised ABUS mass segmentation. IEEE Trans. Med. Imaging **40**(1), 431–443 (2020)
5. Chaitanya, K., Erdil, E., Karani, N., Konukoglu, E.: Contrastive learning of global and local features for medical image segmentation with limited annotations. In: NeurIPS, vol. 33, pp. 12546–12558 (2020)
6. Cichocki, A., Amari, S.I.: Families of alpha-beta-and gamma-divergences: flexible and robust measures of similarities. Entropy **12**(6), 1532–1568 (2010)
7. Fang, K., Li, W.-J.: DMNet: difference minimization network for semi-supervised segmentation in medical images. In: Martel, A.L., et al. (eds.) MICCAI 2020. LNCS, vol. 12261, pp. 532–541. Springer, Cham (2020). https://doi.org/10.1007/978-3-030-59710-8_52
8. Gal, Y., Ghahramani, Z.: Dropout as a Bayesian approximation: representing model uncertainty in deep learning. In: ICML, pp. 1050–1059 (2016)
9. Hadsell, R., Chopra, S., LeCun, Y.: Dimensionality reduction by learning an invariant mapping. In: CVPR, vol. 2, pp. 1735–1742 (2006)
10. Havrda, J., Charvát, F.: Quantification method of classification processes. Concept of structural a-entropy. Kybernetika **3**(1), 30–35 (1967)
11. Hu, L., et al.: Semi-supervised NPC segmentation with uncertainty and attention guided consistency. Knowl.-Based Syst. **239**, 108021 (2022)

12. Hughes, E., et al.: The developing human connectome: announcing the first release of open access neonatal brain imaging. Organ. Human Brain Mapp, 25–29 (2017)
13. Kendall, A., Gal, Y.: What uncertainties do we need in Bayesian deep learning for computer vision? In: NeurIPS, vol. 30 (2017)
14. Kervadec, H., Dolz, J., Granger, É., Ben Ayed, I.: Curriculum semi-supervised segmentation. In: Shen, D., et al. (eds.) MICCAI 2019. LNCS, vol. 11765, pp. 568–576. Springer, Cham (2019). https://doi.org/10.1007/978-3-030-32245-8_63
15. Kervadec, H., Dolz, J., Tang, M., Granger, E., Boykov, Y., Ayed, I.B.: Constrained-CNN losses for weakly supervised segmentation. MedIA 54, 88–99 (2019)
16. Li, X., Yu, L., Chen, H., Fu, C.W., Xing, L., Heng, P.A.: Transformation-consistent self-ensembling model for semisupervised medical image segmentation. IEEE Trans. Neural Netw. Learn. Syst. 32(2), 523–534 (2020)
17. Li, Y., Chen, J., Xie, X., Ma, K., Zheng, Y.: Self-loop uncertainty: a novel pseudo-label for semi-supervised medical image segmentation. In: Martel, A.L., et al. (eds.) MICCAI 2020. LNCS, vol. 12261, pp. 614–623. Springer, Cham (2020). https://doi.org/10.1007/978-3-030-59710-8_60
18. Luo, X., Chen, J., Song, T., Wang, G.: Semi-supervised medical image segmentation through dual-task consistency. In: AAAI, vol. 35, pp. 8801–8809 (2021)
19. Pándy, M., Agostinelli, A., Uijlings, J., Ferrari, V., Mensink, T.: Transferability estimation using Bhattacharyya class separability. arXiv preprint arXiv:2111.12780 (2021)
20. Patel, G., Dolz, J.: Weakly supervised segmentation with cross-modality equivariant constraints. MedIA 77, 102374 (2022)
21. Peng, J., Estrada, G., Pedersoli, M., Desrosiers, C.: Deep co-training for semi-supervised image segmentation. Pattern Recogn. 107, 107269 (2020)
22. Peng, J., Wang, P., Desrosiers, C., Pedersoli, M.: Self-paced contrastive learning for semi-supervised medical image segmentation with meta-labels. In: NeurIPS, vol. 34 (2021)
23. Tarvainen, A., Valpola, H.: Mean teachers are better role models: weight-averaged consistency targets improve semi-supervised deep learning results. In: NeurIPS, vol. 30 (2017)
24. Tsallis, C.: Possible generalization of Boltzmann-Gibbs statistics. J. Stat. Phys. 52(1), 479–487 (1988)
25. Valvano, G., Leo, A., Tsaftaris, S.A.: Learning to segment from scribbles using multi-scale adversarial attention gates. IEEE TMI 40(8), 1990–2001 (2021)
26. Van, P., et al.: Leveraging the Bhattacharyya coefficient for uncertainty quantification in deep neural networks. Neural Comput. Appl. 33(16), 10259–10275 (2021)
27. Wang, K., et al.: Tripled-uncertainty guided mean teacher model for semi-supervised medical image segmentation. In: de Bruijne, M., et al. (eds.) MICCAI 2021. LNCS, vol. 12902, pp. 450–460. Springer, Cham (2021). https://doi.org/10.1007/978-3-030-87196-3_42
28. Wang, P., Peng, J., Pedersoli, M., Zhou, Y., Zhang, C., Desrosiers, C.: Self-paced and self-consistent co-training for semi-supervised image segmentation. Media 73, 102146 (2021)
29. Wang, Y., et al.: Double-uncertainty weighted method for semi-supervised learning. In: Martel, A.L., et al. (eds.) MICCAI 2020. LNCS, vol. 12261, pp. 542–551. Springer, Cham (2020). https://doi.org/10.1007/978-3-030-59710-8_53
30. Wikipedia: Normal distribution. https://en.wikipedia.org/wiki/Normal_distribution#Other_properties. Accessed 29 June 2022
31. Xia, Y., et al.: 3D semi-supervised learning with uncertainty-aware multi-view co-training. In: WACV, pp. 3646–3655 (2020)

32. Xu, X., Sanford, T., Turkbey, B., Xu, S., Wood, B.J., Yan, P.: Shadow-consistent semi-supervised learning for prostate ultrasound segmentation. IEEE TMI **41**, 1331–1345 (2021)

33. Yang, H., Shan, C., Kolen, A.F., de With, P.H.N.: Deep Q-network-driven catheter segmentation in 3D US by hybrid constrained semi-supervised learning and dual-UNet. In: Martel, A.L., et al. (eds.) MICCAI 2020. LNCS, vol. 12261, pp. 646–655. Springer, Cham (2020). https://doi.org/10.1007/978-3-030-59710-8_63

34. Yu, L., Wang, S., Li, X., Fu, C.-W., Heng, P.-A.: Uncertainty-aware self-ensembling model for semi-supervised 3D left atrium segmentation. In: Shen, D., et al. (eds.) MICCAI 2019. LNCS, vol. 11765, pp. 605–613. Springer, Cham (2019). https://doi.org/10.1007/978-3-030-32245-8_67

35. Zhang, Y., Liao, Q., Jiao, R., Zhang, J.: Uncertainty-guided mutual consistency learning for semi-supervised medical image segmentation. arXiv preprint arXiv:2112.02508 (2021)

36. Zhang, Y., Yang, L., Chen, J., Fredericksen, M., Hughes, D.P., Chen, D.Z.: Deep adversarial networks for biomedical image segmentation utilizing unannotated images. In: Descoteaux, M., Maier-Hein, L., Franz, A., Jannin, P., Collins, D.L., Duchesne, S. (eds.) MICCAI 2017. LNCS, vol. 10435, pp. 408–416. Springer, Cham (2017). https://doi.org/10.1007/978-3-319-66179-7_47

37. Zhou, Y., et al.: Semi-supervised 3D abdominal multi-organ segmentation via deep multi-planar co-training. In: WACV, pp. 121–140 (2019)

What Do Untargeted Adversarial Examples Reveal in Medical Image Segmentation?

Gangin Park[1], Chunsan Hong[1], Bohyung Kim[1], and Won Hwa Kim[2(✉)]

[1] CNAI, Seoul, Korea
ssonpull519@snu.ac.kr
[2] AI Graduate School/Computer Science and Engineering at Pohang University
of Technology and Science (POSTECH), Pohang, Korea
wonhwa@postech.ac.kr

Abstract. Recent literature point out overconfidence problems in DNNs which is demonstrated as biased confidences in false predictions in medical image segmentation tasks regardless of the ground truth. To explore and identify the uncertain regions, we propose a post-training method with untargeted adversarial examples where the input image is iteratively perturbed in a direction that maximizes the loss of original and perturbed prediction. The perturbed predictions from these adversarial examples can be seen as unstable areas in terms of input variability; we theoretically observe that the gradient of negative class confidence in terms of input image plays a key role for perturbed outputs, and empirically show that a small adversarial perturbation can help find hidden regions in the output segmentation maps. Compared to previous methods for uncertainty estimation, our method yields competitive results for uncertain region findings on medical image datasets while only requiring one extra inference from a pre-trained model and short iteration of attack. We expect our novel findings can provide insights for future medical image segmentation problems where detection of subtle variations (e.g., lesions) are required.

1 Introduction

Image segmentation is a traditional problem not only in Computer Vision but also in Medical Imaging such as segmentation of brains in neuroimaging [3], lesions in CT and MRI [18,21,22], and tumors in mammography [17]. As opposed to segmenting objects of certain shapes in natural images, the task in medical images is challenging as the variations in the images are typically non-rigid, e.g., tumors are given in different shapes and scales. Recent Deep Learning models have shown successful improvements in medical image segmentation with their representative capabilities for characterizing even complex patterns in the data.

Supplementary Information The online version contains supplementary material available at https://doi.org/10.1007/978-3-031-16749-2_5.

The encoder-decoder architecture such as U-net [23] became a common standard for various image segmentation tasks with outstanding performance. However, recent studies have shown that DNNs for classification are overconfident in a trade-off with their task performance [11], which lead to a mismatch between its confidence values and true probabilities. Segmentation is also not free from those issues, as it is equivalent to a "pixel-wise" classification [20]. Since this could hinder the information of true correctness from users, it is important to know where the uncertainties are with its output confidence.

To highlight the uncertain regions, recent studies worked on uncertainty estimation for the DNN models. Classically, uncertainty estimation was done with Bayesian Neural Networks (BNN), which learn distributions over model parameters. However, such methods are computationally heavy and approximation approached have been adopted. One of the simplest and common approach for the uncertainty estimation can be done through the variance or entropy of multiple samples using Monte-Carlo (MC) dropout at the test time [7]. A popular alternative is Deep Ensembles [14], where multiple training is required for the ensemble of multiple predictions.

Recently, the DNN-based methods are known to be vulnerable to adversarial attacks [24], i.e., a wrong prediction can be made with perturbed input with negligible changes in human perception. Therefore, adversarial examples (AEs) are considered as serious vulnerabilities that one should avoid in modern DNN systems. However, we look at this problem in a different view: If the adversarial attack is untargeted, how does it affect the perturbed segmentation output map? The closest work was previously done by Alarab et al. [1], where adversarial attacks of multiple step sizes of attacks are aggregated as uncertainty by mutual information, which is evaluated only on binary classification tasks related to Bitcoin and blockchain. Galil et al. [9] shows the capability of disrupting output confidence of neural networks with adversarial examples, but does not give insight on the direction of adversarial perturbation. Tuna et al. [25] observe the correlation between the gradient of uncertainty and task loss, to propose an adversarial attack method based on MC dropout.

In this work, we show that a simple adversarial examples with small perturbation can help find uncertain false regions hidden from final outputs for medical image segmentation tasks. A simple theoretical observation on the first order Taylor expansion of perturbed confidence, plus an empirical comparison with other test-time uncertainty estimation methods, are conducted to support our findings. The proposed method can potentially provide the following potential benefits: 1) it does not require any additional supervised data, 2) it does not need to hold-out a separate validation set, and 3) it can control the confidence level such that even subtle variations can be segmented. We extensively validated our idea on various independent medical datasets, and expect to give more insights to feedback the output of segmentation with our findings for future medical imaging tasks.

2   Preliminaries

Let $x \in \mathbb{R}^{H \times W \times C}$ be a C-channel input image of size $H \times W$ with its label $y \in \{0, 1, ..., K\}^{H \times W}$, where K is the number of classes and 0 class corresponds to background. A DNN model f_θ parameterized by trainable weights θ outputs logits $z = f_\theta(x) \in \mathbb{R}^{H \times W \times K}$, leading to a normalized probability prediction of being one of the classes per each pixel in x by a softmax activation σ : $\mathbb{R}^{H \times W \times K} \longrightarrow [0,1]^{H \times W \times K}$, as denoted by

$$\hat{p} = \sigma(z) \tag{1}$$

which is the "confidence" of predictions from the model. The final prediction of the class per each pixel from $\hat{p} \in \mathbb{R}^{H \times W \times K}$ is then given by

$$\hat{y} = \arg \max_c \hat{p}_c. \tag{2}$$

where $p_c \in \mathbb{R}^{H \times W}$ is a probability map of c-th channel that has the same spatial size of $H \times W$, and arg max operation is taken alongside the channel axis.

3   Untargeted Iterative Adversarial Perturbation

In this section, we present how adversarial examples can be utilized for uncertain region identification that many DNNs overlook with overconfidence.

3.1   Adversarial Attack

With the adversarial attack, each image is optimized in a direction that maximizes some loss values while getting only a little perturbation in the original image that human can hardly notice in visual system. One of the most commonly used attack method is Fast Gradient Sign Method (FGSM) [10], where the image is perturbed by the gradient of given loss as denoted by

$$x' = x + \alpha \operatorname{sign} \nabla_x \mathcal{L}(x_t, \hat{y}_0), \tag{3}$$

where $\hat{y}_0$ is the initial prediction from x, $\mathcal{L}$ is a loss function with $\hat{y}_0$ to maximize, and α is a step size for perturbation. Attack with prediction $\hat{y}_0$ as a target makes feasible for application on test-time as there would be no ground-truth mask.

A common iterative version of FGSM is Projected Gradient Descent (PGD) [19], which iteratively updates image by gradient descent (or ascent depending on the objective) of given loss function as

$$x_0 = x, \quad x_{t+1} = \Pi_\epsilon (x_t + \alpha \operatorname{sign} \nabla_x \mathcal{L}(x_t, \hat{y}_0)), \quad t = 0, 1, ..., T \tag{4}$$

where Π_ϵ is a projection function of size ϵ, and T is total number of iterations.

3.2   Adversarial Perturbation for Uncertain Region Identification

Traditionally, adversarial input perturbation has been considered an exploitation, which can cause wrong decision for neural network models. To deal with those risks from malicious input-based attacks, many recent studies have focused on methods for training with adversarial robustness [19, 26, 27].

Stepwise Changes on Perturbed Prediction. We first raise a question for adversarial perturbation, which is considered as a critical vulnerability so far: "How does the output perturbed with untargeted adversarial attacks change as the attack step iterates with a small step size?" To investigate this, we look into the predicted confidence maps from each perturbation step of PGD iteration. The manipulated confidences are given as

$$\hat{p}_t = \sigma\left(f_\theta\left(x_t\right)\right), \quad t = 0; 1, ..., T \tag{5}$$

where x_t is a perturbed image on t-step attack, thus giving a perturbed confidence map $\hat{p}_t$ on t-th iteration.

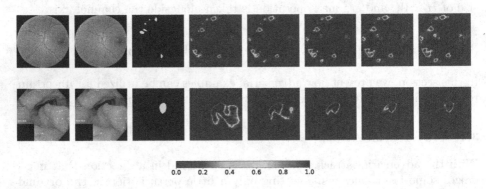

Fig. 1. Softmax confidence maps of each attack iteration. The first row is an example of FGADR [28], and the second row from Kvasir-SEG [13] dataset. Each column corresponds to: first column for original image, second column for perturbed image of 4th iteration, third column for ground-truth masks, and from 4th to 8th columns correspond to $\hat{p}_0$, $\hat{p}_1$, ..., $\hat{p}_4$, respectively.

Figure 1 shows confidence maps of perturbed images on each iteration with the ground truth given in the third column. Here, the first 4 iterations are visualized for identifying their initial changes. Detailed implementations and settings are provided in Sect. 4.2. As shown here, the perturbed prediction regions with an untargeted objective are not just randomly located and inherit some structured outputs that seem to have a visual dependency on their respective input images or original predictions. This is an interesting finding, as the adversarially perturbed predictions have been considered just as a vulnerability that we should avoid in DNN-based medical imaging so far. Motivated by these results, we investigate the capability of adversarially perturbed predictions with small initial steps to reveal unstable regions in terms of output predictions.

Utilizations for Uncertainty Map. We define a simple test-time uncertainty map that utilizes adversarial examples, representing the most unstable areas in terms of adversarial robustness. There are many possible choices, but here we take one of the simplest approaches that uses the absolute difference between original and perturbed prediction. Given a trained model f_θ and an input image x, the unstability map is calculated as

$$U_t\,(x, f_\theta) := |\hat{p_t} - \hat{p_0}|, \tag{6}$$

where $|\hat{p_t} - \hat{p_0}|$ represent the difference of confidences, and $|\cdot|$ denotes the element-wise absolute function.

3.3   Interpretation on First Order Approximation

Bayesian approximation is considered the common approach for uncertainty quantification, but the nonlinearity of f_θ makes hard to derive an explicit connection of it with the perturbed input. Alternatively, we observe how adversarial perturbation of confidence is related to its input variability, with some simple numerical approximation on a single step of FGSM attack.

Let the input perturbation of a single attack as $\delta = \nabla_x \mathcal{L}(f(x), y)$, and the initial positive prediction class on one specific pixel as k. The perturbed output difference on negative class $i \neq k$ is given by

$$|f(x + \delta)_i - f(x)_i|, \tag{7}$$

where $f(x)_i$ is a confidence value on class i. Since the adversarial attack aims to give a small perturbation that corrupts the original confidence, it can be numerically approximated with the first order Taylor expansion of Eq. 7 as

$$|f(x + \delta)_i - f(x)_i| \approx |\nabla_x f(x)_i \cdot \delta|, \tag{8}$$

with small perturbation size $|\delta|$. Here, $\nabla_x f(x)_i$ refers to the direction of an input image to "maximize" the confidence of negative class i, and δ has positive correlation with the direction to "minimize" the confidence of positive class k. The term $\nabla_x f(x)_i \cdot \delta$ thus can be seen as the Euclidean inner product of two gradient vectors, which means that one can break it into the product of magnitudes and angle β of two vectors as

$$|\nabla_x f(x)_i \cdot \delta| = |\,||\nabla_x f(x)_i|| \,||\delta|| \cos \beta|, \tag{9}$$

where $||\cdot||$ is L2-norm.

Equation 9 gives two interpretations to maximize Eq. 7 in terms of magnitude and angle. First, with fixed δ (by the context of untargeted attack), $||\nabla_x f(x)_i||$ itself should be large, which corresponds to the high confidence variability on class i in terms of input change. This can be thought as a main component that makes the adversarial example capable of revealing uncertain false region, with the utilization of input variation. Secondly, $\nabla_x f(x)_i$ and δ should be parallel to each other. This alignment means that two classes i and k have a similar set of input space pixel indices to be manipulated. We hypothesize that it is more affected by the characteristics of image itself in the context of visually hidden adversarial perturbations, and expect more depth of meaningful relationship on β in future works.

4   Experiments

4.1   Datasets

1) FGADR [28] dataset contains 1842 retinal fundus images, with pixel-level annotations of 6 types of lesions: microaneurysms (MA), hemorrhages (HE), hard exudates (EX), soft exudates (SE), intra-retinal microvascular abnormalities (IRMA), and neovascularization (NV). Labels are annotated by three ophthalmologists. Dataset is split into training and test set with 0.9 ratio for training set, and all images are resized to 512×512 pixels.
2) Kvasir-SEG [13] dataset consists of 1000 gastrointestinal polyp images, with their corresponding pixel-level annotations of ground-truth polyp masks by an experienced gastroenterologist. All images are resized to 512×512 pixels, and dataset is split into training and test set with 0.9 ratio for training set.
3) LIDC-IDRI [2,5] dataset contains 1018 lung CT scans from 1010 patients. Abnormal lesions in each scan are annotated by 4 radiologists. Following [16], each patch that contains at least one lesion is resampled to resolution of 0.5 mm, and the slices are cropped to 128×128 pixels. For training, pixels with more than 2 annotators agree positively are considered ground-truth positives. Dataset is split by subjects into training and test set with 0.9 ratio for training set.

4.2   Implementation Details

We use U-net [23] architecture for our segmentation models. A residual network [12] with 18 layers is used as backbones of the encoders. All models are trained for 30 epochs. Dice score and binary cross entropy (BCE) are summed for training loss as $\mathcal{L}_{dice} + \mathcal{L}_{bce}$, and Adam [15] optimizer is used for backpropagation. For FGADR and Kvasir-SEG, a learning rate of 0.001 with a step scheduler of 10 step size and a decay factor of $\gamma = 0.1$ is used. For LIDC-IDRI, a learning rate of 1e−4 with a step scheduler of 20 step size and $\gamma = 0.1$ is used since this yielded better performance.

For PGD, a projection size ϵ is set to $\frac{4}{255}$ as manually chosen. A perturbation rate α is set to 5e−5, and $\mathcal{L}$ is set as same as training loss: $\mathcal{L}_{dice} + \mathcal{L}_{bce}$. We set $T = 5$ for the number of iteration, as 5 was enough to indicate uncertain regions. We investigate the effect of some attack hyperparameters in Sect. 4.3.

We compare our unstability map with other post-training uncertainty estimation methods. For predictive entropy, we take the entropy of the confidences on each pixel, following [8]. For MC dropout [7], we insert a dropout layer before the last convolution layer of U-net with $p = 0.5$, and take multiple inferences with 5 different seeds to aggregate them, with the entropy of the mean of multiple predictions, following [6].

Table 1. Dice scores and False Rates (FR), True Rates (TR) of top 1% and 2% uncertainty on U-net.

Dataset	Method	DSC	Top 1%				Top 2%			
			FNR	FPR	TNR	TPR	FNR	FPR	TNR	TPR
FGADR	MC	0.7079	0.5653	0.4884	0.0076	0.0118	0.6628	0.5904	0.0166	0.0225
	AE		0.4935	0.5484	0.0050	0.0270	0.6048	0.6786	0.0112	0.0534
Kvasir-SEG	MC	0.8390	0.4262	0.2559	0.0098	0.0031	0.5664	0.4067	0.0203	0.0077
	AE		0.2170	0.2168	0.0079	0.0077	0.3465	0.3454	0.0162	0.0157
LIDC-IDRI	MC	0.7509	0.8239	0.7323	0.0117	0.0046	0.9100	0.8422	0.0259	0.0090
	AE		0.8410	0.8186	0.0088	0.0069	0.9195	0.8892	0.0222	0.0122

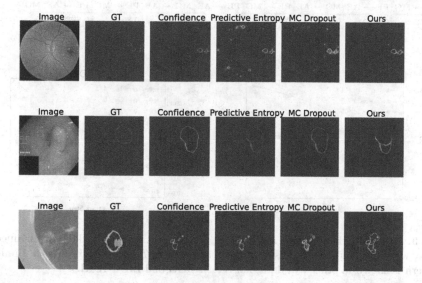

Fig. 2. visualization of uncertainty map from three datasets. Colormap is the same as Fig. 1 except for the ground-truth (GT) from LIDC-IDRI. Our method from adversarial examples show reasonable and a little explorative false region identification.

4.3 Experimental Results

Quantitative Analysis. For quantitative analysis, the number rates of false and true pixels included in high uncertainty area are measured in Table 1. The popular MC dropout [7] (MC) and our method with adversarial examples (AE) are compared on test sets with given Dice score coefficient (DSC) between the ground-truth and prediction. Here, the rates: false positive rate (FPR), false negative rate (FNR), true positive rate (TPR), true negative rate(TNR) are measured by the number of FP/FN/TP/TN pixels in high uncertainty region. The true rate (TR) and false rate (FR) are defined by the sum of TPR, TNR, and FPR, FNR, respectively. For fair comparison, the high uncertainty area is defined by top 1% and 2% uncertain pixels among uncertainty values across all pixels on each image.

As shown in Table 1, our unstability maps of AEs reveal competitive number of false cases compared to widely-used MC dropout method, while requiring only one more inference from trained model plus short T attack iterations. In this regard, adversarial examples can be helpful for quick indication of uncertain area, which could be easily hidden by biased confidence in medical segmentation.

Table 2. Pearson correlations between each uncertainty method.

FGADR			Kvasir-SEG			LIDC-IDRI		
PE ↔ MC	PE ↔ AE	MC ↔ AE	PE ↔ MC	PE ↔ AE	MC ↔ AE	PE ↔ MC	PE ↔ AE	MC ↔ AE
0.6025	0.4231	0.7585	0.9189	0.5500	0.5715	0.8942	0.8512	0.7865

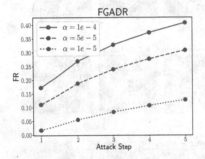 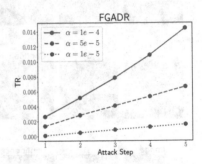

Fig. 3. Pixel and channel-wise False Rates (FR) and True Rates (TR) of our uncertainty with adversarial examples in terms of attack step T for FGADR dataset. Similar pattern is shown in other two datasets: Kvasir-SEG and LIDC-IDRI.

The same experiment is additionally done on DeepLabV3+ [4] architecture, showing similar results with U-net as included in Table 1 from our supplementary material. We also tried larger number of seeds for MC dropout such as $N = 32$, resulting in about 2% increase in FPR or FNR.

In addition, to observe the explorative property of unstability map derived from adversarial examples, we measured linear correlations between each uncertainty estimation method: predictive entropy (PE), MC dropout (MC), and our method (AE). Table 2 shows Pearson correlations of three possible pairs. The correlation values on Kvasir-SEG and LIDC-IDRI shows that adversarial examples have capability to reveal more explorative regions, while keeping competitive TNR and TPR compared to MC dropout as measured in Table 1. The results from FGADR shows the highest correlation on MC and AE, and we hypothesize that this is because the prediction region from FGADR is sparsely distributed, affecting to the exceptional results.

Qualitative Visualizations. For qualitative study, Fig. 2 visualizes the unstability map from U-net with other post-training uncertainty estimation methods. Multiple annotations from LIDC-IDRI are drawn in different colors, and only one class is visualized from FGADR. The perturbed output maps marks uncertain area that were originally categorized as false pixels in their ground-truth. Furthermore, we qualitatively observed that the outputs from AEs tend to highlight in more explorative way, compared to previous methods that indicated the boundary of original predictions, as quantitatively analyzed in Sect. 4.3.

Effect of Attack Hyperparameters. We investigate the effect of attack hyperparameters on finding false regions, such as number of step T and step size α. Figure 3 shows false rate (FR) and true rate (TR) in terms of T derived from U-net, each plot for different value of α. Increasing T or α results in higher FR in a trade-off with increasing TR, supporting the importance of the choice of appropriate T and α for further possible utilization. Experiments on other datasets showed similar tendency, as shown in Fig. 1 from our supplementary material.

References

1. Alarab, I., Prakoonwit, S.: Adversarial attack for uncertainty estimation: identifying critical regions in neural networks. Neural Process. Lett. **54**(3), 1805–1821 (2022)
2. Armato, S.G., III., et al.: The lung image database consortium (LIDC) and image database resource initiative (IDRI): a completed reference database of lung nodules on CT scans. Med. Phys. **38**(2), 915–931 (2011)
3. Bakas, S., et al.: Advancing the cancer genome atlas glioma MRI collections with expert segmentation labels and radiomic features. Sci. Data **4**(1), 1–13 (2017)
4. Chen, L.C., Zhu, Y., Papandreou, G., Schroff, F., Adam, H.: Encoder-decoder with atrous separable convolution for semantic image segmentation. In: Proceedings of the European Conference on Computer Vision (ECCV), pp. 801–818 (2018)
5. Clark, K., et al.: The cancer imaging archive (TCIA): maintaining and operating a public information repository. J. Digit. Imaging **26**(6), 1045–1057 (2013). https://doi.org/10.1007/s10278-013-9622-7
6. Czolbe, S., Arnavaz, K., Krause, O., Feragen, A.: Is segmentation uncertainty useful? In: Feragen, A., Sommer, S., Schnabel, J., Nielsen, M. (eds.) IPMI 2021. LNCS, vol. 12729, pp. 715–726. Springer, Cham (2021). https://doi.org/10.1007/978-3-030-78191-0_55
7. Gal, Y., Ghahramani, Z.: Dropout as a Bayesian approximation: representing model uncertainty in deep learning. In: International Conference on Machine Learning, pp. 1050–1059. PMLR (2016)
8. Gal, Y., Islam, R., Ghahramani, Z.: Deep Bayesian active learning with image data. In: International Conference on Machine Learning, pp. 1183–1192. PMLR (2017)
9. Galil, I., El-Yaniv, R.: Disrupting deep uncertainty estimation without harming accuracy. In: Advances in Neural Information Processing Systems, vol. 34, pp. 21285–21296 (2021)

10. Goodfellow, I.J., Shlens, J., Szegedy, C.: Explaining and harnessing adversarial examples. arXiv preprint arXiv:1412.6572 (2014)
11. Guo, C., Pleiss, G., Sun, Y., Weinberger, K.Q.: On calibration of modern neural networks. In: International Conference on Machine Learning, pp. 1321–1330. PMLR (2017)
12. He, K., Zhang, X., Ren, S., Sun, J.: Deep residual learning for image recognition. In: Proceedings of the IEEE Conference on Computer Vision and Pattern Recognition, pp. 770–778 (2016)
13. Jha, D., et al.: Kvasir-SEG: a segmented polyp dataset. In: Ro, Y.M., et al. (eds.) MMM 2020. LNCS, vol. 11962, pp. 451–462. Springer, Cham (2020). https://doi.org/10.1007/978-3-030-37734-2_37
14. Kendall, A., Gal, Y.: What uncertainties do we need in Bayesian deep learning for computer vision? In: Advances in Neural Information Processing Systems, vol. 30 (2017)
15. Kingma, D.P., Ba, J.: Adam: a method for stochastic optimization. arXiv preprint arXiv:1412.6980 (2014)
16. Kohl, S., et al.: A probabilistic U-Net for segmentation of ambiguous images. In: Advances in Neural Information Processing Systems, vol. 31 (2018)
17. Lee, R.S., Gimenez, F., Hoogi, A., Miyake, K.K., Gorovoy, M., Rubin, D.L.: A curated mammography data set for use in computer-aided detection and diagnosis research. Sci. Data 4(1), 1–9 (2017)
18. Liew, S.L., et al.: A large, curated, open-source stroke neuroimaging dataset to improve lesion segmentation algorithms. medRxiv (2021)
19. Madry, A., Makelov, A., Schmidt, L., Tsipras, D., Vladu, A.: Towards deep learning models resistant to adversarial attacks. arXiv preprint arXiv:1706.06083 (2017)
20. Mehrtash, A., Wells, W.M., Tempany, C.M., Abolmaesumi, P., Kapur, T.: Confidence calibration and predictive uncertainty estimation for deep medical image segmentation. IEEE Trans. Med. Imaging 39(12), 3868–3878 (2020)
21. Menze, B.H., et al.: The multimodal brain tumor image segmentation benchmark (BRATS). IEEE Trans. Med. Imaging 34(10), 1993–2024 (2014)
22. Rister, B., Yi, D., Shivakumar, K., Nobashi, T., Rubin, D.L.: CT-ORG, a new dataset for multiple organ segmentation in computed tomography. Sci. Data 7(1), 1–9 (2020)
23. Ronneberger, O., Fischer, P., Brox, T.: U-Net: convolutional networks for biomedical image segmentation. In: Navab, N., Hornegger, J., Wells, W.M., Frangi, A.F. (eds.) MICCAI 2015. LNCS, vol. 9351, pp. 234–241. Springer, Cham (2015). https://doi.org/10.1007/978-3-319-24574-4_28
24. Szegedy, C., et al.: Intriguing properties of neural networks. arXiv preprint arXiv:1312.6199 (2013)
25. Tuna, O.F., Catak, F.O., Eskil, M.T.: Exploiting epistemic uncertainty of the deep learning models to generate adversarial samples. Multimedia Tools Appl. 81(8), 11479–11500 (2022)
26. Zhang, H., Yu, Y., Jiao, J., Xing, E., El Ghaoui, L., Jordan, M.: Theoretically principled trade-off between robustness and accuracy. In: International Conference on Machine Learning, pp. 7472–7482. PMLR (2019)
27. Zhang, J., et al.: Attacks which do not kill training make adversarial learning stronger. In: International Conference on Machine Learning, pp. 11278–11287. PMLR (2020)
28. Zhou, Y., Wang, B., Huang, L., Cui, S., Shao, L.: A benchmark for studying diabetic retinopathy: segmentation, grading, and transferability. IEEE Trans. Med. Imaging 40(3), 818–828 (2020)

Uncertainty Calibration

Improved Post-hoc Probability Calibration for Out-of-Domain MRI Segmentation

Cheng Ouyang[1]([✉])[iD], Shuo Wang[2][iD], Chen Chen[1][iD], Zeju Li[1][iD], Wenjia Bai[1,3,4][iD], Bernhard Kainz[1,5][iD], and Daniel Rueckert[1,6][iD]

[1] BioMedIA Group, Department of Computing, Imperial College London, London, UK
c.ouyang@imperial.ac.uk
[2] School of Basic Medical Sciences, Fudan University, Shanghai, China
[3] Department of Brain Sciences, Imperial College London, London, UK
[4] Data Science Institute, Imperial College London, London, UK
[5] Friedrich-Alexander-Universität Erlangen-Nürnberg, Erlangen, Germany
[6] Klinikum rechts der Isar, Technical University of Munich, Munich, Germany

Abstract. Probability calibration for deep models is highly desirable in safety-critical applications such as medical imaging. It makes output probabilities of deep networks interpretable, by aligning prediction probability with the actual accuracy in test data. In image segmentation, well-calibrated probabilities allow radiologists to identify regions where model-predicted segmentations are unreliable. These unreliable predictions often occur to out-of-domain (OOD) images that are caused by imaging artifacts or unseen imaging protocols. Unfortunately, most previous calibration methods for image segmentation perform sub-optimally on OOD images. To reduce the calibration error when confronted with OOD images, we propose a novel post-hoc calibration model. Our model leverages the pixel susceptibility against perturbations at the local level, and the shape prior information at the global level. The model is tested on cardiac MRI segmentation datasets that contain unseen imaging artifacts and images from an unseen imaging protocol. We demonstrate reduced calibration errors compared with the state-of-the-art calibration algorithm.

1 Introduction

In safety-critical applications like medical imaging, segmentation models are required to produce accurate predictions on clean input data and are also expected to be *aware* of predictions for which the model has *low confidence*, when confronted with out-of-domain (OOD) data. In medical imaging, OOD data is often caused by imaging artifacts or changes in imaging protocols. The awareness of uncertainty allows to alert radiologists about potentially unreliable predictions. Unfortunately, deep models are found to be generally over-confident about predicted probabilities [1,2].

© The Author(s), under exclusive license to Springer Nature Switzerland AG 2022
C. H. Sudre et al. (Eds.): UNSURE 2022, LNCS 13563, pp. 59–69, 2022.
https://doi.org/10.1007/978-3-031-16749-2_6

Probability calibration corrects over- or under-confident predictions, and makes prediction probability *interpretable*, by aligning it with the accuracy on the test dataset. For example, if a segmentation model yields a *confidence* (the probability of the highest-scored class) of 70% for each pixel in a test image, we say the model to be well-calibrated if 70% of the pixels are correctly predicted [3].

Unfortunately, most existing probability calibration methods cannot be directly applied to medical image segmentation due to the following reasons: First, the majority of existing methods are designed for image classification, which yield a single class probability per image [4–8]. Secondly, most previous methods assume training and testing images are from a same domain. However, we argue that it is the OOD image for which probability calibration is most desirable, while most calibration methods are shown to perform sub-optimally on OOD images [9]. Therefore, in this study we particularly focus on improving calibration for OOD medical images.

In this work, we propose a new learning-based probability calibration model for medical image segmentation on out-of-domain (OOD) data. Particularly, we focus on the most flexible calibration setting: *post-hoc* calibration that can be applied to various frozen feed-forward networks. Specifically, our calibration model outputs a *temperature map* that re-adjusts the prediction probability of the segmentation network [3,6], correcting over- or under-confident probabilities. Unlike the state-of-the-art method [3] that only considers the pixel values of input images and their logits, our model finds unreliable predictions by considering how susceptible the prediction of each pixel is, against small perturbations. Such susceptibility helps to reveal the uncertainty caused by the real-world perturbations that originate from imperfect acquisition process (device noise, patient movement *etc.*) or changes in imaging condition (machine vendors, imaging protocols *etc.*). The proposed model further takes advantage of global prior information about the shapes of segmentation targets. These local-level and global-level sources of information strengthens the calibration performance for OOD images. Our contributions can be summarized as follows:

- We systematically investigate post-hoc probability calibration for the safety-critical medical image segmentation on out-of-domain (OOD) images.
- We propose a new learning-based probability calibration model that incorporates the susceptibility information of pixel-level predictions against perturbations at the local level, and the shape prior information at the global level. The proposed method demonstrates improved performance on OOD testing images compared to the state-of-the-art method.
- We build a comprehensive testing environment for post-hoc calibration, on segmentation for out-of-domain MRI. It incorporates common imaging artifacts: motion artifacts, bias fields, ghosting artifacts, spikes in k-space, and an unseen imaging protocol: late gadolinium enhancement (LGE) sequence for MRI.

2   Related Work

Probability Calibration for Image Segmentation: Most probability calibration methods can be categorized into three types: 1) training strategies that intrinsically improve calibration for the task network (classification, regression, *etc.*). These techniques include focal loss [10], multi-task learning [11], adversarial training [12]; 2) Bayesian methods that carefully model the uncertainties of model parameters, input data and/or labeling process [13–17]; 3) post-hoc methods that post-process the softmax output (probability) of an already-trained task network [3–6]. Our work follows the post-hoc framework due to its superior flexibility: being applicable to most of already-trained task networks.

More recently, several papers have discussed calibration for image segmentation: [16] evaluates the effects of segmentation losses, model ensembling and MC-dropout on calibration. [11] demonstrates that multi-task learning improves calibration. However, neither works contribute further to post-hoc calibration. Our idea of using data augmentation to estimate susceptibility of pixel-level predictions, which can be interpreted as aleatoric uncertainty estimation, is inspired by [15]. However, [15] does not investigate post-hoc calibration itself. Our method is built on the state-of-the-art local temperature scaling (LTS) [3]. To reduce the calibration error on OOD images, we extend LTS by incorporating pixel-level susceptibility and global-level shape prior information.

Segmenting Out-of-Domain Medical Images: A robust image segmentation model can usually be obtained by applying input-level or feature-level data augmentations [18–20], or by enforcing shape priors [21–23]. Unlike these works, our method focuses on the under-explored problem of promoting interpretability of prediction probabilities, especially for those on out-of-domain images.

Segmentation Quality Assessment: Segmentation quality assessment [24–26] predicts a global model performance score, and/or makes corrections to the predicted segmentation labels. Probability calibration is more challenging, as it is required to make continuous, pixel-wise adjustments to prediction probabilities.

3   Method

Model-based Post-hoc Calibration: We aim to align the prediction probability with the accuracy on the test dataset. To this end, in model-based post-hoc calibration, we build a separate calibration model $g_\phi(\cdot)$ for a pre-trained task model (in our case segmentation) $f_\theta(\cdot)$. To train the calibration model, the validation dataset for the task model is re-used for building $g_\phi(\cdot)$. We let $\mathbf{x}_i \in \mathbb{R}^{1 \times M \times N}$ be the image, $\mathbf{y}_i \in \mathbb{R}^{C \times M \times N}$ the ground truth segmentation in the form of one-hot encoding, where (M, N) is the spatial size and C the number of classes. Note, it is usually desirable that the calibration process does not affect the categorical prediction $\hat{\mathbf{y}}_i$ for segmentation (therefore does not change the accuracy of $f_\theta(\cdot)$).

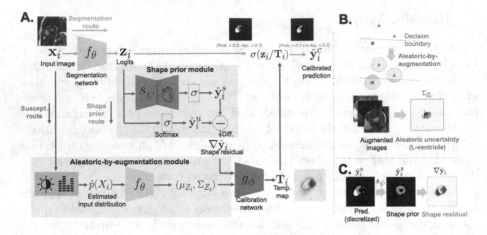

Fig. 1. A. Workflow of the proposed calibration technique: A temperate map $\mathbf{T}_i$ is used to adjust probabilities of a segmentation network. To do this, the image $\mathbf{x}_i$ is sent through a segmentation network $f_\theta(\cdot)$ to obtain the logits $\mathbf{z}_i$. Meanwhile, to obtain $\mathbf{T}_i$, $\mathbf{x}_i$ is sent through two calibration routes: In the susceptibility route, the estimated distribution $\hat{p}(X_i)$ of $\mathbf{x}_i$ is obtained by repeated data augmentations. The uncertainty $(\mu_{Z_i}, \Sigma_{Z_i})$ is computed by sending samples of $\hat{p}(X_i)$ to $f_\theta(\cdot)$. In the shape prior route, $\mathbf{z}_i$ is sent to the shape prior network $s_\psi(\cdot)$ to obtain a shape residual $\nabla\hat{\mathbf{y}}_i$ which high-lights the regions where the prediction differs from the prior knowledge about plausible shapes of segmentation targets. The calibration network $g_\phi(\cdot)$ takes $(\mu_{Z_i}, \Sigma_{Z_i})$ and $\nabla\hat{\mathbf{y}}_i$ as inputs and estimates $\mathbf{T}_i$ for rescaling logits $\mathbf{z}_i$ of the segmentation. **B. Aleatoric uncertainty** reflects the susceptibility (shaded regions trespassing the decision bound-ary) of a prediction under small perturbations. **C. Shape prior and shape residual**, highlighting potentially unreliable predictions. (Color figure online)

Temperature Scaling: Temperature scaling [3,27] is one of the most simple and effective frameworks for probability calibration. It produces a temperature factor (or map) $\mathbf{T}_i > 0$ to weigh over-confident predictions down while boost under-confident ones. Formally, let $\mathbf{z}_i = f_\theta(\mathbf{x}_i)$, $\mathbf{z}_i \in \mathbb{R}^{C \times M \times N}$ be the output logits, let $\sigma(\cdot)$ denote the softmax function along the channel dimension, we nat-urally have the uncalibrated probability $\hat{\mathbf{y}}_i^u = \sigma(\mathbf{z}_i)$. While with the temperature map $\mathbf{T}_i \in \mathbb{R}^{C \times M \times N}$, the calibrated probability $\hat{\mathbf{y}}_i^c$ can be obtained by re-scaling the logits using $\mathbf{T}_i$, *i.e.* $\hat{\mathbf{y}}_i^c = \sigma(\mathbf{z}_i/\mathbf{T}_i)$.[1]

Method Overview: We aim to obtain a temperature-scaling-based calibration network $g_\phi(\cdot)$ that is suitable for out-of-domain (OOD) testing images. Examples of these OOD images are assumed to be *unseen* by the segmentation network $f_\theta(\cdot)$ and the calibration network $g_\phi(\cdot)$ during their training processes. To this

---

[1] To ensure that the calibration does not affect the accuracy of the task network, for each spatial location (m, n) in $\mathbf{T}_i$, it is usually assumed that $\mathbf{T}_i(c_j, m, n) = \mathbf{T}_i(c_k, m, n)$, $\forall (c_j, c_k) \in \{1, 2, 3, ..., C\}$, *i.e.*, temperature values remain the same for different channels/classes [3,6].

end we propose to 1) provide the susceptibility of the prediction of each pixel against small perturbations caused by potential image corruption/artifact or a change in imaging protocol. This susceptibility reflects how likely the prediction of a pixel might be altered when real image artifacts or changes in imaging protocols are present. This is also known as *aleatoric uncertainty*[2] [14,15]. 2) We also provide the calibration network with prior information about the shape of the target segmentation. This shape prior is encoded by a denoising autoencoder $s_\psi(\cdot)$ and it provides a second opinion about the correctness of the prediction.

As shown in Fig. 1-A, to obtain the temperature map $\mathbf{T}_i$, the input $\mathbf{x}_i$ is fed to two modules: The *Aleatoric-by-augmentation* module (colored in purple) estimates the pixel-level susceptibility (aleatoric uncertainty) by repeated data augmentations. The *shape prior module* (colored in green) compares the uncalibrated prediction with the shape prior encoded in the denoising autoencoder $s_\psi(\cdot)$, and provides the calibration network $g_\phi(\cdot)$ with the residual between the uncalibrated prediction and the prior. The calibration network $g_\phi(\cdot)$ takes the outputs of the two modules, and estimates a temperature map for adjusting $\mathbf{z}_i$. Finally, the calibrated prediction is made by passing $\mathbf{z}_i/\mathbf{T}_i$ to a softmax layer.

Aleatoric Uncertainty by Augmentation: The aleatoric-by-augmentation module provides the calibration network $g_\phi(\cdot)$ with information about susceptibility of predictions for each pixel against small perturbations. Intuitively, if the prediction can be easily flipped by a small perturbation, the prediction of that pixel could be unreliable. In medical images, OOD images can also be viewed as being generated by perturbing intra-domain images [23].

To formally model this susceptibility, we resort to the concept of *aleatoric uncertainty* [13–15]. As shown in Fig. 1-B, it models images to have a distribution $p(X_i)$ arising from the acquisition process, rather than treating each image as a single data point (which is instead assumed by the state-of-the-art LTS [3]). This modeled distribution can be written as $p(X_i) = \int p(X_i|a)p(a)da$, where $p(X_i|a)$ represents the image acquisition process and $a \sim p(A)$ denotes the "randomness" within different possible acquisition processes [15]. Then, the susceptibility (uncertainty) can be estimated by propagating $p(X_i)$ through the segmentation model $f_\theta(\cdot)$.

In practice, inspired by [15,20], we employ data augmentation to obtain the estimation $\hat{p}(X_i)$ of the real $p(X_i)$. Specifically, for each image $\mathbf{x}_i$, we perform repeated augmentations to obtain $\{\mathbf{x}'_{i,l}|\mathbf{x}'_{i,l} = \mathcal{T}_{a'_l}(\mathbf{x}_i),\ a'_l \sim p(A')\}$, where $l = 1, 2, 3, ..., N_A$ is the index of augmented samples and $\mathcal{T}_{a'_l}(\cdot)$'s are photometric augmentations parameterized by a'_l's. To ensure fairness, $\mathcal{T}_{a'_l}(\cdot)$'s are configured to be the *same types of* photometric augmentations used for training $f_\theta(\cdot)$ and they *do not* incorporate the corruptions (artifacts) in the testing data. Then, the propagated uncertainty in the logits, in the form of mean μ_{Z_i} and variance Σ_{Z_i}, can be computed by sending $\{\mathbf{x}'_{i,l}\}$ to the segmentation network $f_\theta(\cdot)$. For simplicity, when computing Σ_{Z_i}, each pixel is assumed to be independent.

---

[2] We do not explicitly highlight it as aleatoric uncertainty, since we do not have the ground truth to evaluate the accuracy of this estimation of aleatoric uncertainty.

Shape Prior: To provide a second opinion about the correctness of the segmentation, shape priors [21,24,28] are used. For probability calibration, if the predicted shape deviates largely from the prior information about plausible shapes, the prediction is likely to be unreliable.

Here, we employ a denoising autoencoder as the shape prior model. It memorizes correct shapes of segmentation targets in the validation dataset. As shown in the green block in Fig. 1-A, the autoencoder $s_\psi(\cdot)$ takes the uncalibrated logits $\mathbf{z}_i$ as the input and produces a denoised plausible shape $\hat{\mathbf{y}}_i^s$ of the segmentation target, in the form of probabilities. To highlight regions where the uncalibrated prediction $\hat{\mathbf{y}}_i^u = \sigma(\mathbf{z}_i)$ deviates from the plausible shape $\hat{\mathbf{y}}_i^s$, we send the shape residual $\nabla\hat{\mathbf{y}}_i = \hat{\mathbf{y}}_i^s - \hat{\mathbf{y}}_i^u$ to the calibration network. An example of a shape residual is shown in Fig. 1-C. In practice, to avoid learning an identity mapping, we apply heavy dropout to the encoder part of $s_\psi(\cdot)$ during training.

Unlike the shape priors in [21,23], which directly correct the prediction, we do not expect $s_\psi(\cdot)$ to provide highly accurate segmentations: As shown in Fig. 1-C, the right ventricle has been correctly predicted by $f_\theta(\cdot)$ while $s_\psi(\cdot)$ (erroneously) disagrees. Instead, we only expect the shape prior module to highlight potentially implausible regions. We leave the calibration network to make the final decision.

Calibration Network: The calibration network $g_\phi(\cdot)$ produces a temperature map $\mathbf{T}_i$ that is specific to $\mathbf{x}_i$, by considering the pixel-level susceptibility (uncertainty) $(\mu_{Z_i}, \Sigma_{Z_i})$ and the shape residual $\nabla\hat{\mathbf{y}}_i$. Following the baseline LTS [3], we also send the image $\mathbf{x}_i$ and the uncalibrated logits $\mathbf{z}_i$ to $g_\phi(\cdot)$. After $\mathbf{T}_i$ is computed, the calibrated prediction $\hat{\mathbf{y}}_i^c$ is given by $\hat{\mathbf{y}}_i^c = \sigma(\mathbf{z}_i/\mathbf{T}_i)$, where $\mathbf{T}_i = g_\phi(\mu_{Z_i}, \Sigma_{Z_i}, \nabla\hat{\mathbf{y}}_i, \mathbf{z}_i, \mathbf{x}_i)$, and $\sigma(\cdot)$ denotes the softmax layer.

In practice, we configure $g_\phi(\cdot)$ as a shallow residual network, which we empirically found to yield comparable results to the decision-tree-inspired network in the vanilla LTS [3], but to be more flexible in terms of model architecture. A channel attention layer is used in $g_\phi(\cdot)$ to allow the network to adaptively weigh information from different sources.

Training Objectives: Following the standard setting of post-hoc calibration, both the calibration network $g_\phi(\cdot)$ and the shape prior module $s_\psi(\cdot)$ are trained on the validation dataset used in building the segmentation network $f_\theta(\cdot)$. To avoid shortcut learning from $s_\psi(\cdot)$ to $g_\phi(\cdot)$, two networks are trained one by one. We first train the shape prior module using the cross entropy loss:

$$\mathcal{L}_s(\psi) = -\frac{1}{MN}\sum_{m,n}\sum_c \mathbf{y}_i(c,m,n)\log\left(\sigma(s_\psi(\mathbf{z}_i(c,m,n)))\right), \qquad (1)$$

where $\mathbf{z}_i = f_\theta(\mathbf{x}_i)$, $(\mathbf{x}_i, \mathbf{y}_i) \in \mathcal{D}_{val}$ the validation set, the subscript c denotes the class index. After $s_\psi(\cdot)$ is trained, we close the gradient computation for $s_\psi(\cdot)$. We then train the calibration network $g_\phi(\cdot)$ using the negative log likelihood loss that is commonly used for training post-hoc calibration networks [3,6,27]:

$$\mathcal{L}_g(\phi) = -\frac{1}{MN}\sum_{m,n}\sum_c \mathbf{y}_i(c,m,n)\log\left(\sigma(\mathbf{z}_i(c,m,n)/\mathbf{T}_i(c,m,n))\right), \qquad (2)$$

Table 1. Quantitative results on expected calibration error (ECE) and static calibration error (SCE). Lower the better. Average Dice scores of the segmentation networks are appended for reference.

Method	ECE [%] ↓							SCE [%] ↓						
	Intra-dom.	Bias field	Motion	Ghosting	Spike	Artifact Avg.	Cross Seq.	Intra-dom.	Bias field	Motion	Ghosting	Spike	Artifact Avg.	Cross Seq.
UC	10.29	13.60	22.38	19.68	39.05	23.67	30.29	5.27	6.96	11.45	10.09	19.82	12.08	15.58
Alea. [14,15]	7.74	9.06	16.47	16.78	37.31	19.90	28.50	5.08	8.39	10.11	10.56	21.15	12.55	16.89
TS [6]	10.06	13.31	22.04	19.42	38.87	23.41	29.96	5.17	6.84	11.31	9.99	19.76	11.98	15.47
LTS [3]	3.22	5.46	10.21	10.61	31.60	14.48	16.78	3.63	4.91	7.93	7.80	17.80	9.61	11.52
Proposed	3.12	4.65*	8.88‡	9.23*	28.35†	12.78	15.37†	3.38	4.75*	7.23†	7.14‡	16.45‡	8.89	10.77†
	(−0.10)	(−0.82)	(−1.33)	(−1.38)	(−3.26)	(−1.70)	(−1.41)	(−0.25)	(−0.16)	(−0.70)	(−0.67)	(−1.35)	(−0.72)	(−0.75)

†: p-value < 0.01; ‡: p-value < 0.05; *: p-value > 0.05, compared with the results of LTS [3].

	Dice score [%] ↑						
	Intra-dom	Bias field	Motion	Ghosting	Spike	Artifact Avg.	Cross Seq.
Seg. Net.	85.14	80.29	69.02	79.73	39.02	67.02	62.74

where $\mathbf{T}_i = g_\phi(\mu_{Z_i}, \Sigma_{Z_i}, \nabla\hat{\mathbf{y}}_i, \mathbf{z}_i, \mathbf{x}_i)$, $(\mu_{Z_i}, \Sigma_{Z_i})$'s are obtained by sending multiple augmented versions of $\mathbf{x}_i$ to $f_\theta(\cdot)$. This loss penalizes over-confident erroneous predictions while it encourages high confidence for correct predictions. Although Eq. 2 has similar form as cross-entropy, it essentially optimizes over ϕ via $\mathbf{T}_i$. Since at each location (m, n), $\mathbf{T}_i(c, m, n)$'s remain constant for all the classes c's, this loss does not affect the categorical segmentation result [3,6].

4   Evaluation and Results

Table 2. Ablating key components and the number of test-time augmentations, evaluated on artifact-corrupted images.

Alea.	Shape	ECE [%] ↓	SCE [%] ↓	No. of Aug.	ECE [%] ↓	SCE [%] ↓
×	×	14.48	9.61	15	13.22	9.00
✓	×	13.03	9.20	45	12.94	8.94
×	✓	13.50	9.18	90	12.85	8.92
✓	✓	12.78	8.89	180	12.78	8.89

Dataset: *Training and validation dataset*: We employ the ACDC cardiac MRI segmentation dataset (bSSFP sequence) [29] for building the segmentation model and the proposed calibration model. Specifically, we take the ES fold of ACDC and split it into training, validation and (intra-domain) testing sets of 60/20/20 cases. To simulate data-hungry medical image segmentation [23], each time we take 20 cases out of the training data for building the segmentation network, and 5 out of validation data for validating the segmentation network and for training the calibration model. We repeat this process for 3 times to cover all the training samples, and obtain 3 segmentation models. For each segmentation model, we repeat training the calibration model for 3 times.

66   C. Ouyang et al.

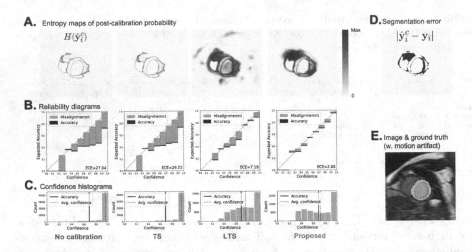

Fig. 2. A. For the proposed method, the entropy map which shows the doubt of the calibration model, agrees well with the actual segmentation error (shown in **D.**). **B.** Reliability map of the proposed method demonstrates the least misalignment (purple bars) between confidence and accuracy. **C.** The confidence histogram shows that the proposed method has corrected over-confident predictions, compared with uncalibrated results. **E.** The motion-corrupted input image and its ground truth segmentation. (Color figure online)

Artifact-Corrupted Testing Dataset: Inspired by [23], we simulate common MRI artifacts: bias field, motion artifact, ghosting artifact and k-space spikes, separately, to the 20 intra-domain testing cases mentioned above, using TorchIO [30]. Using this controlled environment allows us to observe the model behaviors under each type of artifacts.

Cross-Sequence Testing Dataset: We further test the above ACDC-based models on the 40 LGE MRI of the testing fold of the MS-CMRSeg challenge [31]. As ACDC is based on bSSFP sequence, the segmentation and calibration models have never seen images from LGE sequence before testing.

Network Architecture and Training Configurations: We employ a U-Net [32] as the segmentation network. For the calibration network $g_\phi(\cdot)$, we employ a shallow ResNet with 5 input branches for processing $\nabla \hat{y}_i$, μ_{Z_i}, Σ_{Z_i}, z_i, and x_i separately. These branches are merged by a channel attention block, followed by two ResNet blocks. The shape prior model $s_\psi(\cdot)$ is configured as a small U-Net with dropout ($p = 0.5$) in its encoder. The Adam optimizer is used, with an initial learning rate of 1×10^{-3}, 800 epochs separately for $s_\psi(\cdot)$ and $g_\phi(\cdot)$. In each iteration, $(\mu_{Z_i}, \Sigma_{Z_i})$ are computed by repeating augmentations for 6 times.

Photometric transforms: brightness, contrast, gamma transform, random additive noises [23], and geometric transformations: affine transformation and elastic transformation are used as data augmentations for training the segmentation model and the calibration model (also for the LTS [3]). Importantly, these data augmentations *do not* include the corruptions in the testing data.

Quantitative and Qualitative Results: We employ commonly-used expected calibration error (ECE) [33] and static calibration error (SCE) [27] for evaluation (lower the better). Both of them measure the gap between the prediction probability and the accuracy in test time, and the latter is a class-conditional version of the former. To account for the foreground-background class imbalance in ACDC, inspired by [16], these two metrics are computed over the region-of-interests obtained by dilating (expanding) the ground truth segmentations with a kernel size of 10 pixels.

As shown in Table 1, we compare the proposed method with the uncalibrated model (UC) and the state-of-the-art local temperature scaling (LTS) [3]. The proposed method demonstrates overall smaller calibration errors compared with LTS. Calibration errors of the estimated aleatoric uncertainty (Alea.) [14,15] and temperature scaling (TS) [6] are also presented. The segmentation performances measured in Dice scores of the segmentation networks are also attached.

We show in the first row of Fig. 2 the entropy maps $H(\hat{y}_i^c)$'s of the calibrated probabilities, where higher values suggest stronger doubts by the calibration network. The entropy map produced by the proposed method has the best agreement with the actual segmentation error. We further show the reliability map in the second row, where the purple bars represent the gaps between confidence (x-axis) and accuracy (y-axis) at each confidence level. The proposed method also yields the smallest gaps. Confidence histograms of post-calibration probabilities are shown in the third row.

Ablation Studies: We ablate the two key components of the proposed method: the susceptibility (aleatoric uncertainty) estimation and the shape prior. The results in Table 2 left show that the best performances are obtained when two components work together. We also ablate the number of repeated augmentations N_A used for estimating susceptibility during *test time*. As shown in Table 2 right, a larger N_A leads to more precise estimations, yielding less errors.

5   Conclusion

In this work we propose a new calibration method for out-of-domain MRI segmentation. Future works can be done by designing better shape prior models that can account for segmentation targets with more irregular shapes, like blood vessels and tumors.

Acknowledgments. This work was in part supported by EPSRC Programme Grants (EP/P001009/1, EP/W01842X/1) and in part by the UKRI London Medical Imaging and Artificial Intelligence Centre for Value Based Healthcare (No. 104691). S.W. was also supported by the Shanghai Sailing Programs of Shanghai Municipal Science and Technology Committee (22YF1409300).

References

1. Nguyen, A., Yosinski, J., Clune, J.: Deep neural networks are easily fooled: high confidence predictions for unrecognizable images. In: Proceedings of the IEEE CVPR, pp. 427–436 (2015)
2. Gonzalez, C., Gotkowski, K., Bucher, A., Fischbach, R., Kaltenborn, I., Mukhopadhyay, A.: Detecting when pre-trained nnU-Net models fail silently for Covid-19 lung lesion segmentation. In: de Bruijne, M., et al. (eds.) MICCAI 2021. LNCS, vol. 12907, pp. 304–314. Springer, Cham (2021). https://doi.org/10.1007/978-3-030-87234-2_29
3. Ding, Z., Han, X., Liu, P., Niethammer, M.: Local temperature scaling for probability calibration. In: Proceedings of the IEEE/CVF ICCV, pp. 6889–6899 (2021)
4. Platt, J., et al.: Probabilistic outputs for support vector machines and comparisons to regularized likelihood methods. In: Advances in Large Margin Classifiers, vol. 10, no. 3, pp. 61–74 (1999)
5. Zadrozny, B., Elkan, C.: Obtaining calibrated probability estimates from decision trees and naive Bayesian classifiers. In: ICML, vol. 1, pp. 609–616. Citeseer (2001)
6. Guo, C., Pleiss, G., Sun, Y., Weinberger, K.Q.: On calibration of modern neural networks. In: ICML, pp. 1321–1330. PMLR (2017)
7. Tomani, C., Buettner, F.: Towards trustworthy predictions from deep neural networks with fast adversarial calibration. In: Proceedings of the AAAI Conference, vol. 35, pp. 9886–9896 (2021)
8. Ji, B., Jung, H., Yoon, J., Kim, K., et al.: Bin-wise temperature scaling (BTS): improvement in confidence calibration performance through simple scaling techniques. In: IEEE/CVF ICCV Workshop, pp. 4190–4196. IEEE (2019)
9. Ovadia, Y., et al.: Can you trust your model's uncertainty? Evaluating predictive uncertainty under dataset shift. In: Advances in NeurIPS, vol. 32 (2019)
10. Mukhoti, J., Kulharia, V., Sanyal, A., Golodetz, S., Torr, P., Dokania, P.: Calibrating deep neural networks using focal loss. In: Advances in NeurIPS, vol. 33, pp. 15288–15299 (2020)
11. Karimi, D., Gholipour, A.: Improving calibration and out-of-distribution detection in deep models for medical image segmentation. IEEE Trans. Artif. Intell., 1 (2022, early access). https://ieeexplore.ieee.org/document/9735278
12. Kireev, K., Andriushchenko, M., Flammarion, N.: On the effectiveness of adversarial training against common corruptions. arXiv preprint arXiv:2103.02325 (2021)
13. Gal, Y., Ghahramani, Z.: Dropout as a Bayesian approximation: representing model uncertainty in deep learning. In: ICML, pp. 1050–1059. PMLR (2016)
14. Kendall, A., Gal, Y.: What uncertainties do we need in Bayesian deep learning for computer vision? In: Advances in NIPS, vol. 30 (2017)
15. Wang, G., Li, W., Aertsen, M., Deprest, J., Ourselin, S., Vercauteren, T.: Aleatoric uncertainty estimation with test-time augmentation for medical image segmentation with convolutional neural networks. Neurocomputing 338, 34–45 (2019)
16. Mehrtash, A., Wells, W.M., Tempany, C.M., Abolmaesumi, P., Kapur, T.: Confidence calibration and predictive uncertainty estimation for deep medical image segmentation. IEEE Trans. Med. Imaging 39(12), 3868–3878 (2020)
17. Baumgartner, C.F., et al.: PHiSeg: capturing uncertainty in medical image segmentation. In: Shen, D., et al. (eds.) MICCAI 2019. LNCS, vol. 11765, pp. 119–127. Springer, Cham (2019). https://doi.org/10.1007/978-3-030-32245-8_14
18. Zhang, L., et al.: Generalizing deep learning for medical image segmentation to unseen domains via deep stacked transformation. IEEE Trans. Med. Imaging 39(7), 2531–2540 (2020)

19. Chen, C., et al.: Realistic adversarial data augmentation for MR image segmentation. In: Martel, A.L., et al. (eds.) MICCAI 2020. LNCS, vol. 12261, pp. 667–677. Springer, Cham (2020). https://doi.org/10.1007/978-3-030-59710-8_65
20. Ouyang, C., et al.: Causality-inspired single-source domain generalization for medical image segmentation. arXiv preprint arXiv:2111.12525 (2021)
21. Larrazabal, A.J., Martínez, C., Glocker, B., Ferrante, E.: Post-DAE: anatomically plausible segmentation via post-processing with denoising autoencoders. IEEE Trans. Med. Imaging 39(12), 3813–3820 (2020)
22. Liu, Q., Chen, C., Dou, Q., Heng, P.A.: Single-domain generalization in medical image segmentation via test-time adaptation from shape dictionary (2022)
23. Chen, C., Hammernik, K., Ouyang, C., Qin, C., Bai, W., Rueckert, D.: Cooperative training and latent space data augmentation for robust medical image segmentation. In: de Bruijne, M., et al. (eds.) MICCAI 2021. LNCS, vol. 12903, pp. 149–159. Springer, Cham (2021). https://doi.org/10.1007/978-3-030-87199-4_14
24. Robinson, R., et al.: Automatic quality control of cardiac MRI segmentation in large-scale population imaging. In: Descoteaux, M., Maier-Hein, L., Franz, A., Jannin, P., Collins, D.L., Duchesne, S. (eds.) MICCAI 2017. LNCS, vol. 10433, pp. 720–727. Springer, Cham (2017). https://doi.org/10.1007/978-3-319-66182-7_82
25. Li, K., Yu, L., Heng, P.A.: Towards reliable cardiac image segmentation: assessing image-level and pixel-level segmentation quality via self-reflective references. Med. Image Anal. 78, 102426 (2022)
26. Wang, S., et al.: Deep generative model-based quality control for cardiac MRI segmentation. In: Martel, A.L., et al. (eds.) MICCAI 2020. LNCS, vol. 12264, pp. 88–97. Springer, Cham (2020). https://doi.org/10.1007/978-3-030-59719-1_9
27. Nixon, J., Dusenberry, M.W., Zhang, L., Jerfel, G., Tran, D.: Measuring calibration in deep learning. In: CVPR Workshops, vol. 2 (2019)
28. Raju, A., et al.: Deep implicit statistical shape models for 3D medical image delineation. arXiv (2021)
29. Bernard, O., et al.: Deep learning techniques for automatic MRI cardiac multi-structures segmentation and diagnosis: is the problem solved? IEEE Trans. Med. Imaging 37(11), 2514–2525 (2018)
30. Pérez-García, F., Sparks, R., Ourselin, S.: TorchIO: a python library for efficient loading, preprocessing, augmentation and patch-based sampling of medical images in deep learning. Comput. Methods Programs Biomed. 208, 106236 (2021)
31. Zhuang, X., et al.: Cardiac segmentation on late gadolinium enhancement MRI: a benchmark study from multi-sequence cardiac MR segmentation challenge. Med. Image Anal. 81, 102528 (2022)
32. Ronneberger, O., Fischer, P., Brox, T.: U-Net: convolutional networks for biomedical image segmentation. In: Navab, N., Hornegger, J., Wells, W.M., Frangi, A.F. (eds.) MICCAI 2015. LNCS, vol. 9351, pp. 234–241. Springer, Cham (2015). https://doi.org/10.1007/978-3-319-24574-4_28
33. Naeini, M.P., Cooper, G., Hauskrecht, M.: Obtaining well calibrated probabilities using Bayesian binning. In: Twenty-Ninth AAAI Conference (2015)

Improving Error Detection in Deep Learning Based Radiotherapy Autocontouring Using Bayesian Uncertainty

Prerak Mody[1]([✉]), Nicolas F. Chaves-de-Plaza[3], Klaus Hildebrandt[3], and Marius Staring[1,2]

[1] Department of Radiology, Leiden University Medical Centre, Leiden, The Netherlands
{P.P.Mody,M.Staring}@lumc.nl
[2] Department of Radiation Oncology, Leiden University Medical Centre, Leiden, The Netherlands
[3] Computer Graphics and Visualization Lab, TU Delft, Delft, The Netherlands

Abstract. Bayesian Neural Nets (BNN) are increasingly used for robust organ auto-contouring. Uncertainty heatmaps extracted from BNNs have been shown to correspond to inaccurate regions. To help speed up the mandatory quality assessment (QA) of contours in radiotherapy, these heatmaps could be used as stimuli to direct visual attention of clinicians to potential inaccuracies. In practice, this is non-trivial to achieve since many accurate regions also exhibit uncertainty. To influence the output uncertainty of a BNN, we propose a modified accuracy-versus-uncertainty (AvU) metric as an additional objective during model training that penalizes both accurate regions exhibiting uncertainty as well as inaccurate regions exhibiting certainty. For evaluation, we use an uncertainty-ROC curve that can help differentiate between Bayesian models by comparing the probability of uncertainty in inaccurate versus accurate regions. We train and evaluate a FlipOut BNN model on the MICCAI2015 Head and Neck Segmentation challenge dataset and on the DeepMind-TCIA dataset, and observed an increase in the AUC of uncertainty-ROC curves by 5.6% and 5.9%, respectively, when using the AvU objective. The AvU objective primarily reduced false positives regions (uncertain and accurate), drawing less visual attention to these regions, thereby potentially improving the speed of error detection.

Keywords: Radiotherapy · Quality assessment · Organs-at-Risk · Bayesian uncertainty · Deep learning · AvU loss · Uncertainty-ROC · FlipOut

---

Supplementary Information The online version contains supplementary material available at https://doi.org/10.1007/978-3-031-16749-2_7.

1   Introduction

Radiotherapy for cancer treatment requires one to acquire diagnostic scans like CT and contour the boundaries of tumors and organs-at-risk (OARs). This process is time-consuming, prone to human error as well as inter-and intra-annotator disagreement [5,27]. For head-and-neck CT scans, these issues are further exacerbated due to the large OAR count ($\sim$35) and a lack of soft-tissue contrast. Although deep learning has made great leaps in auto-contouring of tumors and OARs [26], the predicted contours still need to be manually verified before treatment. In this paper we investigate the use of Bayesian uncertainty heatmaps to help speed up this quality assessment (QA) by directing visual attention of clinicians to regions potentially containing contouring errors. Specifically, to enable faster error detection, we improve upon literature by incentivizing deep Bayesian models to produce uncertainty heatmaps only in inaccurate and not in accurate regions.

There exists a large body of work on uncertainty estimation for medical image segmentation. Some show that uncertainty heatmaps correspond to erroneous regions [23,24] indicating their potential to be used during autocontouring QA. Others investigate loss functions (c.f. Dice vs cross-entropy) [15,24], uncertainty metrics (e.g. entropy, standard deviation) [6,20,23] or the use of uncertainty for error detection [23], contour refinement [2,25] and training data sampling [12]. The aforementioned works design for epistemic (or model) uncertainty which represents the variation in outputs, given an input. Conversely, other works design for aleatoric (or data) uncertainty [4,11,18] for e.g. inter- and intra-annotator disagreement, a phenomenon common in medical image segmentation. To the extent of our knowledge, Bayesian approaches to medical image segmentation have only explored the direct use of uncertainty and have not attempted to influence its nature. Our approach instead trains Bayesian segmentation models to produce both accurate contours along with uncertainty present only in inaccurate regions. This can potentially speed up autocontouring QA by ensuring that clinicians are not distracted by the uncertainty in accurate regions.

To ensure that accurate regions are certain and inaccurate regions are uncertain, we are inspired by [13] and their use of the Accuracy-vs-Uncertainty (AvU) metric in image classification tasks. Specifically, the AvU metric measures the ratio of the sum of accurate and certain (n_{ac}) and inaccurate and uncertain (n_{iu}) voxels to the total number of voxels (N). Our contribution is to use this metric as a loss term to improve the clinical utility of uncertainty heatmaps by providing a higher signal-to-noise ratio for error detection in a medical image segmentation context. In addition, we propose a loss term to specifically reduce uncertainty in accurate regions, as these regions are largest and may play a major role in influencing the visual attention of clinicians during autocontouring QA. Unlike [13], we maximize AvU across a range of uncertainty thresholds and evaluate our approach using the uncertainty-ROC metric [16].

2   Method

2.1   Dataset and Neural Architecture

We used two public datasets of CT scans of the head-and-neck region which were annotated with 9 organs-at-Risk (OARs). The MICCAI 2015-Head and Neck Segmentation Challenge dataset [22] contains 33 training, 5 validation and 10 test samples. The DeepMindTCIA dataset [21], containing 15 patients, is used as an independent test set.

Building upon literature, we use OrganNet2.5D [7], a non-Bayesian model as our base neural architecture. It follows the encoder-decoder design and uses a combination of both 2D-only and 3D-only convolutions. Its middle layers use dilated convolutions to obtain a sufficient receptive field since it only performs two down-sampling steps to maintain resolution for the smaller optic organs. Inspired by earlier work [1], we add Bayesian layers in the middle of our network.

To perform training for Bayesian models, a prior on the weights is assumed and updated to a posterior using the available dataset. For inference, we perform Monte-Carlo sampling of the posterior weights to estimate the output distribution as follows:

$$p(y|x, D) = \mathbb{E}_{W \sim p(W|D)}[p(y|x, W)]. \qquad (1)$$

Here, x is an input mapped to an output y, $p(y|x, D)$ is the output distribution and $p(W|D)$ is the posterior [3] used to sample model weights W. We use the FlipOut technique [28], a form of variational inference in Bayesian neural nets that enables GPU-efficient sampling of weights from the posterior. Here, the prior is assumed to be a Gaussian factorizable across the Bayesian layers which is initialized with zero mean and identity covariance. FlipOut with a Gaussian prior was chosen over methods like Dropout [9] or DropConnect [16] since they use a Bernoulli distribution that may not be as representative of the neural net weight distribution when compared to a Gaussian. Unlike OrganNet2.5D, we use a lower count of filters in our model to be able to efficiently perform training and inference on its Bayesian version.

2.2   Losses

Segmentation Loss: In 3D segmentation, for each OAR class ($c \in C$) the model produces 3D probability maps (P_c) where each voxel (i) is represented by a probability vector summing to 1. We use the Cross Entropy (L_{CE}) loss and the Dice loss (L_{Dice}) on each P_c to learn organ geometry as also done in [17].

Accuracy-vs-Uncertainty (AvU) Loss: After prediction, each voxel has two properties – accuracy and uncertainty. Uncertainty is calculated on the output distribution $p(y|x, D)$. We chose predictive entropy, a commonly used uncertainty statistic, as it is capable of capturing both epistemic and aleatoric uncertainty [8]. Here, entropy represents the average amount of ambiguity present in the OAR probability vector P_c^i of each voxel i in the probability map P_c and is calculated as shown in [17]. In this work, we use the normalized entropy calculated by dividing the entropy by $\ln|C|$. Each voxel then belongs to one of four categories: n_{ac}, n_{au}, n_{ic} and n_{iu}, where n stands for the number of voxels, a for accurate, i for inaccurate, c for certain and u for uncertain. For QA, it is desirable to have a high n_{ac} when compared to n_{au} to prevent clinicians from spending time investigating accurate regions as well as high n_{iu} when compared to n_{ic} to prevent omission of errors. This requirement leads to the formulation of the AvU metric [19]:

$$\text{AvU} = \frac{n_{ac} + n_{iu}}{n_{ac} + n_{au} + n_{ic} + n_{iu}}, \tag{2}$$

with a range between [0,1]. To maximize AvU, we follow [13] and minimize the negative logarithm of the AvU metric which uses a differentiable version of n_{ac}, n_{au}, n_{ic} and n_{iu}. This loss term is minimal when all accurate voxels are certain and inaccurate voxels are uncertain, i.e. $n_{au} = n_{ic} = 0$. While [13] applies the AvU loss to each image in a classification task, for organ segmentation we apply it on a dilated region around the ground truth and predicted mask since the background usually has low error as well as low uncertainty. In addition, rather than using a fixed uncertainty threshold calculated by the average uncertainty on a held-out validation set, we instead propose penalizing the AvU metric across a range of uncertainty thresholds ($t \in T$) and average their AvU loss values:

$$L_{\text{AvU}} = \frac{1}{T} \sum_{t=1}^{T} \ln\left(1 + \frac{n_{au}^t + n_{ic}^t}{n_{ac}^t + n_{iu}^t}\right). \tag{3}$$

$p(u|a)$ **Loss:** In practice, inaccuracies are usually present along the contour and not in the core. To avoid unnecessary visual inspection, it is desirable to have low uncertainty in the core of such organs. Thus, we investigate an additional loss on the probability of uncertainty in accurate regions, $p(u|a)$:

$$L_{p(u|a)} = \frac{1}{T} \sum_{t=1}^{T} \ln\left(1 + \frac{n_{au}^t}{n_{ac}^t + n_{au}^t}\right). \tag{4}$$

This loss is at its minimum when n_{ac} is 0. Thus, the final model objective is:

$$L = L_{\text{CE}} + L_{\text{Dice}} + \alpha \cdot L_{\text{AvU}} + \beta \cdot L_{p(u|a)}. \tag{5}$$

2.3   Evaluation

As a first measure of evaluation, we evaluate AvU for each uncertainty threshold t in the full range of normalized entropy ($0 \leq t \leq 1$). Then a single Area-under-the-curve (AUC) score is computed for each model using the AvU scores across a range of uncertainty thresholds. However, the AvU score compresses information of all voxels in a single value and does not allow to evaluate uncertainty separately in accurate and inaccurate regions. For faster radiotherapy contour QA, we need high probability of uncertainty in inaccurate regions – $p(u|i)$, and low probability of uncertainty in accurate regions – $p(u|a)$. Let us plot $p(u|i)$ on the y-axis and $p(u|a)$ on the x-axis of a graph and also define n_{iu} as True Positive (TP), n_{au} as False Positive (FP), n_{ac} as True Negative (TN) and n_{au} as False Negative (FN). This makes $p(u|i)$ the True Positive Rate and $p(u|a)$ the False Positive Rate, essentially giving us the commonly used Receiver Operating Characteristic (ROC) curve. We dub this measure as the uncertainty-ROC curve [16]. Calculation of the AUC would provide us with insight into whether the additional AvU loss has been useful. In this work, the $p(u|i)$ and $p(u|a)$ values plotted on the graph are the average across all test samples calculated using a discretized set of uncertainty values. Instead of uncertainty-ROC, [13] uses the Uncertainty Calibration Error (UCE) [14] metric to evaluate the effect of the AvU loss. This metric motivated by model trustworthiness metric Expected Calibration Error (ECE) [10], requires a normalized uncertainty value of x $\in [0, 1]$ to also provide an error percentage of the same value. We believe that this approach of treating the scalar value of uncertainty as a proxy for error percentage is not the correct approach. Finally, we also report ECE where a high score would indicate that the model, on average, produces high confidence probability estimates (i.e. low entropy), even for inaccurate predictions.

Due to inter-observer variation common in radiotherapy contouring [5], we consider voxels with "tolerable" errors within the inaccuracy map as accurate since they do not require clinical intervention [23]. Two morphological operations on the inaccuracy map i.e. erosion (to remove) followed by dilation (to repair partially eroded error regions) help us output an error map consisting only of segmentation failures that require clinical intervention.

3   Experiments and Results

3.1   Experimental Details

For our data, we ensure homogeneity by resampling all CT volumes to a resolution of (0.8, 0.8, 2.5) mm. As is commonly done in radiotherapy anatomical contouring, we trim the Hounsfield units of the CT scan from -125 to $+225$ for improved contrast of soft tissues. Finally, during training, random 3D patches of size $140 \times 140 \times 40$ were extracted and augmented with 3D translations, 3D rotations, 3D elastic deformation and Gaussian noise.

We compare the original FlipOut model to the one with AvU loss (FlipOut-A) and the one with the AvU and $p(u|a)$ loss (FlipOut-AP), by training them on the MICCAI2015 training set and evaluating on the MICCAI2015 and DeepMindT-CIA test sets. Additionally, the FlipOut-A(t1), FlipOut-A(t2) and FlipOut-A models use the following thresholds (Eq. (3)): the median, the mean [13] and the 25th to 75th percentile range in steps of 0.05%, of the uncertainty values in the MICCAI2015 validation set.

All our models are trained for 1000 epochs, with the FlipOut-A and Flipout-AP models having their first 50 epochs dedicated to segmentation losses alone,

Table 1. Comparing Bayesian models for the MICCAI2015 (MIC2015) and Deep-MindTCIA (DMTCIA) datasets. [†] and [‡] represents statistical significant difference ($p < 0.05$) when compared to FlipOut and FlipOut-A respectively. The mean and standard deviation are calculated across all patients.

Dataset	Model	HD95 (mm)	ECE ($\times 10^{-2}$)	AvU ($\times 10^{-1}$)	unc-ROC ($\times 10^{-1}$)
MIC2015	FlipOut	3.30.4	7.30.6	8.50.1	6.50.2
	FlipOut-A(t1)	3.10.3	6.50.7[†‡]	8.70.5[†]	6.70.6[†‡]
	FlipOut-A(t2)	3.20.4	6.40.2[†‡]	8.70.6[†]	6.71.0[†‡]
	FlipOut-A	3.10.4	5.80.6[†]	8.90.1[†]	6.90.2[†]
	FlipOut-AP	3.20.3	5.81.0[†]	9.00.1[†]	6.90.3[†]
DMTCIA	FlipOut	4.41.4	8.21.1	8.10.2	6.10.3
	FlipOut-A(t1)	4.50.9	8.30.5	8.20.9[†]	6.40.7[†]
	FlipOut-A(t2)	4.41.2	8.10.5	8.30.5[†]	6.40.2[†]
	FlipOut-A	4.41.3	8.20.7	8.50.3[†]	6.50.3[†]
	FlipOut-AP	4.51.4	8.20.9	8.60.2[†]	6.60.1[†]

so that they can learn the geometry of individual organs-at-risk prior to tuning their uncertainty. They are further trained till a 1000 epochs when the KL-divergence between the posterior $p(W|D)$ and prior $p(W)$ has stabilized. The loss balancing terms $\alpha = 100$ and $\beta = 100$ (Eq. (5)) are experimentally determined from the training set $\{1, 10, 100\}$ such that the volumetric and surface measures of the newer model are either better or equivalent to the base model. For training we use a fixed learning rate of 10^{-3} with the Adam optimizer. For output distribution estimation, we perform 5 and 30 Monte Carlo sampling steps during training and inference respectively. During training and evaluation, we identify tolerated errors by using a kernel size corresponding to (2.4,2.4,2.5) mm. Code is implemented using Tensorflow version 2.4 on an Nvidia V100 (16 GB). Code to reproduce results is available on https://github.com/prerakmody/hansegmentation-uncertainty-errordetection.

3.2 Results and Analysis

Table 1 shows 95th percentile of Hausdorff Distance (HD95), Expected Calibration Error (ECE) [10], and AUC (Area-under-the-curve) scores for the AvU and uncertainty-ROC (unc-ROC) curves along with their statistical significances, using a Wilcoxon signed-rank test. There are no significant differences between the HD95 scores. For the internal MICCAI2015 dataset, the results show that using even a single threshold in the AvU loss causes a significant decrease in the ECE score, thus leading to more trustworthy probability estimates while a range of thresholds further improves calibration performance. This is in line with the results observed in [13], but the same does not hold for the external dataset. We also observe that upon using the AvU (Eq. (3)) and $p(u|a)$ (Eq. (4)) loss, AUC scores for the AvU and uncertainty-ROC curves have significant improvements in the uncertainty outputs over FlipOut (Fig. 1). Compared to

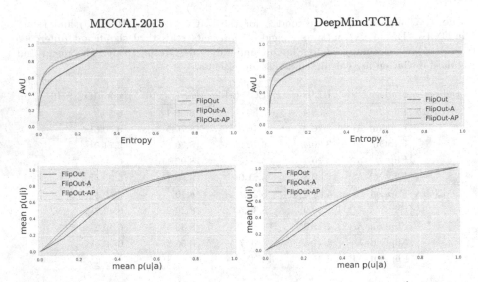

Fig. 1. The top row shows the AvU scores while the bottom row shows the uncertainty-ROC curve for the MICCAI2015 (left) and DeepMindTCIA (right) datasets respectively.

FlipOut-A(t1) and FlipOut-A(t2), FlipOut-A has significantly better unc-ROC scores for the MICCAI dataset, but not for the DeepMindTCIA dataset. Finally, compared to FlipOut-A, FlipOut-AP increases the AvU score slightly, at similar uncertainty-ROC scores.

In Fig. 2, the rows depict CT slices with varying "qualities" of uncertainty maps. The first row shows the mandible bone with both the models having near-perfect contour predictions. Despite this, the FlipOut model still exhibits uncertainty in the core of the mandible bone even though there are no contrast issues. Conversely, the other models show uncertainty only on the contour of the prediction since uncertainty in accurate voxels has been suppressed leading to less visual attention in those regions. The second row shows the left parotid gland with all models having acceptable contours with minor errors (and associated uncertainty) in the medial lobe. The differences in uncertainty lies in the white blob (i.e. a vein) in the core of the gland as well as its lateral boundaries. While the FlipOut model shows uncertainty on both, the FlipOut-A model shows uncertainty only on the white blob and the FlipOut-AP model does not show uncertainty in both due to the use of the $p(u|a)$ loss. In the third row, we show the top-most slice of the brainstem with the FlipOut and FlipOut-AP model showing uncertainty along the predicted contours and the FlipOut-A model showing uncertainty in the core region. Thus, although there may not be significant differences in the uncertainty-ROC metric between the FlipOut-A and Flipout-AP models (Fig. 1), the Flipout-AP may still be useful in certain scenarios. Note here that the slight contour differences are simply a result of the Monte-Carlo sampling as the overall models have similar geometric scores. In

FlipOut Contour   FlipOut-A Contour   FlipOut-AP Contour   FlipOut Uncertainty   FlipOut-A Uncertainty   FlipOut-AP Uncertainty

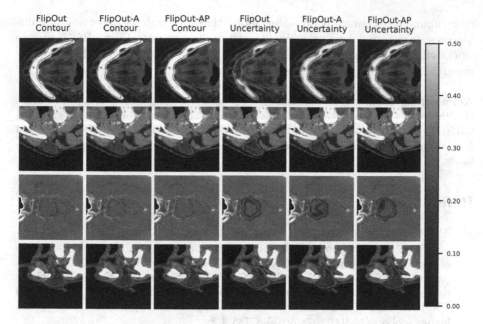

Fig. 2. Comparing the entropy heatmaps for the FlipOut, FlipOut-A and FlipOut-AP models. Here, we see the clinical (green) and predicted (blue) contours (columns 1–3) and the entropy heatmaps (columns 4–6). (Color figure online)

the fourth row, we again show the left parotid gland, but with larger errors on the medial lobe. In all cases, the models do not show any uncertainty in the erroneous region despite textural differences in the same. Such errors in contouring and omission in uncertainty may be attributed to the small size of our training dataset and such false negatives (in context of uncertainty) can be a potential blocker to adoption in the clinic.

4 Conclusion

This work investigates the use of the Accuracy-vs-Uncertainty (AvU) and $p(u|a)$ metrics as an additional objective in deep Bayesian modelling for improving error detection using uncertainty. Specifically, the proposed losses potentially enables faster error detection in radiotherapy contouring by motivating the model to produce accurate voxels which are certain and inaccurate voxels which are uncertain. This can assist clinicians during the mandatory quality assessment (QA) of autocontouring algorithms prior to radiation dosage calculation. We evaluate the effect of the AvU loss by using the uncertainty-ROC curve which shows that we improve the correlation of uncertainty with contouring inaccuracies. Our modified AvU loss does not require a manual choice of the uncertainty threshold, and improves the uncertainty-ROC metric on both an internal and external test dataset. We also explore an uncertainty-based loss specifically designed for the more abundant accurate regions, but found that although we observe visual differences, it does not lead to a significantly improved uncertainty-ROC. Future work will consider exploring the effects of a larger dataset and the utility of uncertainty from our proposed models by conducting trials with clinicians.

Acknowledgements. The research for this work was funded by Varian, a Siemens Healthineers Company, through the HollandPTC-Varian Consortium (grant id 2019022) and partly financed by the Surcharge for Top Consortia for Knowledge and Innovation (TKIs) from the Ministry of Economic Affairs and Climate, The Netherlands.

References

1. Alex Kendall, V.B., Cipolla, R.: Bayesian SegNet: model uncertainty in deep convolutional encoder-decoder architectures for scene understanding. In: Proceedings of the British Machine Vision Conference (BMVC). BMVA Press (2017)
2. Arega, T.W., Bricq, S., Meriaudeau, F.: Leveraging uncertainty estimates to improve segmentation performance in cardiac MR. In: Sudre, C.H., et al. (eds.) UNSURE/PIPPI -2021. LNCS, vol. 12959, pp. 24–33. Springer, Cham (2021). https://doi.org/10.1007/978-3-030-87735-4_3
3. Blundell, C., Cornebise, J., Kavukcuoglu, K., Wierstra, D.: Weight uncertainty in neural network. In: International Conference on Machine Learning. PMLR (2015)
4. Bragman, F.J.S., et al.: Uncertainty in multitask learning: joint representations for probabilistic MR-only radiotherapy planning. In: Frangi, A.F., Schnabel, J.A., Davatzikos, C., Alberola-López, C., Fichtinger, G. (eds.) MICCAI 2018. LNCS, vol. 11073, pp. 3–11. Springer, Cham (2018). https://doi.org/10.1007/978-3-030-00937-3_1
5. Brouwer, C.L., et al.: 3D variation in delineation of head and neck organs at risk. Radiat. Oncol. **7**(1), 1–10 (2012)
6. Camarasa, R., et al.: Quantitative comparison of Monte-Carlo dropout uncertainty measures for multi-class segmentation. In: Sudre, C.H., et al. (eds.) UNSURE/GRAIL -2020. LNCS, vol. 12443, pp. 32–41. Springer, Cham (2020). https://doi.org/10.1007/978-3-030-60365-6_4
7. Chen, Z., et al.: A novel hybrid convolutional neural network for accurate organ segmentation in 3D head and neck CT images. In: de Bruijne, M., et al. (eds.) MICCAI 2021. LNCS, vol. 12901, pp. 569–578. Springer, Cham (2021). https://doi.org/10.1007/978-3-030-87193-2_54
8. Gal, Y.: Uncertainty in deep learning. Ph.D. thesis, University of Cambridge (2016)
9. Gal, Y., Ghahramani, Z.: Dropout as a Bayesian approximation: representing model uncertainty in deep learning. In: International Conference on Machine Learning, pp. 1050–1059. PMLR (2016)
10. Guo, C., Pleiss, G., Sun, Y., Weinberger, K.Q.: On calibration of modern neural networks. In: International Conference on Machine Learning, pp. 1321–1330. PMLR (2017)
11. Islam, M., Glocker, B.: Spatially varying label smoothing: capturing uncertainty from expert annotations. In: Feragen, A., Sommer, S., Schnabel, J., Nielsen, M. (eds.) IPMI 2021. LNCS, vol. 12729, pp. 677–688. Springer, Cham (2021). https://doi.org/10.1007/978-3-030-78191-0_52

12. Iwamoto, S., Raytchev, B., Tamaki, T., Kaneda, K.: Improving the reliability of semantic segmentation of medical images by uncertainty modeling with Bayesian deep networks and curriculum learning. In: Sudre, C.H., et al. (eds.) UNSURE/PIPPI -2021. LNCS, vol. 12959, pp. 34–43. Springer, Cham (2021). https://doi.org/10.1007/978-3-030-87735-4_4
13. Krishnan, R., Tickoo, O.: Improving model calibration with accuracy versus uncertainty optimization. In: Advances in Neural Information Processing Systems (2020)
14. Laves, M.H., Ihler, S., Kortmann, K.P., Ortmaier, T.: Well-calibrated model uncertainty with temperature scaling for dropout variational inference. arXiv preprint arXiv:1909.13550 (2019)
15. Mehrtash, A., Wells, W.M., Tempany, C.M., Abolmaesumi, P., Kapur, T.: Confidence calibration and predictive uncertainty estimation for deep medical image segmentation. IEEE Trans. Med. Imaging **39**, 3868–3878 (2020)
16. Mobiny, A., Yuan, P., Moulik, S.K., Garg, N., Wu, C.C., Van Nguyen, H.: DropConnect is effective in modeling uncertainty of Bayesian deep networks. Sci. Rep. **11**(1), 1–14 (2021)
17. Mody, P.P., de Plaza, N.C., Hildebrandt, K., van Egmond, R., de Ridder, H., Staring, M.: Comparing Bayesian models for organ contouring in head and neck radiotherapy. In: Medical Imaging 2022: Image Processing. International Society for Optics and Photonics, SPIE (2022)
18. Monteiro, M., et al.: Stochastic segmentation networks: modelling spatially correlated aleatoric uncertainty. Adv. Neural Inf. Process. Syst. **33**, 12756–12767 (2020)
19. Mukhoti, J., Gal, Y.: Evaluating Bayesian deep learning methods for semantic segmentation. CoRR arXiv:abs/1811.12709 (2018)
20. Nair, T., Precup, D., Arnold, D.L., Arbel, T.: Exploring uncertainty measures in deep networks for multiple sclerosis lesion detection and segmentation. Med. Image Anal. **59**, 101557 (2020)
21. Nikolov, S., et al.: Clinically applicable segmentation of head and neck anatomy for radiotherapy: deep learning algorithm development and validation study. J. Med. Internet Res. **23**(7), e26151 (2021)
22. Raudaschl, P.F., et al.: Evaluation of segmentation methods on head and neck CT: auto-segmentation challenge 2015. Med. Phys. **44**(5), 2020–2036 (2017)
23. Sander, J., de Vos, B.D., Išgum, I.: Automatic segmentation with detection of local segmentation failures in cardiac MRI. Sci. Rep. **10**, 21769 (2020)
24. Sander, J., de Vos, B.D., Wolterink, J.M., Išgum, I.: Towards increased trustworthiness of deep learning segmentation methods on cardiac MRI. In: Medical Imaging 2019: Image Processing, vol. 10949, pp. 324–330. SPIE (2019)
25. Soberanis-Mukul, R.D., Navab, N., Albarqouni, S.: Uncertainty-based graph convolutional networks for organ segmentation refinement. In: Medical Imaging with Deep Learning, pp. 755–769. PMLR (2020)
26. Van Dijk, L.V., et al.: Improving automatic delineation for head and neck organs at risk by deep learning contouring. Radiother. Oncol. **142**, 115–123 (2020)
27. van der Veen, J., Gulyban, A., Nuyts, S.: Interobserver variability in delineation of target volumes in head and neck cancer. Radiotherapy Oncol. **137**, 9–15 (2019)
28. Wen, Y., Vicol, P., Ba, J., Tran, D., Grosse, R.: Flipout: efficient pseudo- independent weight perturbations on mini-batches. In: Proceedings of the 6th International Conference on Learning Representations (2018)

Stochastic Weight Perturbations Along the Hessian: A Plug-and-Play Method to Compute Uncertainty

Hariharan Ravishankar(✉), Rohan Patil, Deepa Anand, Vanika Singhal, Utkarsh Agrawal, Rahul Venkataramani, and Prasad Sudhakar

GE Healthcare, Bangalore, India
{hariharan.ravishankar,rohan.patil,deepa.anand1,vanika.singhal,
utkarsh.agrawal,rahul.venkataramani,prasad.sudhakar}@ge.com

Abstract. An uncertainty score along with predictions of a deep learning model is necessary for acceptance and often mandatory to satisfy regulatory requirements. The predominant method to generating uncertainty scores is to utilize a Bayesian formulation of deep learning. In this paper, we present a plug-and-play method to obtain samples from an already optimized model. Specifically, we present a simple, albeit principled methodology, to generate a number of models by sampling along the eigen directions of the Hessian of the converged minimum. We demonstrate the utility of our methods on two challenging medical ultrasound imaging problems - cardiac view recognition and kidney segmentation.

Keywords: Uncertainty · Deep learning · Calibration · Medical imaging

1 Introduction

In spite of the burgeoning popularity of deep learning (DL) methods, practical calibration continues to remain a challenge. In this paper, we aim to address the problem of calibration/uncertainty quantification with a novel procedure of *Stochastic weight perturbations using Hessian - SWPH* which has minimal (almost none) training constraints and demonstrate the algorithm on two representative medical imaging problems.

Bayesian formulations for DL methods, or their approximations, have emerged as the algorithm of choice for quantifying uncertainty of a prediction. However, these methods are plagued with a number of issues: constraints while training the neural network and/or computationally prohibitive. Most practical methods of computing uncertainty involve obtaining a multitude of predictions and deriving the desired quantity from them. In this work, we propose a simple principled approach to carefully perturb a model away from the learned local minimum and use these models to obtain predictions. We empirically show that the uncertainty computed using these predictions has impressive calibration error without imposing any training time constraints.

© The Author(s), under exclusive license to Springer Nature Switzerland AG 2022
C. H. Sudre et al. (Eds.): UNSURE 2022, LNCS 13563, pp. 80–88, 2022.
https://doi.org/10.1007/978-3-031-16749-2_8

The contributions of this paper are:

1. A novel method to generate a set of (infinite, if needed) models from a single trained model, with neither training overhead nor architectural constraints, leading to model disagreement based epistemic uncertainty quantification.
2. A practical framework for calibrating a pre-trained medical imaging model post-deployment on a target domain.
3. Demonstration of the efficacy of the method on two challenging medical imaging problems - segmentation and classification, obtaining comparable quantitative calibration performance to state-of-the-art methods.

1.1 Related Work

A principled way of obtaining predictive uncertainty of a model is through Bayesian learning and the following Bayesian model averaging defines it:

$$p(y|\boldsymbol{x}, \mathcal{D}) = \int p(y|\boldsymbol{x}, \boldsymbol{\theta})p(\boldsymbol{\theta}|\mathcal{D})d\boldsymbol{\theta} \approx \frac{1}{S}\sum_{j=1}^{S} p(y|\boldsymbol{x}, \boldsymbol{\theta}^j), \qquad (1)$$

where y is the prediction on an input $\boldsymbol{x}$ with a model $\boldsymbol{\theta}$ trained on a dataset $\mathcal{D}$.

In Bayesian learning, computing the full posterior weight distribution $p(\boldsymbol{\theta}|\mathcal{D})$ is intractable even for simple DL architectures and therefore approximation methods are used. These include sampling methods such as MCMC, Hamiltonian Monte Carlo, Stochastic Langevin Dynamics, etc. The quality of approximation depends on sampling a diverse set of model parameters $\boldsymbol{\theta}$ [4], and the complexity of sampling itself is an important consideration. Alternative to these methods are the variational approximation methods [3,6].

In practice, most deep learning models are learnt in a non-Bayesian way. To address the issue of uncertainty quantification in non-Bayesian learning, several methods have been proposed which enable such models to provide Bayesian type uncertainties. These methods are either motivated by, or have been shown to have striking connections with, the approximation methods used in the Bayesian learning framework. For example, deep ensembles (DE), which has good empirical performance, implements a sampling based approximation to $p(\boldsymbol{\theta}|\mathcal{D})$. Methods such as stochastic weight averaging (SWA), Monte Carlo dropout [5], etc. are shown to perform local approximations to $p(\boldsymbol{\theta}|\mathcal{D})$.

Of interest to the rest of the discussion is the Laplace approximation (LA) where the weight distribution around the MAP solution is approximated by a multivariate Gaussian $p(\boldsymbol{\theta}|\mathcal{D}) \approx \mathcal{N}\left(\boldsymbol{\theta}_{\mathrm{MAP}}, H_{\mathrm{MAP}}^{-1}\right)$, where H_{MAP} is the Hessian of (training) loss with respect to the weights, evaluated at $\boldsymbol{\theta}_{\mathrm{MAP}}$. One can use samples from this distribution to obtain an approximate posterior predictive. Methods employing LA during training [8] or in a post-hoc manner mainly focus on getting computationally efficient approximations to H [1,11]. SWA and its variations empirically estimate the multivariate Gaussian distribution by averaging the iterates of SGD.

Our work, though having a flavour of LA methods, is inspired by the properties of loss landscape around converged weights $\boldsymbol{\theta}^*$. We propose to sample points on the loss surface around $\boldsymbol{\theta}^*$ in the direction of pth top eigenvector of the loss Hessian at $\boldsymbol{\theta}^*$. We restrict the samples to lie within the region where the loss values are comparable to that of $\boldsymbol{\theta}^*$. We describe the details of our method, SWPH - a simple and post-hoc method to obtain uncertainty estimates without requiring any control of training process, in the next section.

2   SWPH

In supervised learning, given a dataset $\mathcal{D} = \{(\boldsymbol{x}_n \in \mathbb{R}^M, \boldsymbol{y}_n \in \mathbb{R}^K)\}_{n=1}^N$, the weights of the neural network $\boldsymbol{\theta} \in \mathbb{R}^D$ are optimized using empirical risk minimization to obtain a point estimate $\boldsymbol{\theta}^*$. To generate a multitude of predictions, instead of estimating a parametric distribution analytically and sampling, we propose to sample different models from the local neighborhood of the point estimate $\boldsymbol{\theta}^*$ using insights from loss landscape geometry at convergence [9]. Guided by insights from [4], a good sample should satisfy: 1) high divergence in the weight space and 2) low functional diversity (all models are approximately as good as $\boldsymbol{\theta}^*$). Models that satisfy the above properties can be sampled from a region within the *s-flatness* of $\boldsymbol{\theta}^*$, a quantity we will define below.

s-Flatness: Given a dataset $\mathcal{D}$, for any direction $\boldsymbol{v}_j \in \mathbb{R}^D$ in the weight space, s is defined as follows:

$$s := \underset{t \in S}{\operatorname{argmax}}(\boldsymbol{\theta}^* + t \cdot \boldsymbol{v}_j), \text{ such that, } \mathcal{L}_{\mathcal{D}}(\boldsymbol{\theta}^* + t \cdot \boldsymbol{v}_j) \leq \mu \cdot \mathcal{L}_{\mathcal{D}}(\boldsymbol{\theta}^*), \qquad (2)$$

where $S \subset \mathbb{R}$, $\mathcal{L}_{\mathcal{D}}(\cdot)$ is the loss and $\mu \geq 1$ is the allowance for loss divergence.

2.1   Generating High Quality Samples

We utilize a small portion $\mathcal{D}_{\texttt{calib}}$ of the validation dataset to estimate the *s-flatness* of a given model, unlike many post-hoc methods that require access to full training data [2]. To obtain the highest diversity of models while retaining a high accuracy (small μ), one should sample in the subspace spanned by the eigenvectors corresponding to the smallest eigenvalues of the loss Hessian. This is also evident in the LA approach where the covariance matrix of the Gaussian is the inverse of the Hessian. However, owing to the numerical instabilities and computational overhead, we take the intermediate path of choosing the eigenvectors $\{\boldsymbol{v}_1, \boldsymbol{v}_2, \cdots, \boldsymbol{v}_P\}$ corresponding to the top P eigenvalues of the Hessian at $\boldsymbol{\theta}^*$ and then use the trailing subset $\mathbb{V} := \{\boldsymbol{v}_{P-(p-1)}, \cdots, \boldsymbol{v}_{P-1}, \boldsymbol{v}_P\}$ of p eigenvectors to obtain new weights:

$$\boldsymbol{\theta}_i = \boldsymbol{\theta}^* + \alpha_i \cdot \boldsymbol{v}_j, \ \boldsymbol{v}_j \in \mathbb{V}, \qquad (3)$$

where α_i is uniformly sampled in $[s_j^-, s_j^+] - \{0\}$, with $s_j^- < 0 < s_j^+$ computed using (2) for each $\boldsymbol{v}_j \in \mathbb{V}$. For a given budget of M models, we obtain approximately $\lfloor M/p \rfloor$ models per $\boldsymbol{v}_j$. To compute the Hessian and its eigenspace, we use the PyHessian package [13].

2.2 Uncertainty as a Function of SWPH Members Disagreement

Let $f_\theta(x)$ denote the forward pass of the input sample through the model resulting in a prediction vector of length k, for a k−way classification problem. Assuming $f_\theta(x)$ includes the soft-max, it is then indeed the predictive class distribution

$$p(y|\theta, x) = f_\theta(x). \tag{4}$$

Predictions from each of the member models is given by $f_{\theta_i}(x)$, with $\{\theta_i\}_i$ defined in (3). Denoting y_i as the predicted class label from θ_i, the predictive confidence from SWPH method is defined as the average number of sampled member models out of $\{\theta_i\}_i$ that agree with predicted class label y from the unperturbed model θ^*. That is, with $y_i = \mathrm{argmax} f_{\theta_i}(x)$, we have

$$\mathrm{Conf}_{SWPH} := \frac{1}{M} \sum_{i=1}^{M} \mathbb{I}(y = y_i), \tag{5}$$

where $\mathbb{I}$ is the indicator function capturing agreement between a member (y_i) and original model's predictions (y).

2.3 Estimation of *s-Flatness*

We provide a practical method to estimate s with a two step procedure. Recall that the loss surface is a function of the model weights, and each point of the calibration loss surface provides the value of loss of the model computed on $\mathcal{D}_{\texttt{calib}}$. Around the converged weights, along v_p, we fit a parabola $p_{\theta^*}(\alpha)$ for the calibration loss surface. We then choose an initial $\hat{s}$ as that point on the abscissa where the absolute value of the slope of $p_\theta(\alpha)$ reaches a certain fixed value c. With abused notation, $\hat{s} := \arg_\alpha (|p'_\theta(\alpha)| == c)$. Then, we solve (2) numerically, setting $S = [\frac{\hat{s}}{4}, \frac{\hat{s}}{2}, \hat{s}, 2\hat{s}, 3\hat{s}, \cdots]$ for obtaining s^+ and $-S$ for s^-.

3 Experiments on Medical Imaging Problems

3.1 Cardiac View Classification on B-Mode Ultrasound Images

Problem: We consider the problem of identifying eight standard cardiac views from B-mode ultrasound cine loops - (i) 4chamber (4ch), (ii) 2chamber (2ch), (iii) 5chamber (5ch), (iv) Paresternal Long Axis (PLAX), (v) Apical Long Axis (APLAX), (vi) Paresternal Short Axis (PSAX), (vii) Aortic Valve Shot Axis (SAX) and (viii) Subcostal views. This is a challenging due to the combination of subject diversity, acquisition settings differences and operator variability.

Data and Architecture Details: We used the standard ResNet-18 architecture for the 8-way classification problem. All the models were trained on 60 B-mode cine loops for every class. Total number of training images were ~23500 frames, with ~50 frames per loop. Test data consisted of 30 independent subject loops per class (~14000 images). The ResNet-18 models were built with SGD optimizer and in PyTorch using NVIDIA GPUs.

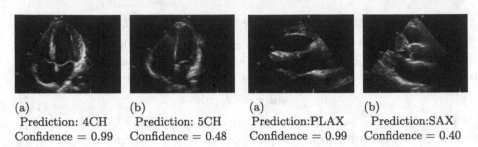

(a)   (b)   (a)   (b)
Prediction: 4CH   Prediction: 5CH   Prediction:PLAX   Prediction:SAX
Confidence = 0.99 Confidence = 0.48 Confidence = 0.99 Confidence = 0.40

Fig. 1. Examples from 4Ch views.   Fig. 2. Examples from PLAX views.

3.2 Segmentation of Kidney Morphology from Ultrasound Scans

Problem: Automated measurement of kidney volume from B-mode ultrasound images helps in early diagnosis of potential renal illnesses leading to improved patient outcomes and also accelerated clinical work-flow. However, obtaining accurate segmentation is often extremely challenging due to wide diversity in kidney morphology, presence of pathology or acquisition differences. Additionally, the boundaries of the kidney are often blurred and affected by shadows making it challenging even for expert sonographers (Fig. 5a).

Data and Architecture Details: We built a standard U-Net [12] with 5 encoder and decoder blocks with skip connections. Data utilized were obtained from subject data coming from multi-site acquisitions. Training data consisted of 576 images and test data had 149 images.

The problems chosen are extremely challenging yet widely relevant medical imaging problems, which make them suitable to evaluate the proposed method.

3.3 Competing Methods and Performance Metrics

We compare the proposed method with four popular/state-of-the-art methods.

1. **SGD-Likelihood (SGD)** - Vanilla method where likelihood of winning class is treated as predictive confidence.
2. **MC-dropout (DP)** - A popular approach for epistemic uncertainty based on varying drop-out during test-time and ensembling the predictions.
3. **Deep ensembles (DE)** - state-of-the-art for both performance and uncertainty quantification - Ensembling M models built from M initializations.
4. **Test-time-Augmentation (TTA)** - A popular aleatoric uncertainty method; predictions on augmented copies of input are ensembled during test-time.

We compare the quality of uncertainty modeling using the metrics listed below.

1. **Expected Calibration Error (ECE) and Maximum Calibration Error (MCE)** - The standard ways of quantifying the quality of uncertainty computation [10]. By binning the confidence and accuracy into B non-overlapping bins, ECE measures the expected absolute difference between them while MCE measures worst-case calibration error.

$$\text{ECE} = \sum_{b=1}^{B} \frac{n_b}{B} |\text{Acc}(b) - \text{Conf}(b)|, \ \text{MCE} = \max_b |\text{Acc}(b) - \text{Conf}(b)|. \quad (6)$$

2. **Accuracy and Dice overlap scores** - To ensure that the well-calibrated models are also useful, we report relevant performance metrics - accuracy and Dice overlap in classification and segmentation problems respectively.
3. **Reliability diagrams** - We also visually capture the quality of uncertainty quantification through modified reliability diagrams used in [7].

4   Results

For both the problems, we ensembled predictions from six different models in DE method ($M = 6$). For TTA, we used standard augmentations of flipping, rotations, color jitter for view classification and geometric translations for kidney segmentation. For MC-dropout method, we added dropout layers after every convolutional layer and test-time dropout factor of 0.1 and 0.2 was used in classification and segmentation problems respectively. The major take-aways from our experiments are as follows.

1. **SWPH achieves very good calibration performance:** For the kidney segmentation problem (Table 2), the proposed approach achieves ***state-of-the-art*** calibration performance amongst all compared methods, beating DE method too across all defined metrics. Note that we report average ECE computed at image level: ECE-Image, as well as pixel-wise calibration errors: ECE-Pixel and MCE-Pixel.

   In view classification problem (Table 1), SWPH achieves third best ECE and MCE, being very competitive to DE method, clearly highlighting the merit of

Table 1. Accuracy and ECE comparisons for ultrasound cardiac view classification.

Method	Accuracy %	ECE %	MCE %	Average absolute CE %
SGD likelihood	86.9	8.4	39.12	14.04
MC-dropout	88.6	2.04	**7.29**	**1.2**
Deep ensembles	**90.4**	**1.33**	18.98	3.37
TTA	87.28	9.0	42.30	19
SWPH (proposed)	87	3.61	14.63	3.45

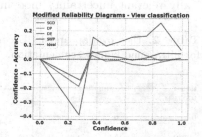

Fig. 3. Calibration comparisons across different methods.

SWPH. We point out that MC-dropout had extremely high variance in performance and calibration for even small changes in test-time dropout factor and we have chosen not to penalize this and still reported its best performance (Table 1).

2. **SWPH achieves consistent calibration for all confidence ranges:** ECE can often be less informative with skewed confidence distribution, hence it is crucial to analyze the calibration across all confidence ranges. This is captured in modified reliability diagram, plotting $(confidence - accuracy)$ versus confidence for all ranges. Ideally, $(confidence - accuracy)$ should be as close to zero as possible for all ranges of confidence values. The superiority of the proposed approach is highlighted in Fig. 3 and Fig. 4, where SWPH achieves the best reliability being most close to zero for both problems.

3. **SWPH produces clinically significant uncertainty maps:** Figure 5 captures pixel-wise uncertainty map produced by SWPH for kidney segmentation problem. It is striking that the uncertainty maps shown in Fig. 5e correlates extremely well with Fig. 5d. In row 1, we show a near-perfect segmentation with negligible error, which is also captured in uncertainty map - being confident everywhere. In row 2, we show a challenging case with input image (Fig. 5a) having blurry right pole regions as well unclear lower boundary impacted by shadows. It is fascinating that the proposed method has highlighted exactly these regions as uncertain regions. Finally, in row 3, we show a complete wrong segmentation where the model has extremely over-segmented the kidney regions. Again, the uncertainty map captures the error with the correct kidney regions being certain. Figures 1 and 2 demonstrate the clinical utility in classification problem - low confidence on challenging and wrongly classified examples and vice-versa on good images.

4. **SWPH achieves calibration with negligible inference overhead:** We point out that the sampler defined in Sect. 2.1 is extremely simple and inference time for SWPH is almost same as all the other methods.

5. **SWPH achieves slight improvement in performance:** Even though the aim of the method is to provide reliable uncertainty modeling, we also achieve minor performance improvement. We report that DE method significantly outperforms on both problems, which is consistent with literature.

Overall, the proposed method achieves quantitatively excellent (best) and clinically relevant uncertainty modeling on both the problems. This is significant

Table 2. Dice overlap and ECE comparisons for ultrasound kidney segmentation.

Method	Dice overlap %	ECE-Image %	ECE-Pixel %	MCE-Pixel %
SGD likelihood	85.52	1.80	1.80	21.89
MC-dropout	85.55	2.44	2.31	28.99
Deep ensembles	**86.48**	1.36	1.30	15.16
TTA	86.40	1.31	1.18	6.03
SWPH (proposed)	85.80	1.26	0.70	3.23

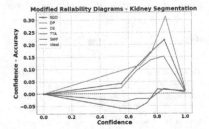

Fig. 4. Calibration comparisons across different methods.

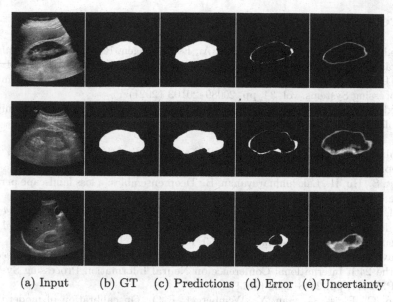

(a) Input   (b) GT   (c) Predictions   (d) Error   (e) Uncertainty

Fig. 5. Uncertainty modeling using SWPH for kidney segmentation. The proposed method's uncertainty map in (e) correlates excellently with error in (d).

because these improvements in calibration are achieved without any additional training of models or constraints.

5   Discussion

Uncertainty quantification of predictions and calibration of deep learning models is a very important factor for their deployment, especially in critical applications such as medical imaging. Most methods for computing predictive uncertainty can be linked to computing approximations to the weight posterior in the Bayesian setting. This paper proposes a novel principled method of obtaining a collection of models without placing any constraint on either the model architecture or training procedure. Using predictions from these models, we compute uncertainty and experimentally show on two challenging medical imaging problems that our method achieves the least calibration error, evaluated using a set of standard calibration metrics.

It is well known that one can approximate a posterior distribution around a point estimate (MLE, MAP, etc.) using a multivariate Gaussian through Laplace approximation. However, our work considers a different but related object, the calibration loss surface, and empirically shows that a principled way of sampling on the loss surface provides useful models that are sufficient to obtain good uncertainty, leading to small calibration error.

It remains to be seen how the samples obtained using the loss surface are exactly related to the posterior distribution or to their local approximations.

References

1. Daxberger, E., Kristiadi, A., Immer, A., Eschenhagen, R., Bauer, M., Hennig, P.: Laplace redux - effortless Bayesian deep learning. In: Ranzato, M., Beygelzimer, A., Dauphin, Y., Liang, P., Vaughan, J.W. (eds.) Advances in Neural Information Processing Systems. vol. 34, pp. 20089–20103 (2021)
2. Daxberger, E., Kristiadi, A., Immer, A., Eschenhagen, R., Bauer, M., Hennig, P.: Laplace redux-effortless Bayesian deep learning. Adv. Neural. Inf. Process. Syst. **34**, 20089–20103 (2021)
3. Dinh, L., Sohl-Dickstein, J., Bengio, S.: Density estimation using real NVP. arXiv preprint arXiv:1605.08803 (2016)
4. Fort, S., Hu, H., Lakshminarayanan, B.: Deep ensembles: a loss landscape perspective. Cite arXiv:1912.02757 (2019)
5. Gal, Y., Ghahramani, Z.: Dropout as a Bayesian approximation: representing model uncertainty in deep learning. In: Proceedings of the 33rd International Conference on Machine Learning, pp. 1050–1059 (2016). JMLR.org
6. Graves, A.: Practical variational inference for neural networks. In: Proceedings of the 24th International Conference on Neural Information Processing Systems, NIPS 2011, pp. 2348–2356 (2011)
7. Guo, C., Pleiss, G., Sun, Y., Weinberger, K.Q.: On calibration of modern neural networks. In: International Conference on Machine Learning, pp. 1321–1330. PMLR (2017)
8. Kristiadi, A., Hein, M., Hennig, P.: Learnable uncertainty under Laplace approximations. In: Proceedings of the Thirty-Seventh Conference on Uncertainty in Artificial Intelligence. Proceedings of Machine Learning Research, vol. 161, pp. 344–353. PMLR, 27–30 July 2021
9. Li, H., Xu, Z., Taylor, G., Studer, C., Goldstein, T.: Visualizing the loss landscape of neural nets. In: Advances in Neural Information Processing Systems, vol. 31. Curran Associates, Inc. (2018)
10. Naeini, M.P., Cooper, G., Hauskrecht, M.: Obtaining well calibrated probabilities using Bayesian binning. In: Twenty-Ninth AAAI Conference on Artificial Intelligence (2015)
11. Ritter, H., Botev, A., Barber, D.: A scalable Laplace approximation for neural networks. In: International Conference on Learning Representations (2018). https://openreview.net/forum?id=Skdvd2xAZ
12. Ronneberger, O., Fischer, P., Brox, T.: U-Net: convolutional networks for biomedical image segmentation. In: International Conference on Medical Image Computing and Computer-Assisted Intervention, pp. 234–241 (2015)
13. Yao, Z., Gholami, A., Keutzer, K., Mahoney, M.W.: PyHessian: neural networks through the lens of the Hessian. In: 2020 IEEE International Conference on Big Data (Big Data), pp. 581–590. IEEE (2020)

Calibration of Deep Medical Image Classifiers: An Empirical Comparison Using Dermatology and Histopathology Datasets

Jacob Carse[iD], Andres Alvarez Olmo[iD], and Stephen McKenna[✉][iD]

CVIP, School of Science and Engineering, University of Dundee, Scotland, UK
{j.carse,s.j.z.mckenna}@dundee.ac.uk

Abstract. As deep learning classifiers become ever more widely deployed for medical image analysis tasks, issues of predictive calibration need to be addressed. Mis-calibration is the deviation between predictive probability (confidence) and classification correctness. Well-calibrated classifiers enable cost-sensitive and selective decision-making. This paper presents an empirical investigation of calibration methods on two medical image datasets (multi-class dermatology and binary histopathology image classification). We show the effect of temperature scaling with temperature optimized using various measures of calibration replacing the standard negative log-likelihood. We do so not only for networks trained using one-hot encoding and cross-entropy loss, but also using focal loss and label smoothing. We compare these with two Bayesian methods. Results suggest little or no advantage to the use of alternative calibration metrics for tuning temperature. Temperature scaling of networks trained using focal loss (with appropriate hyperparameters) provided strong results in terms of both calibration and accuracy across both datasets.

Keywords: Calibration · Classification · Uncertainty · Deep learning

1 Introduction

Deep learning classifiers have been widely adopted for medical image analysis tasks such as diagnostic decision support, in certain restricted settings even outperforming medical specialists, e.g., binary classification of dermoscopic melanoma and nevi images [22]. Such promising results notwithstanding, further improvements are desirable to enable robust translation to the clinic. A known problem with deep neural network classifiers is that they can be poorly calibrated, typically resulting in over-confident predictions. Mis-calibration represents deviation between confidence and correctness. A model that is not well-calibrated cannot correctly identify the amount of uncertainty in its prediction. Well-calibrated probabilistic outputs are needed to support cost-sensitive and selective clinical decision-making [5], providing information helpful for avoiding adverse outcomes. Calibrated predictions are relevant for active learning [4], reinforcement learning [8] and out-of-distribution detection [31].

C. H. Sudre et al. (Eds.): UNSURE 2022, LNCS 13563, pp. 89–99, 2022.
https://doi.org/10.1007/978-3-031-16749-2_9

Several methods have been reported to improve the calibration of deep classifiers in medical image classification. However, their performance can be inconsistent and evidence for which to adopt for any given task and dataset is somewhat lacking. We present an empirical study that adds to this evidence base, focusing on classification datasets from dermatology and histopathology.

Temperature scaling [13] is the most popular method for calibrating modern neural networks due to its post-hoc nature, simple implementation, and effectiveness. It works by scaling output logits using a temperature parameter that is optimized on a validation set. The original implementation called for optimizing temperature using negative log-likelihood. Other researchers have mentioned using calibration metrics to optimize temperature and have stated in passing that this led to improved calibration [11,23]. In this paper, we investigate this claim empirically using a density-based estimator for expected calibration error, and an estimator for maximum calibration error. Section 2 briefly discusses these calibration measures. We explore the effect of the use of different metrics for temperature optimization. We do this not only for neural networks trained by minimizing cross-entropy with one-hot encoded target labels but also for networks trained using focal loss and label smoothing. We also compare these with two Bayesian neural networks, based on Bayes-by-Backprop and a Laplace approximation method. These methods are described in Sect. 3. Details of our experiment design are provided in Sect. 4. Results on the ISIC 2019 multiclass dermatology dataset and the large Patch-Camelyon binary histopathology dataset are given in Sect. 5, providing evidence on the relative performance of the methods in terms of calibration and accuracy on two contrasting tasks.

2 Measures of Calibration

Various metrics can be used to evaluate model calibration. The expected calibration error (ECE) [13] is a measure of the difference in expectation between the predictive confidence and classification accuracy. A commonly used estimator for ECE splits the probability interval into equally spaced bins. It then takes a weighted average of the absolute differences between the accuracy of the predictions in a bin and the mean of the probabilities in that bin. If we instead compute the maximum of this error over the bins, we obtain the maximum calibration error (MCE). This measure can be useful in high-risk situations where the worst-case calibration is relevant.

While histogram-based estimation of ECE has proven useful for evaluating calibration [24], others have criticized the use of equally spaced histogram binning because of inherent bias and statistical inefficiency. To address these criticisms, methods for adapting the number and sizes of bins have been proposed [27]. An alternative is to replace the use of histograms with continuous density estimators [33]. KDE-ECE uses kernel density estimation [25] to estimate the densities of accuracy and confidence, achieving better data-efficiency. In this paper, we use KDE-ECE with a triweight kernel.

The negative log-likelihood is often utilized as a loss function for optimizing deep neural network classifiers, measuring a probabilistic model's quality by assessing its ability to recover the ground-truth conditional distribution. Negative log-likelihood can also be used as an indicator of a model's calibration.

3 Calibration Methods

Methods that try to improve calibration can be roughly categorized into three broad approaches: regularization methods, post-processing methods, and methods designed to cope inherently with model uncertainty, such as Bayesian neural networks [12].

3.1 Model Regularization

Model regularization is performed by modifying the objective function used to optimize a model or by altering the dataset to encourage a model to be more robust and better calibrated. Dataset regularization methods have become commonplace with strategies such as data augmentation [15] or adding out-of-distribution data to the training data [14]. We make use of data augmentation. In our experiments, we compare label smoothing and focal loss, two methods that can improve calibration.

Neural network classifiers are usually trained using a one-hot label encoding. This involves minimizing the expected cross-entropy between target outputs t_k and the network outputs y_k, where $t_k = 1$ for the true class and $t_k = 0$ for the other classes. **Label smoothing** instead trains a network by minimizing the expected cross-entropy using modified targets $\hat{t} = (1 - \alpha)t + \frac{\alpha}{C}$ where C is the number of classes and α is a free parameter [28]. Label smoothing thus modifies the target class distribution and α controls the level of smoothing. At the extremes, $\alpha = 1$ results in a uniform distribution and $\alpha = 0$ recovers one-hot encoding. Label smoothing has been used in medical image analysis to improve calibration and robustness to out-of-distribution data [16]. Its popularity is partly due to ease of implementation and negligible computational overhead.

Focal Loss [19] is a loss function that was originally introduced to improve the performance of object detection by encouraging a model to focus on samples with lower confidence. It has been shown to improve model calibration [23]. It weights predictions based on their confidence to encourage the model to learn more from examples closer to the decision boundary. This can reduce overconfidence, improve calibration, and lead to better results with unbalanced datasets. Focal loss can be written as $FL(y) = -\alpha(1 - y)^\gamma \log(y)$. It adds the factor $(1 - y)^\gamma$ to cross-entropy to weight the predictions. There are two hyper parameters: $\gamma > 0$ determines the weighting of less confident examples, and $\alpha \in [0, 1]$ is used to improve the numerical stability.

3.2   Post-hoc Calibration

Temperature Scaling [13] is the most popular post-hoc calibration method for modern neural networks and has been used successfully in medical image analysis [18]. It is a single-parameter version of Platt logistic scaling [26]. It applies a learned temperature parameter, $T > 0$, to rescale the output logits z of a neural network before a softmax activation function is applied to output probabilistic predictions $\hat{y}$ (1). $T = 1$ recovers the standard softmax activation.

$$\hat{y} = \frac{e^{z/T}}{\sum_{j=1}^{J} e^{z_j/T}} \tag{1}$$

Since T is used to scale all the logits, the output $\hat{y}$ has a monotonic relationship with the unscaled output. For this reason, classification accuracy is unaffected by temperature scaling.

The original implementation of temperature scaling optimizes T by minimizing the negative log-likelihood of the predictions (expected cross-entropy) on a validation set. We have chosen to experiment with the use of alternative metrics for optimizing T. It seems reasonable to expect that optimizing T for a calibration measure on a validation set will lead to better test calibration using that measure. Further details will be given in Sect. 4.2.

3.3   Bayesian Approximations

Bayesian neural networks infer distributions over their weight parameters rather than the usual point estimates. Monte Carlo sampling can then be used to approximate predictive distributions and obtain estimates of predictive means and uncertainty measures such as variance. Bayesian neural nets have been used in medical applications for improved calibration and uncertainty estimation [17].

Bayes by Backprop [2] trains a Bayesian neural network whilst using back-propagation to calculate gradients. It uses variational inference to approximate a posterior distribution over weights $q(w|\theta)$. The parameters for the distribution θ can be computed by minimizing the KL-Divergence between a variational posterior and the true posterior. As there is no way of knowing the true posterior, it is estimated using Monte Carlo sampling of the evidence lower bound. This is shown in Eq. (2) where D is the dataset and N is the number of Monte Carlo samples.

$$\text{ELBO}(D, \theta) \approx \sum_{n=1}^{N} \log q(w^i|\theta) - \log p(w^i) - \log p(D|w^i) \tag{2}$$

To train the Bayesian neural network the ELBO is used as part of a loss function alongside cross-entropy. The ELBO is weighted when combined with cross-entropy with the weighting of $\pi_m = \frac{2^{M-m}}{2^M-1}$ where M is the number of batches and m is the current batch. This weighting means that the first few batches are more influenced by the Bayesian complexity and the later batches learn more from the data.

Laplace Approximation [21] is a cost-effective method for training a Bayesian neural network by approximating the posterior as a Gaussian centered at a local maximum. This local maximum is obtained by training using a gradient-based optimiser in the usual way. Curvature is estimated using approximations to the Hessian matrix [3] at the maximum. Thus a Laplace approximation is fitted post-hoc onto a trained neural network so that probabilistic predictions can be sampled. Laplace approximation has become increasingly popular for Bayesian inference due to its ability to be added post-hoc and its low computational expense compared to other approximations such as Bayes by Backprop [9].

4 Experiments

4.1 Datasets

Our experiments utilize two datasets, the ISIC 2019 challenge dataset [6,7,30] and the Patch Camelyon (PCam) dataset [32]. The ISIC 2019 dataset consists of 25,331 dermoscopic skin lesion images of 8 diagnostic classes: melanoma, melanocytic nevus, basal cell carcinoma, actinic keratosis, benign keratosis, dermatofibroma, vascular lesion, and squamous cell carcinoma. The PCam dataset is comprised of 327,680 96×96 pixel image patches extracted from whole-slide images of H&E-stained lymph node sections from the Camelyon16 dataset [1]. The datasets were split into training, validation and testing sets with proportions 6:2:2. The ISIC images were pre-processed by center-cropping their width to be equal to their height and then resizing to 256×256 pixels. Both datasets were augmented by normalizing each of the image channels, randomly flipping both horizontally and vertically, and randomly rotating by multiples of $90°$.

4.2 Experiment Design

We trained seven different types of CNN classifier on both the ISIC 2019 and the PCam datasets. In the case of ISIC 2019, each classifier was trained three times using different random seeds that altered the training, validation and testing data splits as well as the neural network weights initialization. The first classifier type, which we refer to as the baseline model, was trained using a standard cross-entropy function with one-hot label encoding. The next two classifiers used label smoothing (LS) with cross-entropy, with α set to 0.1 and 0.2, respectively. A further two classifiers types were trained using focal loss (FL) with γ set to 2.0 and 5.0, respectively. We applied temperature scaling to each of these model types after training. In each case, we optimized the temperature parameter for various measures of calibration. These were the negative log-likelihood (nll), KDE-ECE (ece), and MCE (mce), as well as additive combinations of these three measures. We denote these using TS followed by an abbreviation for the measure used to optimize temperature, e.g., *TS nll+mce*. The temperature parameter was optimized using a Limited-memory BFGS optimizer [20]. For comparison, two types of Bayesian neural networks were also trained. These used Bayes-by-Backprop and Laplace approximation, respectively.

4.3   Model Architecture and Training

We used an EfficientNet [29] encoder with a compound coefficient of 7, pre-trained on ImageNet [10] followed by a fully connected hidden layer with a width of 512 neurons before the output layer. For Bayesian convolutional neural networks, the final hidden and output fully-connected layers are replaced with Bayesian fully-connected layers that learn distributions for the weights and biases to be sampled from. All training used a cyclical learning rate scheduler with scheduling between 10^{-4} and 10^{-1}. The batch size was 16 for the ISIC 2019 data and 64 for the PCam data. Bayes by backprop used a weighted loss function combining the expected lower bound from 10 forward-propagation passes and cross-entropy of the 10 predictions. The Laplace approximation was optimized post-hoc to a trained convolutional neural network model fitting the approximation on the output layer of the model using a full Hessian structure. Each model was trained for 40 epochs and the model with the best validation loss was used for evaluation. All code used for experiments can be downloaded from the project GitHub repository[1] along with reproduction instructions, trained models and expanded testing metrics.

5   Results and Discussion

Table 1 reports results for both the ISIC 2019 and the PCam datasets. It is divided into sections showing results for each trained model (with the temperature set to one) followed by results with temperature optimized for different measures of calibration. Note that temperature scaling will never affect accuracy. Each ISIC 2019 result is reported as a mean and standard deviation estimated from three runs.

5.1   ISIC 2019

On the multi-class skin lesion classification task, temperature scaling always improved calibration. The largest improvement in mean KDE-ECE when using the baseline CNN model was from 0.046 to 0.012; other temperature scaling measures achieved similar results.

Label smoothing achieved better accuracy but resulted in calibration inferior to temperature scaling with one-hot labels. Adding temperature scaling to label smoothing tended to improve calibration but was not as effective as temperature scaling without label smoothing in this regard. Optimizing for MCE was ineffective.

Focal loss ($\gamma = 2.0$) with temperature optimized for KDE-ECE achieved calibration and accuracy competitive with, and perhaps slightly better than, the cross-entropy model with temperature scaling. Both of the focal loss models showed behavior more akin to that reported in [23] in the sense that temperature optimized for KDE-ECE led to better calibration with a significant impact on KDE-ECE compared to temperature optimized for NLL.

---

[1] GitHub Repository: https://github.com/UoD-CVIP/Medical_Calibration.

Table 1. Calibration and accuracy results for ISIC 2019 and PCam datasets. ISIC 2019 results are means and standard deviations over three iterations. Each section reports results from a single model type; TS denotes temperature scaling.

	ISIC 2019				PCam			
	KDE-ECE	MCE	NLL	ACC	KDE-ECE	MCE	NLL	ACC
Baseline CNN	0.046 ± 0.017	0.112 ± 0.042	0.514 ± 0.015	0.836 ± 0.012	0.123	0.187	0.543	0.848
TS nll	0.015 ± 0.002	0.037 ± 0.014	0.471 ± 0.017	0.836 ± 0.012	0.123	0.187	0.543	0.848
TS ece	0.017 ± 0.007	0.038 ± 0.010	0.472 ± 0.017	0.836 ± 0.012	0.123	0.204	0.585	0.848
TS mce	0.016 ± 0.004	0.042 ± 0.009	0.471 ± 0.018	0.836 ± 0.012	0.123	0.197	0.567	0.848
TS nll+ece	0.012 ± 0.002	0.043 ± 0.012	0.471 ± 0.017	0.836 ± 0.012	0.122	0.210	0.603	0.848
TS nll+mce	0.018 ± 0.002	0.038 ± 0.010	0.472 ± 0.018	0.836 ± 0.012	0.123	0.210	0.605	0.848
TS ece+mce	0.014 ± 0.021	0.041 ± 0.014	0.472 ± 0.017	0.836 ± 0.012	0.123	0.193	0.557	0.848
TS nll+ece+mce	0.015 ± 0.003	0.042 ± 0.011	0.472 ± 0.017	0.836 ± 0.012	0.123	0.187	0.543	0.848
LS $\alpha = 0.1$	0.039 ± 0.001	0.065 ± 0.001	0.495 ± 0.011	0.855 ± 0.005	0.116	0.146	0.398	0.848
TS nll	0.028 ± 0.003	0.087 ± 0.021	0.483 ± 0.013	0.855 ± 0.005	0.123	0.244	0.536	0.848
TS ece	0.029 ± 0.003	0.134 ± 0.023	0.504 ± 0.013	0.855 ± 0.005	0.124	0.346	1.112	0.848
TS mce	0.053 ± 0.016	0.070 ± 0.016	0.505 ± 0.004	0.855 ± 0.005	0.121	0.198	0.423	0.848
TS nll+ece	0.028 ± 0.003	0.086 ± 0.020	0.048 ± 0.013	0.855 ± 0.005	0.123	0.237	0.551	0.848
TS nll+mce	0.033 ± 0.006	0.071 ± 0.016	0.490 ± 0.015	0.855 ± 0.005	0.121	0.198	0.423	0.848
TS ece+mce	0.032 ± 0.006	0.072 ± 0.016	0.489 ± 0.016	0.855 ± 0.005	0.121	0.198	0.423	0.848
TS nll+ece+mce	0.031 ± 0.004	0.070 ± 0.010	0.488 ± 0.014	0.855 ± 0.005	0.121	0.199	0.424	0.848
LS $\alpha = 0.2$	0.105 ± 0.005	0.173 ± 0.050	0.562 ± 0.015	0.862 ± 0.009	0.097	0.142	0.370	0.852
TS nll	0.037 ± 0.001	0.145 ± 0.006	0.503 ± 0.013	0.862 ± 0.009	0.118	0.307	0.601	0.852
TS ece	0.036 ± 0.001	0.134 ± 0.023	0.504 ± 0.013	0.862 ± 0.009	0.113	0.226	0.396	0.852
TS mce	0.095 ± 0.018	0.129 ± 0.032	0.553 ± 0.015	0.862 ± 0.009	0.113	0.226	0.396	0.852
TS nll+ece	0.036 ± 0.001	0.148 ± 0.009	0.503 ± 0.013	0.862 ± 0.009	0.117	0.284	0.508	0.852
TS nll+mce	0.051 ± 0.006	0.099 ± 0.006	0.514 ± 0.012	0.862 ± 0.009	0.113	0.226	0.396	0.852
TS ece+mce	0.047 ± 0.003	0.106 ± 0.019	0.511 ± 0.011	0.862 ± 0.009	0.113	0.226	0.396	0.852
TS nll+ece+mce	0.046 ± 0.007	0.113 ± 0.012	0.510 ± 0.010	0.862 ± 0.009	0.114	0.243	0.409	0.852
FL $\gamma = 2.0$	0.057 ± 0.020	0.097 ± 0.027	0.491 ± 0.013	0.840 ± 0.004	0.122	0.101	0.356	0.854
TS nll	0.031 ± 0.004	0.078 ± 0.018	0.484 ± 0.007	0.840 ± 0.004	0.100	0.155	0.371	0.854
TS ece	0.011 ± 0.003	0.061 ± 0.021	0.492 ± 0.004	0.840 ± 0.004	0.101	0.180	0.388	0.854
TS mce	0.014 ± 0.002	0.062 ± 0.021	0.497 ± 0.010	0.840 ± 0.004	0.101	0.180	0.392	0.854
TS nll+ece	0.014 ± 0.003	0.062 ± 0.018	0.489 ± 0.007	0.840 ± 0.004	0.100	0.170	0.385	0.854
TS nll+mce	0.013 ± 0.003	0.063 ± 0.018	0.490 ± 0.008	0.840 ± 0.004	0.101	0.180	0.393	0.854
TS ece+mce	0.012 ± 0.003	0.062 ± 0.021	0.494 ± 0.008	0.840 ± 0.004	0.101	0.179	0.391	0.854
TS nll+ece+mce	0.026 ± 0.020	0.085 ± 0.034	0.497 ± 0.013	0.840 ± 0.004	0.101	0.179	0.392	0.854
FL $\gamma = 5.0$	0.180 ± 0.007	0.250 ± 0.010	0.615 ± 0.011	0.823 ± 0.002	0.229	0.289	0.530	0.835
TS nll	0.061 ± 0.010	0.123 ± 0.022	0.551 ± 0.011	0.823 ± 0.002	0.068	0.063	0.382	0.835
TS ece	0.024 ± 0.005	0.084 ± 0.026	0.589 ± 0.016	0.823 ± 0.002	0.070	0.077	0.391	0.835
TS mce	0.031 ± 0.009	0.074 ± 0.007	0.621 ± 0.046	0.823 ± 0.002	0.069	0.069	0.387	0.835
TS nll+ece	0.032 ± 0.008	0.101 ± 0.026	0.561 ± 0.011	0.823 ± 0.002	0.069	0.071	0.387	0.835
TS nll+mce	0.031 ± 0.009	0.102 ± 0.024	0.562 ± 0.010	0.823 ± 0.002	0.069	0.069	0.387	0.835
TS ece+mce	0.025 ± 0.005	0.079 ± 0.012	0.593 ± 0.029	0.823 ± 0.002	0.069	0.069	0.387	0.835
TS nll+ece+mce	0.028 ± 0.007	0.094 ± 0.025	0.569 ± 0.009	0.823 ± 0.002	0.069	0.069	0.387	0.835
Bayes-by-B'prop	0.118 ± 0.006	0.260 ± 0.021	0.886 ± 0.062	0.795 ± 0.069	0.115	0.208	0.551	0.857
Laplace approx.	0.041 ± 0.016	0.101 ± 0.037	0.507 ± 0.010	0.837 ± 0.012	0.122	0.210	0.603	0.848

5.2 Patch Camelyon (PCam)

On the binary classification task using the larger PCam dataset, we observe different behavior when using temperature scaling. The baseline CNN model gained no calibration benefit from temperature scaling, whichever calibration measure was used to optimize the temperature.

Calibration using label smoothing appears to be better than that obtained by the baseline without temperature scaling. Adding temperature scaling to label smoothing appears to worsen calibration performance slightly on this dataset. We observed that calibration measures as functions of temperature had shallow minima; optimized temperature values obtained using the validation set differed from those that would have been optimal for the test set.

Focal loss with $\gamma = 2.0$ had higher accuracy and similar calibration to the baseline without temperature scaling. However, unlike the baseline, both focal loss models' calibration was helped by temperature scaling. Focal loss ($\gamma = 5.0$) combined with temperature scaling achieved the best calibration of any of the models on the PCam dataset. Which measure was used to optimize temperature made little or no difference.

5.3 Comparison with Bayesian Inference Methods

Bayes-by-Backprop performed relatively poorly on the ISIC 2019 dataset both in terms of calibration and accuracy. This could be due to the extra complexity involved with training a multi-class Bayesian neural network using backpropagation. On the other hand, Bayes-by-Backprop achieved the highest accuracy on the PCam dataset and had a lower KDE-ECE than the baseline network. Nevertheless, temperature scaling of networks trained with focal loss achieved comparable accuracy and better calibration in terms of both KDE-ECE and MCE. Laplace approximation outperformed Bayes-by-Backprop on ISIC 2019; it is also computationally less expensive. However, it was not competitive with temperature scaling in terms of calibration. On the larger PCam dataset, the Laplace approximation did not yield advantage over the baseline model.

6 Conclusion

This study has investigated deep neural network calibration for medical image classification and adds to the evidence base on the effectiveness of various calibration methods on two differing tasks and datasets. The results highlight the need to consider the choice of calibration method for each specific task. On ISIC2019, temperature scaling nearly always helped, giving a marked improvement in calibration with cross-entropy loss and focal loss trained networks. In contrast, temperature scaling did not improve calibration when used with cross-entropy trained networks on the PCam dataset, whereas it yielded improved calibration when combined with focal loss. While it is reasonable to expect that the use of calibration measures to tune temperature on validation data would improve calibration measured in that way, we have shown in our experimental results that this is not always the case. In most situations, the calibration performance is not significantly impacted by the measure used for optimization. We found that overall, focal loss combined with temperature scaling could achieve strong calibration performance.

Acknowledgments. J. Carse was supported by the UK Engineering and Physical Sciences Research Council (EPSRC Training Grant EP/N509632/1). This paper also reports independent research partly funded by the National Institute for Health Research (Artificial Intelligence, Deep learning for effective triaging of skin disease in the NHS, AI AWARD01901) and NHSX. The views expressed in this publication are those of the authors and not necessarily those of the National Institute for Health Research, NHSX or the Department of Health and Social Care.

References

1. Bejnordi, B.E., et al.: Diagnostic assessment of deep learning algorithms for detection of lymph node metastases in women with breast cancer. J. Am. Med. Assoc. **318**(22), 2199–2210 (2017)
2. Blundell, C., Cornebise, J., Kavukcuoglu, K., Wierstra, D.: Weight uncertainty in neural networks. In: Proceedings of the 32nd International Conference on Machine Learning, pp. 1613–1622. PMLR (2015)
3. Botev, A., Ritter, H., Barber, D.: Practical Gauss-Newton optimisation for deep learning. In: Proceedings of the 34th International Conference on Machine Learning, pp. 557–565. PMLR (2017)
4. Carse, J., McKenna, S.: Active learning for patch-based digital pathology using convolutional neural networks to reduce annotation costs. In: Reyes-Aldasoro, C.C., Janowczyk, A., Veta, M., Bankhead, P., Sirinukunwattana, K. (eds.) ECDP 2019. LNCS, vol. 11435, pp. 20–27. Springer, Cham (2019). https://doi.org/10.1007/978-3-030-23937-4_3
5. Carse, J., et al.: Robust selective classification of skin lesions with asymmetric costs. In: Sudre, C.H., Licandro, R., Baumgartner, C., Melbourne, A., Dalca, A., Hutter, J., Tanno, R., Abaci Turk, E., Van Leemput, K., Torrents Barrena, J., Wells, W.M., Macgowan, C. (eds.) UNSURE/PIPPI -2021. LNCS, vol. 12959, pp. 112–121. Springer, Cham (2021). https://doi.org/10.1007/978-3-030-87735-4_11
6. Codella, N.C., et al.: Skin lesion analysis toward melanoma detection: a challenge at the 2017 international symposium on biomedical imaging (ISBI), hosted by the international skin imaging collaboration (ISIC). In: 2018 IEEE 15th International Symposium on Biomedical Imaging, pp. 168–172. IEEE (2018)
7. Combalia, M., et al.: BCN20000: dermoscopic lesions in the wild. arXiv preprint arXiv:1908.02288 (2019)
8. Dai, Z., Low, B.K.H., Jaillet, P.: Federated Bayesian optimization via Thompson sampling. Adv. Neural Inf. Process. Syst. **33**, 9687–9699 (2020)
9. Daxberger, E., Kristiadi, A., Immer, A., Eschenhagen, R., Bauer, M., Hennig, P.: Laplace redux-effortless Bayesian deep learning. Adv. Neural Inf. Process. Syst. **34**, 20089–20103 (2021)
10. Deng, J., Dong, W., Socher, R., Li, L.J., Li, K., Fei-Fei, L.: ImageNet: a large-scale hierarchical image database. In: 2009 IEEE Conference on Computer Vision and Pattern Recognition, pp. 248–255. IEEE (2009)

11. Frenkel, L., Goldberger, J.: Network calibration by class-based temperature scaling. In: 2021 29th European Signal Processing Conference, pp. 1486–1490. IEEE (2021)
12. Gawlikowski, J., et al.: A survey of uncertainty in deep neural networks. arXiv preprint arXiv:2107.03342 (2021)
13. Guo, C., Pleiss, G., Sun, Y., Weinberger, K.Q.: On calibration of modern neural networks. In: Proceedings of the 34th International Conference on Machine Learning, pp. 1321–1330. PMLR (2017)
14. Hendrycks, D., Mazeika, M., Dietterich, T.: Deep anomaly detection with outlier exposure. arXiv preprint arXiv:1812.04606 (2018)
15. Hendrycks, D., Mu, N., Cubuk, E.D., Zoph, B., Gilmer, J., Lakshminarayanan, B.: AugMix: a simple data processing method to improve robustness and uncertainty. arXiv preprint arXiv:1912.02781 (2019)
16. Islam, M., Glocker, B.: Spatially varying label smoothing: capturing uncertainty from expert annotations. In: Feragen, A., Sommer, S., Schnabel, J., Nielsen, M. (eds.) IPMI 2021. LNCS, vol. 12729, pp. 677–688. Springer, Cham (2021). https://doi.org/10.1007/978-3-030-78191-0_52
17. Kwon, Y., Won, J.H., Kim, B.J., Paik, M.C.: Uncertainty quantification using Bayesian neural networks in classification: application to biomedical image segmentation. Comput. Stat. Data Anal. **142**, 106816 (2020)
18. Liang, G., Zhang, Y., Wang, X., Jacobs, N.: Improved trainable calibration method for neural networks on medical imaging classification. arXiv preprint arXiv:2009.04057 (2020)
19. Lin, T.Y., Goyal, P., Girshick, R., He, K., Dollár, P.: Focal loss for dense object detection. In: Proceedings of the IEEE International Conference on Computer Vision, pp. 2980–2988 (2017)
20. Liu, D.C., Nocedal, J.: On the limited memory BFGS method for large scale optimization. Math. Program. **45**, 503–528 (1989)
21. MacKay, D.J.: Bayesian interpolation. Neural Comput. **4**(3), 415–447 (1992)
22. Maron, R.C., et al.: Systematic outperformance of 112 dermatologists in multiclass skin cancer image classification by convolutional neural networks. Eur. J. Cancer **119**, 57–65 (2019)
23. Mukhoti, J., Kulharia, V., Sanyal, A., Golodetz, S., Torr, P., Dokania, P.: Calibrating deep neural networks using focal loss. Adv. Neural Inf. Process. Syst. **33**, 15288–15299 (2020)
24. Müller, R., Kornblith, S., Hinton, G.E.: When does label smoothing help? In: Advances in Neural Information Processing Systems, vol. 32 (2019)
25. Parzen, E.: On estimation of a probability density function and mode. Ann. Math. Stat. **33**(3), 1065–1076 (1962)
26. Platt, J., et al.: Probabilistic outputs for support vector machines and comparisons to regularized likelihood methods. Adv. Large Margin Classifiers **10**(3), 61–74 (1999)
27. Roelofs, R., Cain, N., Shlens, J., Mozer, M.C.: Mitigating bias in calibration error estimation. In: International Conference on Artificial Intelligence and Statistics, pp. 4036–4054. PMLR (2022)
28. Szegedy, C., Vanhoucke, V., Ioffe, S., Shlens, J., Wojna, Z.: Rethinking the inception architecture for computer vision. In: Proceedings of the IEEE Conference on Computer Vision and Pattern Recognition, pp. 2818–2826 (2016)
29. Tan, M., Le, Q.: EfficientNet: rethinking model scaling for convolutional neural networks. In: Proceedings of the 36th International Conference on Machine Learning International Conference on Machine Learning, pp. 6105–6114. PMLR (2019)

30. Tschandl, P., Rosendahl, C., Kittler, H.: The HAM10000 dataset, a large collection of multi-source dermatoscopic images of common pigmented skin lesions. Sci. Data **5**(1), 1–9 (2018)
31. Ulmer, D., Meijerink, L., Cinà, G.: Trust issues: uncertainty estimation does not enable reliable OOD detection on medical tabular data. In: Machine Learning for Health, pp. 341–354. PMLR (2020)
32. Veeling, B.S., Linmans, J., Winkens, J., Cohen, T., Welling, M.: Rotation equivariant CNNs for digital pathology. In: Frangi, A.F., Schnabel, J.A., Davatzikos, C., Alberola-López, C., Fichtinger, G. (eds.) MICCAI 2018. LNCS, vol. 11071, pp. 210–218. Springer, Cham (2018). https://doi.org/10.1007/978-3-030-00934-2_24
33. Zhang, J., Kailkhura, B., Han, T.Y.J.: Mix-n-Match: ensemble and compositional methods for uncertainty calibration in deep learning. In: Proceedings of the 37th International Conference on Machine Learning, pp. 11117–11128. PMLR (2020)

Annotation Uncertainty and Out of Distribution Management

nnOOD: A Framework for Benchmarking Self-supervised Anomaly Localisation Methods

Matthew Baugh[1]([✉])(iD), Jeremy Tan[1](iD), Athanasios Vlontzos[1](iD),
Johanna P. Müller[2](iD), and Bernhard Kainz[1,2](iD)

[1] Imperial College London, London SW7 2AZ, UK
matthew.baugh17@imperial.ac.uk
[2] Friedrich–Alexander University Erlangen–Nürnberg, Erlangen, Germany

Abstract. The wide variety of in-distribution and out-of-distribution data in medical imaging makes universal anomaly detection a challenging task. Recently a number of self-supervised methods have been developed that train end-to-end models on healthy data augmented with synthetic anomalies. However, it is difficult to compare these methods as it is not clear whether gains in performance are from the task itself or the training pipeline around it. It is also difficult to assess whether a task generalises well for universal anomaly detection, as they are often only tested on a limited range of anomalies. To assist with this we have developed nnOOD, a framework that adapts nnU-Net to allow for comparison of self-supervised anomaly localisation methods. By isolating the synthetic, self-supervised task from the rest of the training process we perform a more faithful comparison of the tasks, whilst also making the workflow for evaluating over a given dataset quick and easy. Using this we have implemented the current state-of-the-art tasks and evaluated them on a challenging X-ray dataset.

Keywords: Anomaly localisation · Self-supervised learning

1 Introduction

Out-of-distribution detection, *i.e.* learning a normative distribution from a single class and classifying anomalous test samples without supervised training, is a notoriously challenging task. Many methods struggle in scenarios where humans can easily detect an outlier. For example, failures in detecting potholes under different lighting conditions [4], a jet ski in a road scene [7] or determining whether a picture of a cat is a dog [9]. It becomes even more difficult in medical imaging, where abnormalities frequently go unseen by expert observers, often because of inattentional blindness [8]. This issue worsens in high-pressure environments such as emergency and trauma care. There, the main cause of misdiagnosis is the misinterpretation of radiographs, with miss rates of up to 80% [18]. In these

C. H. Sudre et al. (Eds.): UNSURE 2022, LNCS 13563, pp. 103–112, 2022.
https://doi.org/10.1007/978-3-031-16749-2_10

situations an automated tool that acts as a second reader, alerting clinicians to any unusual features, would be useful.

Many publications in the field of medical anomaly detection limit their experiments to datasets with a narrow range of abnormalities [3,15,20,24], raising questions regarding their ability to generalise to anomalies seen in other medical applications or modalities. Recently there has been a trend of training end-to-end anomaly detection models using synthetic anomalies to alter healthy data. These methods exhibit good performance on both manufacturing [21] and medical tasks [24,25], with the majority of the top submissions to the recent MICCAI 2021 Medical Out-of-Distribution challenge (MOOD) [29] being trained in this manner. However, as these tasks are synthetic by nature, it is even more important that they are thoroughly tested, as there is a risk of the task being overly tuned to the target evaluation dataset.

Contribution: In this paper we present the nnOOD framework. It builds on top of the nnU-Net framework [12], maintaining the core principle of adapting the architecture to the provided dataset, but gearing it toward self-supervised anomaly localisation. This makes validating a synthetic anomaly task on a given dataset as simple as organising a dataset for nnU-Net. We also provide a common interface for self-supervised tasks, simplifying the process of creating and applying a new method. We hope that making this paradigm of anomaly detection more accessible can encourage more interest in this research area. Ultimately, we hope that nnOOD provides a standardised framework for comparing these methods fairly. Another goal is to gain insight into what makes a synthetic task useful and elucidate why a certain task fails or succeeds in different situations. Source code, including a guide on applying the framework to a new dataset, is available at https://github.com/matt-baugh/nnOOD.

Related Work: A common way to perform anomaly localisation is by measuring the difference between an image and its reconstruction. The assumption is that a model trained on normal data will not be able to reproduce anomalous regions, leading them to larger deviations. This method lends itself most easily to autoencoder-based architectures [3,15], but has also been applied by using generative adversarial networks [11,20]. However, reconstruction loss often fails as models are not always able to reconstruct healthy regions in potentially unhealthy samples [2], and anomalies with extreme textures but a normal intensity distribution are difficult to identify [16]. Sample-level anomaly detection can be done as an auxiliary task using a classification network, although performance can vary greatly between training epochs [28]. Methods using normalizing flows [10,27] are currently the state-of-the-art benchmarks on the MVTec [6] dataset. Unfortunately, these strategies require pre-trained model which is often not possible for medical imaging tasks, and high performance on computer vision tasks does not guarantee similar performance on medical imaging tasks [5].

Foreign Patch Interpolation (FPI) [24] was the first method to train end-to-end models for out-of-distribution localisation using synthetic anomalies. FPI creates subtle anomalies by interpolating a patch of the current sample with a patch extracted from the same location of a different sample. The model is then trained to predict the pixel-wise interpolation factor, causing the model to learn a score correlated with how anomalous the pixel was. This had good performance on both brain MRI and abdominal CT data, winning the MICCAI 2020 MOOD challenge [29] in both the sample-wise and pixel-wise categories. Poisson image interpolation (PII) was introduced to mitigate the discontinuities at the edges of FPI's patches [25], allowing for a more seamless blend between the patch and its surroundings. However, there was still limited variation in the synthetic anomalies, due to the interpolated patches being extracted from the same location in the secondary image. Independently, CutPaste [13] used a similar sort of augmentation by copying a patch from one place and pasting it at a random different location within the same image. The patches are sometimes altered through rotation or jitter in the pixel values. Rather than training end-to-end, [13] trained a one-class classifier, using a Gaussian density estimator on the output to enable outlier detection, and applying GradCAM [22] for anomaly localisation. Natural synthetic anomalies (NSA) [21] combines the aforementioned image augmentations, further increasing the variety of synthetic samples by resizing the patches and randomising the number of patches introduced in an image. Arguing that in previous methods the difference between the distributions of the blended patches can cause the same label to be applied to vastly different levels of abnormality, they opted to use a scaled logistic function applied to the mean absolute intensity difference across each channel.

The results of the MICCAI 2021 MOOD challenge [29] displayed the success of these techniques, with the majority of the presented works being models trained end-to-end with synthetic anomalies. Despite their achievements, many of those methods faced practical challenges in engineering the synthetic task. For example, many 3D methods used image resizing which leads to loss of information and obscures small anomalies. In addition, some methods apply non-overlapping patches to the larger abdominal data, resulting in prediction artefacts around the edges.

We see the structure of nnU-Net [12] as a natural solution to these issues. The nnU-Net framework uses a set of heuristic rules to dynamically adapt a U-Net [19] to a given biomedical image segmentation dataset. Combining these architectural decisions with a solid pipeline of adaptive preprocessing, extensive data augmentation, model ensembling and aggregating tiled predictions, nnU-Net consistently performs well across a wide range of tasks. The ease with which the framework can be applied has made semantic segmentation more accessible, even to those without machine learning expertise.

2   Method

In this section we discuss adaptations to the well-known nnU-Net pipeline that make it suitable for anomaly detection. Graphically summarized in Fig. 1, our method differs significantly from others such as nnDetection [1] because we aim for pixel-wise predictions, allowing for a greater overlap with the original nnU-Net pipeline.

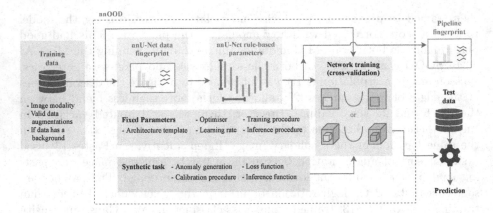

Fig. 1. Overview of the nnOOD framework. The green components are entirely new to nnOOD, orange components differ significantly from their nnU-Net counterparts and grey components have only minor changes. (Color figure online)

One of the primary challenges of applying the nnU-Net framework to anomaly detection is overfitting *to the synthetic task*. This is expected, as nnU-Net is intended for use on the same task at training and test time. Therefore, it is designed to perform its training task as accurately as possible, using heavy data augmentation to avoid overfitting to the specific training data. One way we reduce overfitting to a synthetic task is in model selection. Originally, nnU-Net uses a five-fold cross-validation process across three different network configurations: a 2D U-Net, a 3D U-Net, and, if the data is sufficiently large, a 3D U-Net cascade. Then the final model is chosen as the model or ensemble of two models which achieves the highest mean foreground dice score on the training set cross-validation. In our framework we do not assume we have access to a validation set of real anomalies, and we do not want to select a model based on performance on synthetic data. Instead, we select a model which matches the dimensionality of the data, i.e. using n-dimensional models for n-dimensional data, which performed well in nnU-Net's experiments. We also omit the cascade setting because the dynamic nature of self-supervised tasks is less amenable to cascaded training.

Another area that requires restrictions is the training regime. The original nnU-Net training schedule is much longer than the training duration seen in many self-supervised methods. For instance, the training schedule in Schlüter et al. [21] terminates well before the earliest stopping point of nnU-Net, after less than a third of the number of iterations. To mitigate this we add early stopping based on a moving average of the average precision score (AP) on the synthetic data validation set. We found that a threshold of 0.875 allows the models to learn useful features without overfitting to the fine-grain details of the synthetic tasks. If a model fails to reach this threshold we utilise the original nnU-Net early stopping based on the loss plateauing as a backup. We train each method to an equal level of validation performance (on its own task) so that we always learn each task to the same extent, regardless of it's difficulty. By contrast, using a set number of epochs for every task would likely lead to overtraining for simple tasks, while undertraining on more complex ones.

Although data augmentation is one of the key factors for nnU-Net's success, we cannot naïvely apply it, as many of the augmentations carry the risk of moving the sample out of the distribution of the normal data. By learning invariance to an augmentation, the representation is trained to ignore it, preventing it from being identified as anomalous. For example, a model trained with random rotations and translations would see misaligned data as normal. Instead we opt to allow the user to define which augmentations are "safe" as part of the dataset description. This allows us to utilise as much data augmentation as possible within valid parameters for the given dataset.

The appearance of normal data can vary vastly depending on the location within the image. This leads to an inconsistent training signal for the model when attempting to learn to identify normality within incomplete patches. This is particularly true when applying synthetic tasks such as CutPaste, where the patch is anomalous specifically because it appears at a different location within the image. To allow the model to perceive the spatial context when evaluating a patch we incorporate a positional encoding, similar to ConvCoord [14]. An additional channel is concatenated per spatial dimension of the data, with values ranging from -1 to 1, representing the coordinate value of that pixel for that dimension. This has been shown to assist convergence in other anomaly detection tasks [23].

When selecting a patch to train on, nnU-Net chooses uniformly from all patches that lie fully within the image bounds. This leads to the model rarely learning from regions towards the edges of the images, as only a small proportion of valid locations include them. This is an issue at inference time where many patches are taken from the boundaries of the image, which are then more likely to be considered anomalous, due to the infrequency of observing them during training. To rectify this, we simply randomly select from the inference patch locations at training time. As the synthetic anomalies are often quite small relative to the size of the image, during training we oversample the anomalies. For 30% of each batch we choose the random patch location such that the centre of at least one anomaly was present within the patch.

When integrating the synthetic task into the framework we want to be as flexible as possible, to avoid pigeonholing future tasks into the structure of the current ones. Formally, we define a synthetic anomaly task as:

$$\tilde{x}_i, \tilde{y}_i = f_\theta(x_i, x_j, [m_i, m_j]) \qquad\qquad \theta = g(X, P) \qquad (1)$$

where f is the anomaly generating function, producing an augmented sample $\tilde{x}_i$ with pixel-wise label $\tilde{y}_i$ from two samples of the distribution of normal data x_i and x_j. m_i and m_j denote the foreground masks for the corresponding samples, which are provided if present. These are created by applying a simple Sobel operator on the image, calculating the magnitude of the gradient and using region growing from a number of locations around the image corners. We chose to use the image gradient to determine the background as different modalities have different background intensities, but most will be uniform with a low gradient magnitude. Hence we only apply this if the dataset description indicates that the dataset has a consistent, uniform background. An example of this would be in brain MRI, where the background occupies a large portion of the image, but we would not attempt to generate foreground masks for X-ray data, such as ChestX-ray14, as they are normally already cropped to the region of interest. The parameters of the task, θ, are determined by a calibration function g when applied to the dataset of normal data X and the current experiment plan P. The calibration function is necessary because although some tasks have constant parameters, others (such as NSA [21]) use different parameters depending on the dataset. We place no further restrictions on the implementation of these functions, allowing users to utilise or ignore the provided arguments as they see fit to produce a useful synthetic anomaly task.

To provide more flexibility, we allow the user to define the loss function $\mathcal{L}_\theta$ used when training with their task, which is given the raw network logits and the synthetic label $\widehat{y}_i$ as input. They can similarly define the inference function h_θ, which is applied to the network logits at test time to produce pixel-wise anomaly scores.

Finally, if the synthetic task happens to follow the structure of patch-based methods such as FPI and CutPaste, we provide a compartmentalised framework to build such tasks. This divides the task into the initial creation of the patch shape, a sequence of patch transformations, which can be spatial or alter the pixel values, the blending of the patch into the destination image and the labelling of the resulting image. This makes it much easier to tweak existing tasks and isolate the factors that contribute the most to performance.

3   Experiments and Results

Synthetic Tasks: As an initial baseline for future methods we have implemented the FPI [24], CutPaste [13], PII [25] and NSA [21] tasks using our framework. Due to their simplicity, FPI and PII can be directly generalised to arbitrary dimensions and applied to any sort of input, however the specialised nature of the other two methods requires some changes. For CutPaste this is primarily due to their use of colour jitter, which applied brightness, contrast, saturation and hue transformations. We omit the saturation and hue operations as the concepts do not translate to other modalities. For contrast, we move the pixel intensity values to the mean across each channel (as opposed to the weighted average used for colour images) and for brightness we take the global minimum of the dataset as the zero value for scaling. Adapting NSA was a more involved task due to the number of hyperparameters that were originally chosen for each dataset by visual inspection of the generated anomalies. At a high level, we base the maximum number of anomalies, bounds on the size of each dimension, and the minimum object area included in the extracted patch on the average foreground dimensions (treating the entire image as foreground if no background is present). NSA also converts absolute intensity differences into labels that conform to a logistic function. To automate this, we create 100 anomalies and calculate shape and scale parameters such that anomalous regions translate to labels with a lower bound of 0.1 that saturate at the 40th percentile. We experimented with using both source and mixed gradients, denoted as NSA and NSA_{Mixed} respectively.

Data: We evaluate these tasks on ChestX-ray14 [26], a public chest X-ray dataset covering 14 common thorax disease categories as well as healthy samples. We use the same training distribution as [25]: posteroanterior (PA) views of healthy adult patients, divided by gender to create two healthy training datasets, with 17,852 male and 14,720 female samples respectively. For the test dataset we perform the same filtering on the unhealthy data, but further restrict it to samples that provide pathology bounding boxes. This leaves us with 245 male and 217 female test samples. As there are no pixel-wise annotations provided we treat the bounding boxes as anomaly masks. For preprocessing each sample is normalised to have zero mean and unit standard deviation. Note that we did not need to resize the images due to the patch-based nature of our framework.

Results: Table 1 shows our comparison of the different self-supervised tasks, with Fig. 2 displaying example test images and their predicted anomaly maps. These scores demonstrate the challenging nature of the dataset. Inexact ground truth bounding boxes and class imbalance make it difficult to achieve high pixel-level average precision (calculated using `scikit-learn` [17]). For reference, a random classifier (0.5 AUROC) would achieve 0.074 and 0.063 AP for the male and female datasets respectively.

Table 1. Pixel-wise metrics comparing models trained with different anomaly tasks using the nnOOD framework. AUROC - Area Under the Receiver Operating Characteristic curve, AP - Average Precision score.

Dataset	Male PA					Female PA				
Task	FPI	CutPaste	PII	NSA	NSA_{Mixed}	FPI	CutPaste	PII	NSA	NSA_{Mixed}
AUROC ↑	0.515	0.484	0.554	0.718	0.714	0.490	0.446	0.615	0.699	0.698
AP ↑	0.075	0.071	0.084	0.162	0.167	0.064	0.060	0.086	0.139	0.133

The FPI and CutPaste tasks do not seem to help the models identify medical anomalies. This is most likely because sharp, image-aligned discontinuities are unlikely to appear in real pathologies. Both of these methods generally predict low scores across the images (Fig. 2), resulting in performance similar to that of a random classifier. On the other hand, tasks which seamlessly blend their synthetic anomalies into the target image (PII, NSA, NSA_{Mixed}) help more. Although these approaches may not reach supervised performance, they are able to learn useful features without any exposure to real anomalies.

Interestingly, the use of different synthetic tasks massively altered the time taken to reach the AP threshold. The difference in average training times reflects how easily the anomalies can be seen: CutPaste uses very obvious anomalies (27.3 epochs), NSA and NSA$_{Mixed}$ blend their patches more seamlessly (88.5 and 119.7 epochs), by not moving the extracted patch FPI's anomalies are more subtle (272.5 epochs), and PII's addition of Poisson image blending to that formula increases the subtlety even further (312.7 epochs).

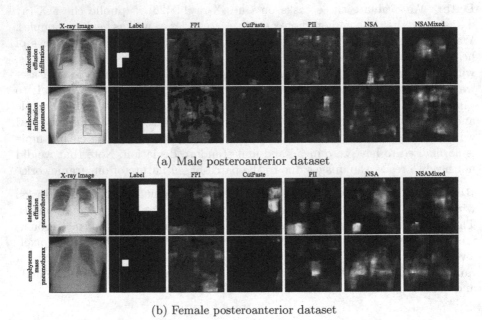

(a) Male posteroanterior dataset

(b) Female posteroanterior dataset

Fig. 2. Examples of test predictions on each X-ray dataset. The disease labels are keywords extracted from the sample's radiologist report [26].

4   Conclusion

In this paper we present a framework that makes self-supervised anomaly local-isation more accessible and facilitates evaluation on a unified platform. By automating the training configuration independently from the synthetic task, we are able to compare the true ability of each method under more controlled settings and free from unequal hyperparameter tuning. Using this framework, we compare the current state-of-the-art methods and show that there is still much room for improvement. We hope that nnOOD will enable further investigation of self-supervised, synthetic anomaly localisation methods across a wider variety of modalities. Our modular design also serves as a foundation for continued research in paradigms other than patch blending, such as using deformations.

In our experiments, we focused on anomaly localisation at the pixel level. Although sample-level detection is often reported, these scores sometimes inflate performance. We believe that pixel-level evaluation better reflects the usefulness of these methods in clinical practice. For example, an accurate sample-level score with poor localisation may actually mislead a clinician to pursue a tangential diagnosis. This is particularly concerning in anomaly detection, where scores do not correspond to any specific disease classes. We hope that nnOOD will help facilitate future developments in anomaly detection and hold them to a higher standard, so that the field as a whole can move closer to real, beneficial tools.

Acknowledgements. This work was supported by the UKRI London Medical Imaging and Artificial Intelligence Centre for Value Based Healthcare.

References

1. Baumgartner, M., Jäger, P.F., Isensee, F., Maier-Hein, K.H.: nnDetection: a self-configuring method for medical object detection. In: de Bruijne, M., et al. (eds.) MICCAI 2021. LNCS, vol. 12905, pp. 530–539. Springer, Cham (2021). https://doi.org/10.1007/978-3-030-87240-3_51
2. Baur, C., Denner, S., Wiestler, B., Navab, N., Albarqouni, S.: Autoencoders for unsupervised anomaly segmentation in brain MR images: a comparative study. Med. Image Anal. **69**, 101952 (2021) https://doi.org/10.1016/j.media.2020.101952
3. Baur, C., Wiestler, B., Albarqouni, S., Navab, N.: Scale-space autoencoders for unsupervised anomaly segmentation in brain MRI. In: Martel, A.L., et al. (eds.) MICCAI 2020. LNCS, vol. 12264, pp. 552–561. Springer, Cham (2020). https://doi.org/10.1007/978-3-030-59719-1_54
4. Bello-Salau, H., Onumanyi, A.J., Salawudeen, A.T., Mu'azu, M.B., Oyinbo, A.M.: An examination of different vision based approaches for road anomaly detection. In: 2019 2nd International Conference of the IEEE Nigeria Computer Chapter (NigeriaComputConf), pp. 1–6 (2019). https://doi.org/10.1109/NigeriaComputConf45974.2019.8949646
5. Berger, C., Paschali, M., Glocker, B., Kamnitsas, K.: Confidence-based out-of-distribution detection: a comparative study and analysis. In: Sudre, C.H., et al. (eds.) UNSURE/PIPPI -2021. LNCS, vol. 12959, pp. 122–132. Springer, Cham (2021). https://doi.org/10.1007/978-3-030-87735-4_12
6. Bergmann, P., Batzner, K., Fauser, M., Sattlegger, D., Steger, C.: The MVTEC anomaly detection dataset: a comprehensive real-world dataset for unsupervised anomaly detection. Int. J. Comput. Vis. **129**(4), 1038–1059 (2021). https://doi.org/10.1007/s11263-020-01400-4
7. Chan, R., et al.: Segmentmeifyoucan: A benchmark for anomaly segmentation. arXiv preprint arXiv:2104.14812 (2021)
8. Drew, T., Võ, M.L.H., Wolfe, J.M.: The invisible gorilla strikes again: sustained inattentional blindness in expert observers. Psychol. Sci. **24**(9), 1848–1853 (2013)
9. Golan, I., El-Yaniv, R.: Deep anomaly detection using geometric transformations. Adv. Neural Inf. Process. Syst. **31** (2018)
10. Gudovskiy, D., Ishizaka, S., Kozuka, K.: Cflow-ad: real-time unsupervised anomaly detection with localization via conditional normalizing flows. In: Proceedings of the IEEE/CVF Winter Conference on Applications of Computer Vision, pp. 98–107 (2022)
11. Han, C., et al.: MADGAN: unsupervised medical anomaly detection GAN using multiple adjacent brain MRI slice reconstruction. BMC Bioinf. **22**(2), 1–20 (2021)
12. Isensee, F., Jaeger, P.F., Kohl, S.A.A., Petersen, J., Maier-Hein, K.H.: nnu-net: a self-configuring method for deep learning-based biomedical image segmentation. Nat. Method. **18**(2), 203–211 (2021). https://doi.org/10.1038/s41592-020-01008-z

13. Li, C.L., Sohn, K., Yoon, J., Pfister, T.: Cutpaste: self-supervised learning for anomaly detection and localization. In: Proceedings of the IEEE/CVF Conference on Computer Vision and Pattern Recognition, pp. 9664–9674 (2021)
14. Liu, R., et al.: An intriguing failing of convolutional neural networks and the coord-conv solution. Adv. Neural Inf. Process. Syst. **31** (2018)
15. Marimont, S.N., Tarroni, G.: Anomaly detection through latent space restoration using vector quantized variational autoencoders. In: 2021 IEEE 18th International Symposium on Biomedical Imaging (ISBI), pp. 1764–1767 (2021). https://doi.org/10.1109/ISBI48211.2021.9433778
16. Meissen, F., Wiestler, B., Kaissis, G., Rueckert, D.: On the pitfalls of using the residual as anomaly score. In: Medical Imaging with Deep Learning (2022). https://openreview.net/forum?id=ZsoHLeupa1D
17. Pedregosa, F., et al.: Scikit-learn: machine learning in python. J. Mach. Learn. Res. **12**, 2825–2830 (2011)
18. Pinto, A., et al.: Errors in imaging patients in the emergency setting. Br. J. Radiol. **89**, 20150914 (2016). https://doi.org/10.1259/bjr.20150914
19. Ronneberger, O., Fischer, P., Brox, T.: U-Net: convolutional networks for biomedical image segmentation. In: Navab, N., Hornegger, J., Wells, W.M., Frangi, A.F. (eds.) MICCAI 2015. LNCS, vol. 9351, pp. 234–241. Springer, Cham (2015). https://doi.org/10.1007/978-3-319-24574-4_28
20. Schlegl, T., Seeböck, P., Waldstein, S.M., Langs, G., Schmidt-Erfurth, U.: f-anogan: fast unsupervised anomaly detection with generative adversarial networks. Med. Image Anal. **54**, 30–44 (2019). https://doi.org/10.1016/j.media.2019.01.010
21. Schlüter, H.M., Tan, J., Hou, B., Kainz, B.: Self-supervised out-of-distribution detection and localization with natural synthetic anomalies (NSA). arXiv preprint arXiv:2109.15222 (2021)
22. Selvaraju, R.R., Cogswell, M., Das, A., Vedantam, R., Parikh, D., Batra, D.: Grad-cam: visual explanations from deep networks via gradient-based localization. In: Proceedings of the IEEE International Conference on Computer Vision, pp. 618–626 (2017)
23. Song, J., Kong, K., Park, Y.I., Kim, S.G., Kang, S.J.: Anomaly segmentation network using self-supervised learning. In: AAAI 2022 Workshop on AI for Design and Manufacturing (ADAM) (2021)
24. Tan, J., Hou, B., Batten, J., Qiu, H., Kainz, B.: Detecting outliers with foreign patch interpolation. arXiv preprint arXiv:2011.04197 (2020)
25. Tan, J., Hou, B., Day, T., Simpson, J., Rueckert, D., Kainz, B.: Detecting outliers with poisson image interpolation. In: de Bruijne, M., et al. (eds.) MICCAI 2021. LNCS, vol. 12905, pp. 581–591. Springer, Cham (2021). https://doi.org/10.1007/978-3-030-87240-3_56
26. Wang, X., Peng, Y., Lu, L., Lu, Z., Bagheri, M., Summers, R.: Chestx-ray8: hospital-scale chest x-ray database and benchmarks on weakly-supervised classification and localization of common thorax diseases. In: 2017 IEEE Conference on Computer Vision and Pattern Recognition (CVPR), pp. 3462–3471 (2017)
27. Yu, J., et al.: Fastflow: unsupervised anomaly detection and localization via 2d normalizing flows. arXiv preprint arXiv:2111.07677 (2021)
28. Zhang, O., Delbrouck, J.-B., Rubin, D.L.: Out of distribution detection for medical images. In: Sudre, C.H., et al. (eds.) UNSURE/PIPPI -2021. LNCS, vol. 12959, pp. 102–111. Springer, Cham (2021). https://doi.org/10.1007/978-3-030-87735-4_10
29. Zimmerer, D., et al.: Medical out-of-distribution analysis challenge 2021 (2021). https://doi.org/10.5281/zenodo.4573948

Generalized Probabilistic U-Net
for Medical Image Segementation

Ishaan Bhat[1]([✉])(iD), Josien P.W. Pluim[1,2](iD), and Hugo J. Kuijf[1](iD)

[1] Image Sciences Institute, University Medical Center Utrecht, Heidelberglaan 100,
3584 CX Utrecht, The Netherlands
{i.r.bhat,h.kuijf}@umcutrecht.nl

[2] Department of Biomedical Engineering, Eindhoven University of Technology,
Groene Loper 3, 5612 AE Eindhoven, The Netherlands
j.pluim@tue.nl

Abstract. We propose the Generalized Probabilistic U-Net, which
extends the Probabilistic U-Net [14] by allowing more general forms of
the Gaussian distribution as the latent space distribution that can better
approximate the uncertainty in the reference segmentations. We study
the effect the choice of latent space distribution has on capturing the
uncertainty in the reference segmentations using the LIDC-IDRI dataset.
We show that the choice of distribution affects the sample diversity of
the predictions and their overlap with respect to the reference segmentations. For the LIDC-IDRI dataset, we show that using a mixture of
Gaussians results in a statistically significant improvement in the generalized energy distance (GED) metric with respect to the standard Probabilistic U-Net. We have made our implementation available at https://
github.com/ishaanb92/GeneralizedProbabilisticUNet.

Keywords: Image segmentation · Uncertainty estimation · Variational
inference

1 Introduction

Image segmentation may be posed as a supervised classification task with a
deep learning system trained using manually created expert labels producing a
segmentation map by estimating per-voxel class probabilities. A shortcoming of
standard deep learning approaches is that they produce point estimate predictions and not an output distribution from which multiple plausible predictions
can be sampled [10]. This disadvantage is highlighted when multiple annotations per image are available, which standard deep learning approaches cannot
leverage. Inter-observer variability reflects the disagreement among experts and
ambiguity present in the image, and ideally, a supervised learning approach needs
to reflect these for unseen test cases [9].

C. H. Sudre et al. (Eds.): UNSURE 2022, LNCS 13563, pp. 113–124, 2022.
https://doi.org/10.1007/978-3-031-16749-2_11

Recent works such as the Probabilistic U-Net [14] and PHISeg framework [2] were developed to handle segmentation of ambiguous images by using multiple annotations per image during training. They used variational inference [26] to produce multiple spatially coherent predictions per image by sampling from a distribution over a (learned) latent space. Key to their approach is modelling the latent space distribution as an axis-aligned Gaussian, i.e. a multivariate Gaussian distribution with a diagonal covariance matrix. It has been hypothesized that the choice of a simple distribution reduces sample diversity and a more expressive distribution might be required for producing more realistic segmentations [23,25].

In this paper, we extend the Probabilistic U-Net framework by using more general forms of the Gaussian distribution to study the effect the choice of the latent space distribution has on capturing the uncertainty in medical images.

2   Related Work

In [14] the authors combine the conditional variational autoencoder (cVAE) [24] framework with the popular U-Net [22] architecture to create the Probabilistic U-Net. Different variants of the prediction are computed by sampling from the (learned) latent space and combining this sample with the highest resolution feature map of the U-Net. In [5] the authors extend the Probabilistic U-Net to capture model uncertainty by using variational dropout [13] over the model weights. The PHISegNet [2] and Hierarchical Probabilistic U-Net [15] show a further improvement in sample diversity by using a series of hierarchical latent spaces from which samples are combined with the U-Net feature maps at different resolutions. The Probabilistic U-Net and its hierarchical variants use an axis-aligned Gaussian distribution to model the distribution over the latent space. However, techniques such as normalizing flows [21], that convert simple distributions into complex ones via invertible transformations, have been shown to be a promising alternative to model the latent space distribution. The cFlowNet [23] uses normalizing flows to model the latent space distribution to produce plausible and diverse outputs.

3   Contributions

In an image segmentation problem, we typically have an image $x \in \mathbb{R}^{H \times W \times C}$ and label $y \in \{0, 1\}^{H \times W}$ and our goal is to produce accurate and coherent samples from the distribution $p_\theta(y|x)$ using a deep neural network parameterized by θ. To enable tractable sampling from $p_\theta(y|x)$, simple parameterizable distributions $p_\phi(z|x)$ and $q_\psi(z|x, y)$ are used as approximations for the true prior and posterior distributions over the latent space z respectively. The distributional parameters for $q_\psi(z|x, y)$ and $p_\phi(z|x)$ are learned by neural (sub-)networks paramterized by ψ and, ϕ respectively.

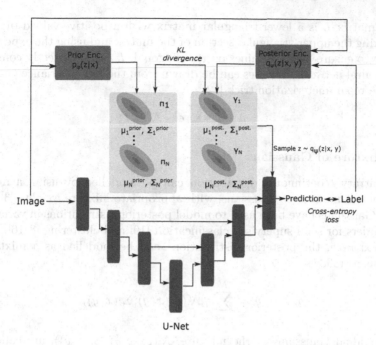

Fig. 1. Generalized Probabilistic U-Net framework. During training, the model learns prior and posterior distribution parameters $\{\mu_i^{\text{prior}}, \Sigma_i^{\text{prior}}, \pi_i\}_{i=1}^{N}$ and $\{\mu_i^{\text{post.}}, \Sigma_i^{\text{post.}}, \gamma_i\}_{i=1}^{N}$. In the most general case, the prior and posterior distributions are modelled as a mixture of N Gaussians. Similarly, different variants of the multivariate Gaussian distribution can be modelled by constructing the covariance matrix in the different ways described in Sect. 3. By setting $N = 1$ and restricting the covariance matrix to be diagonal, we recover the original Probabilistic U-Net. During inference, the posterior encoder is discarded, and different plausible outputs can be computed by sampling from the prior distribution and combining this sample with the last U-Net layer.

To produce predictions that better approximate the uncertainty in the reference segmentations, we propose two extensions to the Probabilistic U-Net framework by using more general forms of the Gaussian distribution as choices for the latent space distributions. Our Generalized Probabilistic U-Net framework is shown in Fig. 1.

3.1 Full-Covariance Gaussian

For a matrix to be a valid covariance matrix, it must be positive semidefinite. Since this constraint is difficult to impose while training a neural network, the covariance matrix Σ is built using its Cholesky decomposition L [27]:

$$\Sigma = LL^T$$

The matrix L is a lower-triangular matrix with a positive-valued diagonal. By masking the upper-triangular section of the matrix and using the exponential operator to ensure positive values on the diagonal, L can be directly computed by the neural network. Samples can be drawn from the full-covariance Gaussian using the reparameterization trick [12]:

$$z = \mu + L * \epsilon, \ \epsilon \sim \mathcal{N}(0, I)$$

3.2 Mixture of Gaussians

Any arbitrary (continuous) distribution can be modelled by using a mixture of a sufficient number of Gaussians, with appropriate mixture weights [3]. Mixtures of Gaussians have been used to model posterior distributions in variational autoencoders for semi-supervised classification [19] and clustering [8, 16].

For example, the posterior distribution[1] can be modelled as a mixture of Gaussians as follows:

$$q_\psi(z|x, y) = \sum_{i=1}^{N} \gamma_i \mathcal{N}(\mu_i(x, y), \Sigma_i(x, y))$$

The individual Gaussians in the mixture, $\mathcal{N}(\mu_i(x, y), \Sigma_i(x, y))$, are called the component distributions and the weights for the component distributions, $\{\gamma_i\}_{i=1}^{N}$, are the mixing coefficients. The individual Gaussians can be modelled using a diagonal or full covariance matrix. For the distribution to be valid, the mixing coefficients must be greater than or equal to 0 and sum to 1. Therefore, a categorical distribution can be used to define the mixture distribution.

A distribution chosen to model the posterior must support differentiable sampling so that optimization of the loss function may be performed via backpropagation. To sample from a mixture of Gaussians, first a component index is sampled from the categorical distribution defined by the mixture coefficients and then a value is sampled from the corresponding component (Gaussian) distribution.

$$i \sim \text{Cat}(N; \gamma)$$
$$z \sim \mathcal{N}(\mu_i(x, y), \Sigma_i(x, y))$$

The second step in the sampling process is differentiable and supports the reparameterization trick, however, the first step i.e. sampling from a categorical distribution is not differentiable. To make sampling fully differentiable, we used the Gumbel-Softmax (GS) distribution [7, 18] to model the mixture distribution. The Gumbel-Softmax distribution is a continuous relaxation (controlled by the temperature parameter, τ) of the discrete categorical distribution, that supports differentiable sampling via the reparameterization trick. To obtain a discrete component index, we perform Straight-Through(ST) sampling [7], where

---

[1] This subsection holds true for the cVAE prior distribution as well. The only difference is the dependence on the label, y, is dropped.

we used the argmax operation in the forward pass and used the continuous relaxation in the backward pass while computing gradients. With this, we used the following two-step process to sample from the mixture of Gaussians:

$$i \sim GS(N; \gamma, \tau)$$
$$z \sim \mathcal{N}(\mu_i(x,y), \Sigma_i(x,y))$$

Unlike for a pair of Gaussians, the KL divergence for a pair of Gaussian mixtures, which is a part of the neural network loss function, does not have a closed-form expression. We estimated the KL divergence via Monte Carlo integration, which provides a good approximation [4].

4 Methodology

4.1 Data

The LIDC-IDRI dataset [1] consists of 1018 thoracic CT scans with lesion segmentations from four experts. Similar to [2,14] we use a pre-processed version of the dataset, consisting of 128×128 patches containing lesions.

We obtained a total of $15,096$ patches. We used a $60:20:20$ split to get 9058, 3019, and 3019 patches for training, validation, and testing respectively. The intensity of the patches was scaled to $[0,1]$ range and no data augmentation was used. We used the publicly available version of the pre-processed dataset available at https://github.com/stefanknegt/Probabilistic-Unet-Pytorch.

4.2 Neural Network Training

For all models we used the ADAM [11] optimizer with a learning rate of 10^{-4}. Training was stopped when the validation loss did not improve for more than 20 epochs, and the model parameters with the minimum loss were saved.

We used the Tune [17] package to choose optimal hyperparameters via a random search strategy. Depending on the number of hyperparameters, the best performing model was chosen among $4-24$ instances. The hyperparameters for all models are shown in Appendix A.

To ensure comparability between models with different latent space distributions, we maintain the same number of layers for the U-Net, the prior encoder, and the posterior encoder. Furthermore, in accordance with the original Probabilistic U-Net architecture, the prior and posterior encoder have the same architecture as the U-Net encoder. Each convolution block in the model consisted of convolution with a 3×3 kernel, a ReLU nonlinearity and batch normalization [6]. Downsampling is performed via average pooling and upsampling is performed via bilinear interpolation.

The code for the neural network training and inference was developed using the PyTorch [20] library.

4.3   Experiments

We study the following variants of the Probabilistic U-Net by using different distributions (Sect. 3) to model the latent space distributions(s):

– Axis-aligned Probabilistic U-Net (AA) [14]
– Full covariance Probabilistic U-Net (FC)
– Mixture AA Probabilistic U-Net
– Mixture FC Probabilistic U-Net

We used the *generalized energy distance* (GED) metric [14] to compare how well the distribution of neural network predictions P_s matched the distribution of ground truth labels P_{gt}.

$$D_{GED}^2(P_{gt}, P_s) = 2\mathbb{E}[d(S, Y)] - \mathbb{E}[d(S, S')] - \mathbb{E}[d(Y, Y')] \tag{1}$$

The distance metric between a pair of segmentations, $d(x, y)$, is defined as $1 - \mathrm{IoU}(x, y)$ [2,14]. In Eq. 1, S, S' are samples from the prediction distribution and Y, Y' are samples from the ground truth distribution. The expectation terms in Eq. 1 are computed via Monte Carlo estimation. We used 16 samples from the prediction distribution to compute the GED. A lower GED implies a better match between prediction and ground truth distributions. To check for statistical significance in the differences between the GED metric for models, we performed the Wilcoxon signed-rank test at a significance of 0.05.

We also looked at the trends in the component terms of the GED metric. The first term $\mathbb{E}[d(S, Y)]$ signifies the extent of overlap between samples from the prediction and ground truth distribution, while the second term $\mathbb{E}[d(S, S')]$ is the sample diversity. By looking at trends in these terms in conjunction with the GED metric, we studied the interplay between overlap and diversity that lead to a better (or worse) match between distributions.

5   Results and Discussion

Figure 2 and Table 1 show the trend in the GED metric for the LIDC-IDRI dataset. We see that the Probabilistic U-Net using a mixture of full covariance Gaussians (Mixture FC) performs best w.r.t the GED metric. We also see that the models, using a full covariance Gaussian as the latent space distribution, did better than the standard Probabilistic U-Net (AA).

In Fig. 3, our results show that the Mixture FC variant achieves an optimal combination between overlap and diversity to emerge as the best performing model with respect to the GED metric. The Mixture FC predictions matched the distribution of reference segmentations closest, with a higher overlap and a sample diversity closer to the inter-observer variability. We also observed that models using a Gaussian mixture distribution had better overlap but produced less diverse predictions than single Gaussian variants, for both axis-aligned and full covariance distributions. This has been illustrated visually with examples in Appendix B.

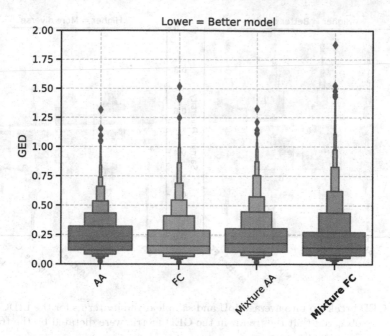

Fig. 2. Trends in the GED metric for LIDC-IDRI dataset using a letter-value plot. The median is shown by a horizontal line segment, and the innermost box is drawn at the upper and lower fourths, i.e. 25th and 75th percentiles. The other boxes are drawn at the upper and lower eighths, sixteenths and so on. The GED was computed using 16 prediction samples. We found all pairwise differences to be statistically significant, with Mixutre FC to be the best performing model.

Table 1. Mean and standard deviation of the GED metric for the LIDC-IDRI test-set.

Model	GED (mean ± std-dev)
AA	0.242 ± 0.168
FC	0.220 ± 0.188
Mixture AA	0.238 ± 0.191
Mixture FC	0.218 ± 0.220

A limitation in our generalized Probabilistic U-Net framework is the increase in the number of hyperparameters that need to be tuned for the distributions used. For example, mixture models need to find the optimal number of components (N), and the temperature (τ) for the Gumbel-Softmax distribution, used to control the relaxation of the discrete categorical distribution. Therefore, finding the optimal model for a particular dataset could potentially be a time-consuming task. An interesting research direction could be treating the number of mixture components as a learned parameter, instead of it being fixed at the start of training.

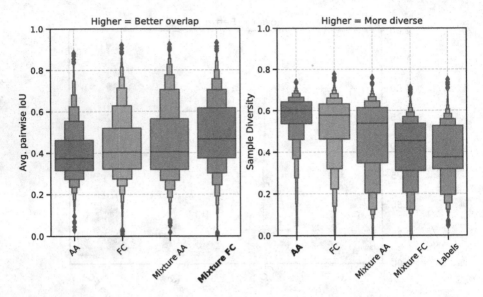

Fig. 3. GED break-up into average IoU and sample diversity terms for the LIDC-IDRI dataset. We observed that the trends in the GED metric were dictated by the tradeoff between overlap and diversity.

6   Conclusion

Our work focused on extending the Probabilistic U-Net framework by going beyond the axis-aligned Gaussian distribution as the de facto choice for the variational distribution. Our results showed that the choice of model (or distribution) is dictated by the optimal overlap-diversity combination. Therefore, investigating the suitability of different latent space distributions is beneficial. The distributions studied in this paper can be used as a drop-in replacement for the axis-aligned Gaussian in other extensions to the Probabilistic U-Net framework, like the class of models using hierarchical latent spaces [2,15], or as base distributions for normalizing flow based segmentation models [23].

Acknowledgements. This work was financially supported by the project IMPACT (Intelligence based iMprovement of Personalized treatment And Clinical workflow supporT) in the framework of the EU research programme ITEA3 (Information Technology for European Advancement).

A   Neural Network Hyperparameters

We used the Tune [17] package to perform hyperparameters optimization. The number of hyperparameters changed based on the model/latent distribution. The number of U-Net encoder and decoder blocks was fixed at 3, and the filter depths used were $32, 64, 128$ for the first, second and third blocks respectively.

The bottleneck layer had a filter depth of 512. β is the weight assigned to the KL-divergence term in the Probabilistic U-Net loss function.

Table 2 contains the search space used to perform hyperparameter optimization.

B   Example Predictions

To support the quantitative results in Sect. 5, we present example predictions, along with images and reference segmentations, in Fig. 4.

(a) This example shows the reduced sample diversity (and improved overlap) of the mixture models (M-AA, M-FC) with respect to the full-covariance (FC) and axis-aligned (AA) Gaussians. Specifically, the AA predictions are diverse but do not match the distribution of the reference segmentations (poor overlap).

(b) This example shows an instance where the Mixture FC (M-FC) and FC predictions perfectly match the distribution of the reference segmentations, with 75% of its predictions containing a lesion.

Fig. 4. Example image, labels, and predictions for the LIDC-IDRI dataset. The first row contains the image and the reference segmentations. The following rows show 16 samples drawn from the prediction distribution (used to compute the GED).

Table 2. Hyperparameter search space.

Hyper-parameter	Search space	
	Range	Search type
Latent space dimension	$[2, 4, 6, 8]$	Grid search
β	$[1, 10, 100]$	Grid search
Rank	$[1, 5]$	Random sampling
Mixture components	$[1, 10]$	Random sampling
Temperature	$[0.1, 0.5]$	Random sampling

Table 3. LIDC-IDRI hyperparameters.

Model	Hyperparameters				
	Latent space dimension	β	Rank	Mixture components	Temperature
AA	6	1	–	–	–
FC	2	1	–	–	–
AA Mixture	4	1	–	5	0.36
FC Mixture	2	1	–	9	0.28

References

1. Armato, III, S.G., et al.: The lung image database consortium (LIDC) and image database resource initiative (IDRI): a completed reference database of lung nodules on CT scans. Med. Phys. **38**(2), 915–931 (2011). https://doi.org/10.1118/1.3528204
2. Baumgartner, C.F., et al.: PHiSeg: capturing uncertainty in medical image segmentation. In: Shen, D., et al. (eds.) MICCAI 2019. LNCS, vol. 11765, pp. 119–127. Springer, Cham (2019). https://doi.org/10.1007/978-3-030-32245-8_14
3. Bishop, C.M.: Pattern Recognition and Machine Learning (Information Science and Statistics). Springer, Heidelberg (2006)
4. Hershey, J.R., Olsen, P.A.: Approximating the Kullback Leibler divergence between gaussian mixture models. In: 2007 IEEE International Conference on Acoustics, Speech and Signal Processing - ICASSP 2007, vol. 4, pp. IV-317–IV-320 (2007). https://doi.org/10.1109/ICASSP.2007.366913
5. Hu, S., Worrall, D., Knegt, S., Veeling, B., Huisman, H., Welling, M.: Supervised uncertainty quantification for segmentation with multiple annotations. In: Shen, D., et al. (eds.) MICCAI 2019. LNCS, vol. 11765, pp. 137–145. Springer, Cham (2019). https://doi.org/10.1007/978-3-030-32245-8_16
6. Ioffe, S., Szegedy, C.: Batch normalization: accelerating deep network training by reducing internal covariate shift. In: Bach, F., Blei, D. (eds.) Proceedings of the 32nd International Conference on Machine Learning. Proceedings of Machine Learning Research, vol. 37, pp. 448–456. PMLR, Lille (2015). https://proceedings.mlr.press/v37/ioffe15.html
7. Jang, E., Gu, S., Poole, B.: Categorical Reparameterization with Gumbel-Softmax. arXiv preprint arXiv:1611.01144 (2017). version: 2

8. Jiang, Z., Zheng, Y., Tan, H., Tang, B., Zhou, H.: Variational Deep Embedding: An Unsupervised and Generative Approach to Clustering. arXiv preprint arXiv:1611.05148 (2017)
9. Jungo, A., et al.: On the effect of inter-observer variability for a reliable estimation of uncertainty of medical image segmentation. In: Frangi, A.F., Schnabel, J.A., Davatzikos, C., Alberola-López, C., Fichtinger, G. (eds.) MICCAI 2018. LNCS, vol. 11070, pp. 682–690. Springer, Cham (2018). https://doi.org/10.1007/978-3-030-00928-1_77
10. Kendall, A., Gal, Y.: What uncertainties do we need in Bayesian deep learning for computer vision? In: Guyon, I., et al. (eds.) Advances in Neural Information Processing Systems, vol. 30. Curran Associates, Inc. (2017). https://proceedings.neurips.cc/paper/2017/file/2650d6089a6d640c5e85b2b88265dc2b-Paper.pdf
11. Kingma, D.P., Ba, J.: Adam: a method for stochastic optimization. In: 3rd International Conference on Learning Representations, ICLR 2015, San Diego, 7–9 May 2015, Conference Track Proceedings (2015)
12. Kingma, D.P., Welling, M.: An introduction to variational autoencoders. Found. Trends Mach. Learn. **12**(4), 307–392 (2019). https://doi.org/10.1561/2200000056
13. Kingma, D.P., Salimans, T., Welling, M.: Variational dropout and the local reparameterization trick. In: Cortes, C., Lawrence, N., Lee, D., Sugiyama, M., Garnett, R. (eds.) Advances in Neural Information Processing Systems, vol. 28. Curran Associates, Inc. (2015). https://proceedings.neurips.cc/paper/2015/file/bc7316929fe1545bf0b98d114ee3ecb8-Paper.pdf
14. Kohl, S., et al.: A probabilistic U-Net for segmentation of ambiguous images. In: Advances in Neural Information Processing Systems, vol. 31. Curran Associates, Inc. (2018). https://papers.nips.cc/paper/2018/hash/473447ac58e1cd7e96172575f48dca3b-Abstract.html
15. Kohl, S.A.A., et al.: A Hierarchical Probabilistic U-Net for Modeling Multi-Scale Ambiguities. arXiv preprint arXiv:1905.13077 (2019)
16. Kopf, A., Fortuin, V., Somnath, V.R., Claassen, M.: Mixture-of-experts variational autoencoder for clustering and generating from similarity-based representations on single cell data. PLOS Comput. Biol. **17**(6), e1009086 (2021) https://doi.org/10.1371/journal.pcbi.1009086
17. Liaw, R., Liang, E., Nishihara, R., Moritz, P., Gonzalez, J.E., Stoica, I.: Tune: a research platform for distributed model selection and training. arXiv preprint arXiv:1807.05118 (2018)
18. Maddison, C.J., Mnih, A., Teh, Y.W.: The Concrete Distribution: A Continuous Relaxation of Discrete Random Variables. arXiv preprint arXiv:1611.00712 (2017)
19. Nalisnick, E.T., Hertel, L., Smyth, P.: Approximate inference for deep latent gaussian mixtures (2016)
20. Paszke, A., et al.: Pytorch: an imperative style, high-performance deep learning library. In: Wallach, H., Larochelle, H., Beygelzimer, A., d'Alché-Buc, F., Fox, E., Garnett, R. (eds.) Advances in Neural Information Processing Systems, vol. 32, pp. 8024–8035. Curran Associates, Inc. (2019)
21. Rezende, D.J., Mohamed, S.: Variational Inference with Normalizing Flows. arXiv preprint arXiv:1505.05770 (2016)
22. Ronneberger, O., Fischer, P., Brox, T.: U-Net: convolutional networks for biomedical image segmentation. In: Navab, N., Hornegger, J., Wells, W.M., Frangi, A.F. (eds.) MICCAI 2015. LNCS, vol. 9351, pp. 234–241. Springer, Cham (2015). https://doi.org/10.1007/978-3-319-24574-4_28

23. Selvan, R., Faye, F., Middleton, J., Pai, A.: Uncertainty quantification in medical image segmentation with normalizing flows. In: Liu, M., Yan, P., Lian, C., Cao, X. (eds.) MLMI 2020. LNCS, vol. 12436, pp. 80–90. Springer, Cham (2020). https://doi.org/10.1007/978-3-030-59861-7_9

24. Sohn, K., Lee, H., Yan, X.: Learning structured output representation using deep conditional generative models. In: Cortes, C., Lawrence, N., Lee, D., Sugiyama, M., Garnett, R. (eds.) Advances in Neural Information Processing Systems, vol. 28. Curran Associates, Inc. (2015)

25. Valiuddin, M.M.A., Viviers, C.G.A., van Sloun, R.J.G., de With, P.H.N., van der Sommen, F.: Improving aleatoric uncertainty quantification in multi-annotated medical image segmentation with normalizing flows. In: Sudre, C.H., et al. (eds.) UNSURE/PIPPI -2021. LNCS, vol. 12959, pp. 75–88. Springer, Cham (2021). https://doi.org/10.1007/978-3-030-87735-4_8

26. Wainwright, M.J., Jordan, M.I.: Graphical models, exponential families, and variational inference. Found. Trends Mach. Learn. 1(1–2), 1–305 (2007). https://doi.org/10.1561/2200000001

27. Williams, P.M.: Using neural networks to model conditional multivariate densities. Neural Comput. 8(4), 843–854 (1996). https://doi.org/10.1162/neco.1996.8.4.843

Joint Paraspinal Muscle Segmentation and Inter-rater Labeling Variability Prediction with Multi-task TransUNet

Parinaz Roshanzamir[1]($\boxtimes$), Hassan Rivaz[1,2], Joshua Ahn[3], Hamza Mirza[3], Neda Naghdi[4], Meagan Anstruther[4], Michele C. Battié[5], Maryse Fortin[2,4], and Yiming Xiao[2,6]

[1] Department of Electrical and Computer Engineering, Concordia University, Montreal, Canada
parinaz.roshanzamir@concordia.ca
[2] PERFORM Centre, Concordia University, Montreal, Canada
[3] Faculty of Health Sciences, Western University, London, Canada
[4] Health, Kinesiology, and Applied Physiology, Concordia University, Montreal, Canada
[5] School of Physical Therapy and Western's Bone and Joint Institute, Western University, London, Canada
[6] Department of Computer Science and Software Engineering, Concordia University, Montreal, Canada

Abstract. Recent studies have associated morphological and composition changes in paraspinal muscles with low back pain (LBP), which is the most common, but poorly understood musculoskeletal disorder in adults. Accurate paraspinal muscle segmentation from MRI is crucial to enable new image-based biomarkers for the diagnosis and prognosis of LBP. Manual segmentation is laborious and time-consuming. In addition, high individual anatomical variations also pose challenges, resulting in inconsistent segmentation across different raters. While automatic segmentation algorithms can help mitigate the issues, techniques that predict and visualize inter-rater segmentation variability will be highly instrumental to help interpret reliability of automatic segmentation, but they are rarely attempted. In this paper, we propose a novel multi-task TransUNet model to accurately segment paraspinal muscles while predicting inter-rater labeling variability visualized using a variance map of three raters' annotations. Our technique is validated on MRIs of paraspinal muscles at four different disc levels from 118 LBP patients. Benefiting from the transformer mechanism and convolution neural networks, our algorithm is shown to perform better or similar to the state-of-the-art methods and a newly proposed multi-task U-Net model while predicting and visualizing multi-rater annotation variance per muscle group in an intuitive manner.

Keywords: Paraspinal muscle segmentation · TransUNet · Inter-rater variability · Uncertainty estimation · Multi-task learning · MRI

1   Introduction

Paraspinal muscles are critical to stabilizing the spinal column [17] and many recent studies [4, 19] have suggested a link between the morphological and composition (e.g., fatty infiltration) changes of these muscles and painful spinal disorders that lead to low back pain (LBP), such as disc herniation and lumbar spinal stenosis (LSS), with a high prevalence in the adult population worldwide. With superior soft tissue contrast, magnetic resonance imaging (MRI) has become a staple for the relevant investigations, with the new trend to leverage recent computational and imaging techniques to explore image-based biomarkers for more accurate diagnosis and prognosis. To achieve this, good MRI segmentation of paraspinal muscles, especially at different spinal levels plays a critical role. While manual image segmentation is known to be time- and labor-consuming, the high variations in muscle morphology and composition across individuals and spinal levels create additional challenges for segmentation in comparison to other anatomical structures such as the brain. While automatic segmentation algorithms, especially deep learning (DL) methods [12, 14] have been shown to mitigate these issues, only a few were proposed for paraspinal muscle segmentation. Furthermore, most DL methods only offer deterministic outcomes, making it impossible to assess the reliability of their results, which is important in practice. Different from epistemic and aleatoric uncertainties that are used to evaluate the reliability of automatic segmentation [3, 11], methods that predict and visualize inter-rater disagreement in DL-based segmentation, which also offer important insights regarding the reliability of the results, are unfortunately often overlooked. Thus, new techniques are necessary to address this gap.

Automatic paraspinal muscle segmentation has its unique challenges, and only a few techniques [5, 9, 18] were proposed, focusing primarily on deep learning techniques using a single rater's annotation. Earlier, Li *et al.* [9] proposed a U-Net based model with additional residual blocks at each layer and a feature pyramid attention module added to the bottleneck. They obtained a Dice score coefficient (DSC) of 94.9% in multifidus segmentation at three spinal levels. Xia *et al.* [18] combined conditional random fields as recurrent neural networks with a U-Net model to add spatial constraints for labels and achieved a DSC of 95% on the segmentation of the multifidus and erector spinae. Most recently, Huang *et al.* [5] proposed a two-stage coarse-to-fine segmentation framework with attention gates and achieved the best DSC of $94.4 \pm 3.5\%$ on multifidus identification. However, none of the relevant existing works explored the prediction and visualization of inter-rater segmentation variabilities, and all used convolutional neural networks (CNNs). While advantageous in extracting low-level image features, CNNs often fail to capture long-range dependencies in the input data, which can be leveraged to improve segmentation performance, especially in the context of high anatomical variabilities. To address this concern, attention gates have been employed to improve U-Net [12]. Most recently, exploiting self-attention and long-range dependencies, Transformers, which were first proposed in machine translation [16] also lend their powers in vision tasks [2]. To benefit from both CNNs and Vision Transformers (ViT), TransUNet [1] is a recent encoder-decoder-style model that combines a U-Net with a Transformer. This DL model can capture long-range dependencies while extracting the high-resolution features captured by a CNN. To the best of our knowledge, it has not been used for paraspinal muscle segmentation.

To enhance the quality of segmentation ground truths, it is often desirable to employ multiple raters, and a number of techniques have been proposed to explore inter-rater variability. Mirikharaji *et al.* [10] used an ensemble of DL models for lesion segmentation, with each trained on a single rater's annotation, and averaged the results to produce the final output. Ji *et al.* [7] proposed a CNN with embedded modules for encoding raters' expertise levels, generating one prediction per rater and then fusing the predictions based on their uncertainties. Finally, Lemay *et al.* [8] explored the advantages of soft segmentation for training segmentation models to reflect inter-rater variability. They concluded that relying solely on discrete labels as outputs will generate overconfident results and, in these cases, soft segmentation performs better. These prior works often train an ensemble of DL models or use a large model with many learnable parameters, which could be costly. Furthermore, they employed soft or probabilistic segmentation through averaging to represent the inter-rater annotation variability, which may not be visually intuitive or informative.

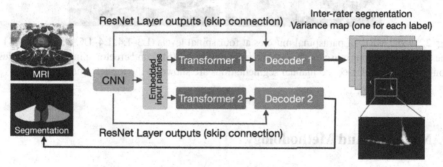

Fig. 1. An overview of the proposed multi-task TransUNet

In this paper, we proposed a novel multi-task deep learning technique (see Fig. 1) to address the aforementioned issues and allow accurate segmentation of paraspinal muscles (i.e., multifidus muscles and erector spinae, left and right separated as shown in Fig. 2) and prediction and visualization of inter-rater segmentation inconsistency. As a design choice, we require the representation of variability across multiple raters to allow efficient training through deep learning models and be easily interpreted. Therefore, instead of averaging multiple segmentations to reflect the inconsistency, we decided to estimate the variance across multi-rater segmentations. Thus, our final algorithm consists of a multi-task TransUNet with shared convolutional layers to produce the patch embeddings from the input images, which are then fed into two task-specific transformers to produce the desired outputs. In Task 1, the features are decoded and up-sampled to produce the segmentations, and a similar decoding process is repeated for Task 2 to produce the pixel-wise variance map of multi-rater annotations.

Our work has four major contributions: <u>First</u>, we use the TransUNet model for paraspinal muscle segmentation for the first time. <u>Second</u>, the proposed algorithm was trained and validated using a large dataset of paraspinal muscle MRIs with multi-rater annotations, and it has shown excellent segmentation performance in comparison to the state-of-the-art techniques and a newly proposed multi-task U-Net model. <u>Third</u>, we proposed to use variance maps of soft labels from multiple raters to offer intuitive and easily comprehensible measures and visualization of inter-rater variability. Lastly and most importantly, to the best of our knowledge, we are the first to propose a multi-task DL model for joint paraspinal muscle segmentation and prediction of inter-rater variability, with the framework easily adaptable to other anatomical segmentation tasks.

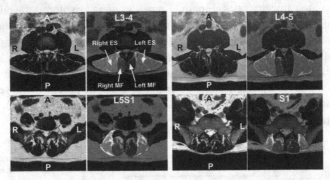

Fig. 2. Axial MRIs of paraspinal muscles at four spinal levels (L3–L4, L4–L5, L5–S1, and S1). The names of the four muscles, the left and right multifidus (MF) and erector spinae (ES) muscles, along with their color-coded manual segmentations are shown in the top left image.

2   Materials and Methodology

2.1   Image Pre-processing and Multi-rater Annotation

From the European research consortium project, Genodisc, on commonly diagnosed lumbar pathologies (physiol.ox.ac.uk/genodisc), lumbosacral T2-weighted (T2w) MR images of 118 patients (59 male, age = 30–59 y) were selected, with the factors of sex and age roughly equally distributed among the subjects. Axial MRI slices of the L3–L4, L4–L5, L5–S1, and S1 spinal levels that are often affected by painful spinal disorders were acquired for analysis. In total, we have 444 MRI slices, including 105 scans at L3–L4, 117 scans at L4–L5, 118 scans at L5–S1, and finally 104 scans at S1. Note that due to imaging artifacts and cropping, not all patients have usable axial slices at all spinal levels. All axial MR images were first processed with N4 inhomogeneity correction [15] to remove field non-uniformity in the image. Then, the multifidus (MF) and erector spinae (ES) muscles were manually segmented for all patients (using the software ITK-SNAP (itksnap.org)) independently by three different raters, who have good knowledge in musculoskeletal anatomy and ITK-SNAP. As all raters have similar levels of expertise and experience in paraspinal muscle segmentation, we decided to use a majority voting scheme to fuse multi-rater annotations, and the final results were used for training and testing the proposed algorithm in terms of discrete anatomical segmentation. To produce the variance maps of multi-rater segmentations for inter-rater variability, instead of directly using discrete labels, we decided to first generate soft label maps by following the steps in [13]. In short, for a multi-class segmentation (4 classes in our case), each class was first binarized, and then transformed into a signed distance map. Then, a sigmoid function was applied to convert the signed distance map into a soft probabilistic label, and the variance across three raters was computed in a pixel-by-pixel manner. Thus, for each image, there are four variance maps, one for each muscle group. The steps for generating the variance map are shown in Fig. 3.

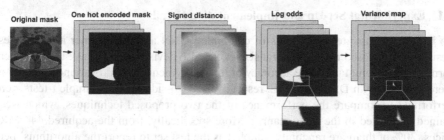

Original mask   One hot encoded mask   Signed distance   Log odds   Variance map

Fig. 3. The steps of calculating the variance maps for assessing inter-rater variability.

2.2 Model Architecture

In this section, we provide a detailed description of the proposed TransUNet model which consists of 3 main parts: (1) The convolutional network (CNN) (2) Transformer and (3) Decoder. The goal of the CNN is to encode important image features and produce the most relevant flattened patch embeddings that can be fed to the task-specific transformers. In our model, the CNN has a ResNet34 backbone with 3 skip connections that feed the ResNet layer outputs to the decoders. In summary, the CNN produces N flattened $P \times P$ patches for each image of dimensions $C \times H \times W$ where $N = (HW)/P^2$ and C is the number of channels. As the encoded information is usable in both segmentation and variance map prediction, the two tasks in our model share the CNN layers. Next, the patches are simultaneously fed into two transformers. Similar to the encoder-decoder architecture of U-Net, the output of each transformer then goes through an up-sampler, where the task-specific information is decoded with the help of the feature maps provided by the skip connections from the ResNet. Finally, the discrete muscle segmentation is generated, as well as a 4-channel output, with each channel corresponding to the variance of the rater annotations of one muscle (left and right multifidus & erector spinae). The schematic of the proposed model is shown in Fig. 1.

As previously mentioned, we trained our model in a multi-task manner. The cost function for model training is a weighted sum of the losses of the individual tasks. For segmentation, we use a combination of Dice and cross-entropy loss and for variance estimation, we use the mean squared error (MSE). In summary, the total model loss is:

$$L_{model} = 0.4\ L_{DiceCE} + 0.6\ L_{MSE} \qquad (1)$$

where L_{MSE} is the mean squared loss of Task 2 and L_{DiceCE} is the segmentation loss which is a weighted sum of Dice loss and cross-entropy:

$$L_{DiceCE} = 0.5\ L_{Dice} + 0.5\ L_{CE} \qquad (2)$$

As TransUNet performs better in terms of generalization and capturing the global context, it can be more resistant to overfitting compared to other models like U-Net. This is especially helpful for both muscle segmentation and variance map estimation.

3 Experiments and Results

3.1 Experimental Set-Up and Implementation Details

To better demonstrate the benefits of combining CNN and transformer architectures, besides the proposed multi-task TransUNet, we also devised a multi-task U-Net to perform the same joint tasks. The accuracy of image segmentation and variance prediction were assessed with DSC and MSE, respectively. Two-sided paired-sample t-tests were performed to compare the performance of the two proposed techniques, which were trained and tested in the same manner. More specifically, from the acquired 444 MRI slices, 20% of them are randomly sampled as the test set to report the algorithms' performance. For the remaining data, 80% and 20% served as training and validation sets, respectively. To improve the robustness of the networks, data augmentation was performed for the training data, where we applied random rotation, image mirroring (label IDs were also swapped accordingly), Gaussian noise, and Gaussian blurring, resulting in 1420 MRI slices in total. Furthermore, in each of the train, validation, and testing sets, there are approximately the same proportion of images from each spinal level. Finally, all MRI scans, discrete manual segmentation, and variance maps are resized to 256 × 256 pixels for network training. We trained the proposed multi-task DL models on an Alienware Aurora PC with Intel(R) Core(TM) i7-8700 CPU and 12 GB NVIDIA TITAN V GPU for 150 epochs, with a batch size of 2 and stochastic gradient descent (SGD) optimization. The initial learning rate was 0.00125, and it was decreased gradually after each iteration. As mentioned in the previous section, a loss function (Eqs. 1 and 2) that integrates cross-entropy and Dice losses, as well as MSE was used.

3.2 Quantitative and Qualitative Results

The quantitative assessments of the two proposed techniques (multi-task TransUNet and U-Net), as well as two recent paraspinal segmentation methods [5, 18] are listed in Table 1 for both the paraspinal muscle segmentation and the associated multi-rater variance map prediction. As shown in Table 1, the Dice scores of the proposed multi-task TransUNet are higher than the U-Net counterpart for 3 of the 4 muscles (p < 0.01). Compared with previous reports [5, 9, 18], the proposed TransUNet has better or nearly similar accuracy in automatic identification of paraspinal muscles on average. For inter-rater segmentation variance map estimation, the multi-task TransUNet outperforms the U-Net for the left multifidus (p < 0.01) and has lower mean errors for the left and right erector spinae muscles. To further demonstrate the results qualitatively, the outcomes of segmentation and variance prediction for one subject are shown in Figs. 4 and 5, respectively. For the segmentation, we can see that TransUNet provides smoother tissue boundaries without "island labels" (see L5-S1 level segmentation of Fig. 4) produced in U-Net segmentations. Furthermore, U-Net produces variance maps with overall higher errors within the target muscle and background than the multi-task TransUNet.

Table 1. Quantitative evaluation of automatic segmentation (in DSC) and inter-rater labeling variance prediction (in MSE) for the proposed techniques. Here, superior performance of Multi-task TransUnet than the Multi-task U-Net is indicated by *(p < 0.01). L = Left and R = Right.

Metric	Task 1 – segmentation (DSC (%))				Task 2 – variance prediction (MSE $\times 10^5$)			
	L MF	R MF	L ES	R ES	L MF	R MF	L ES	R ES
Multi-task U-Net	93.3 ± 4.5	93.6 ± 3.7	92.4 ± 3.9	91.8 ± 4.5	7.37 ± 10.60	5.37 ± 6.67	11.20 ± 16.54	9.81 ± 18,02
Multi-task TransUNet	*94.3 ± 4.1	*94.5 ± 3.4	92.8 ± 4.5	*92.8 ± 4.1	*6.41 ± 9.62	5.57 ± 8.62	10.83 ± 16.03	9.66 ± 17.87
Xia et al. (2019) [18]	95.0 ± 2.3	94.5 ± 1.9	90.6 ± 5.8	91.3 ± 4.6	N/A	N/A	N/A	N/A
Huang et al. (2020) [5]	94.4 ± 3.5	94.9 ± 3.0	94.4 ± 3.4	94.4 ± 3.4	N/A	N/A	N/A	N/A

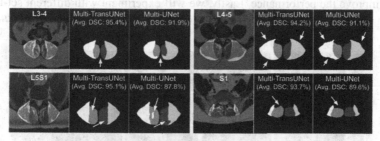

Fig. 4. Automatic paraspinal muscle segmentation results at different spinal levels of a LBP patient, with arrows indicating the differences between results from the TransUNet and U-Net.

4 Discussion

With both quantitative and qualitative assessments, we can see that it is advantageous to combine CNN and Transformer architectures in comparison to using CNNs alone. More specifically, TransUNet offers smoother tissue boundaries in segmentation while nicely handles individual anatomical variabilities (see S1 level segmentation in Fig. 4). On the other hand, the U-Net model can introduce island labels and rough tissue borders. Previous approaches leverage additional conditional random fields as a post-processing step [18] or devise more complex hierarchical processing pipelines [5]. The capacity to encode long-range spatial information while extracting local features allows the proposed technique to achieve similar or better outcomes for tissue labeling with a simpler setup. This benefit also extends to the estimation of inter-rater annotation variability. Compared with the U-Net, the proposed method has significantly lower prediction error for the left multifidus and lower mean errors for the erector spinae muscles. In general, higher rater disagreements usually occur at the borders of the muscles, especially at the borders of muscles vs. bones, the posterior borders of erector spinae, and the posterior division between erector spinae and multifidus. This is because these regions have higher individual variability. For both proposed multi-task TransUNet and U-Net models, the mean errors in the predicted variance maps are higher for the erector spinae than the multifidus, likely because the anatomical variabilities are greater. For the same reason, the automatic segmentation for the erector spinae also has lower Dice scores than that of the multifidus. For this study, multi-task learning allows us to estimate inter-rater disagreement without the need for model ensembles or other complex additional modules. Previous studies [6] also showed that multi-task learning is beneficial to enhance the training and performance of the DL tasks involved. The inter-rater variance maps have low pixel values that lead to small MSEs in the loss function, making training challenging for Task 2. We solved this by scaling the metric to a greater range (multiplying the values by 70) in the training process and received good results. The outputs are re-scaled to their original range at test time.

There are still several aspects of the proposed framework that can be improved in the future. First, more data will be incorporated to further enhance the performance against anatomical variabilities due to individual differences and diseases. Second, we will further investigate the composition of different loss functions and the weights involved to help improve the performance. Lastly, we will experiment with different set-ups for the main architecture to verify their impacts on the accuracy of the desired tasks.

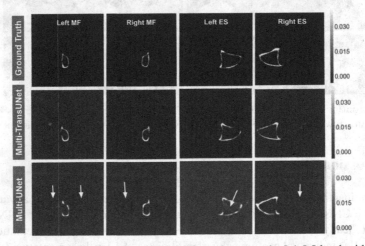

Fig. 5. Results of the variance map estimation of one image at the L4–L5 level with different models. The arrows point to the areas with errors in inter-rater variance map prediction. The overall errors from multi-task U-Net are higher than those from multi-task TransUNet.

5   Conclusion

In this paper, we proposed a novel multi-task TransUNet for simultaneous paraspinal muscle segmentation at multiple spinal levels and prediction of the variance from multiple raters' annotations. While demonstrating the benefit of combining CNN and transformer architectures for the target tasks against the popular U-Net, the proposed technique offers similar or better segmentation accuracy than previous works. The resulting framework offers user-friendly and complementary information in addition to conventional uncertainty estimation, and can be easily extended to other segmentation tasks.

Acknowledgments. We acknowledge the support of the Natural Sciences and Engineering Research Council of Canada (NSERC) and NVIDIA for donation of the GPU.

References

1. Chen, J., et al.: Transunet: transformers make strong encoders for medical image segmentation. arXiv preprint arXiv:2102.04306 (2021)
2. Dosovitskiy, A., et al.: An image is worth 16x16 words: transformers for image recognition at scale. arXiv preprint arXiv:2010.11929 (2020)
3. Durasov, N., Bagautdinov, T., Baque, P., Fua, P.: Masksembles for uncertainty estimation. In: Proceedings of the IEEE/CVF Conference on Computer Vision and Pattern Recognition, pp. 13539–13548 (2021)
4. Fortin, M., Lazáry, A., Varga, P.P., Battié, M.C.: Association between paraspinal muscle morphology clinical symptoms and functional status in patients with lumbar spinal stenosis. Eur. Spine J. **26**, 2543–2551 (2017)
5. Huang, J., Shen, H., Chen, B., Wang, Y., Li, S.: Segmentation of paraspinal muscles at varied lumbar spinal levels by explicit saliency-aware learning. In: Martel, A.L., et al. (eds.) MICCAI 2020. LNCS, vol. 12266, pp. 652–661. Springer, Cham (2020). https://doi.org/10.1007/978-3-030-59725-2_63
6. Kokkinos, I.: Ubernet: training a universal convolutional neural network for low-, mid-, and high-level vision using diverse datasets and limited memory. arXiv preprint arXiv:1609.02132 (2016)
7. Ji, W., et al.: Learning calibrated medical image segmentation via multi-rater agreement modeling. In: 2021 IEEE/CVF Conference on Computer Vision and Pattern Recognition (CVPR), pp. 12336–12346 (2021). https://doi.org/10.1109/CVPR46437.2021.01216
8. Lemay, A., Gros, C., Cohen-Adad, J.: Label fusion and training methods for reliable representation of inter-rater uncertainty. arXiv preprint arXiv:2202.07550 (2022)
9. Li, H., Luo, H., Liu, Y.: Paraspinal muscle segmentation based on deep neural network. Sensors **19**, 2650 (2019). https://doi.org/10.3390/s19122650
10. Mirikharaji, Z., Abhishek, K., Izadi, S., Hamarneh, G.: D-LEMA: deep learning ensembles from multiple annotations-application to skin lesion segmentation. In: Proceedings of the IEEE/CVF Conference on Computer Vision and Pattern Recognition, pp. 1837–1846 (2021)
11. Mukhoti, J., van Amersfoort, J., Torr, P.H., Gal, Y.: Deep deterministic uncertainty for semantic segmentation. arXiv preprint arXiv:2111.00079 (2021)
12. Oktay, O., et al.: Attention u-net: Learning where to look for the pancreas. arXiv preprint arXiv:1804.03999 (2018)
13. Pohl, K.M., et al.: Using the logarithm of odds to define a vector space on probabilistic atlases. Med. Image Anal. **11**(5), 465–77 (2007). https://doi.org/10.1016/j.media.2007.06.003
14. Schlemper, J., et al.: Attention gated networks: learning to leverage salient regions in medical images. Med. Image Anal. **53**, 197–207 (2019)
15. Tustison, N.J., Avants, B.B., Cook, P.A., et al.: N4ITK: improved N3 bias correction. IEEE Trans. Med. Imaging **29**(6), 1310 (2010)
16. Vaswani, A., et al.: Attention is all you need. In: Advances in Neural Information Processing Systems, pp. 5998–6008 (2017)
17. Ward, S.R., Kim, C.W., Eng, C.M., Gottschalk, L.J., Tomiya, A., Garfin, S.R.: Architectural analysis and intraoperative measurements demonstrate the unique design of the multifidus muscle for lumbar spine stability. J. Bone Joint Surg. Am. **91**, 176–185 (2009)

18. Xia, W., et al.: Automatic paraspinal muscle segmentation in patients with lumbar pathology using deep convolutional neural network. In: Shen, D., et al. (eds.) MICCAI 2019. LNCS, vol. 11765, pp. 318–325. Springer, Cham (2019). https://doi.org/10.1007/978-3-030-32245-8_36
19. Xiao, Y., Fortin, M., Ahn, J., et al.: Statistical morphological analysis reveals characteristic paraspinal muscle asymmetry in unilateral lumbar disc herniation. Sci. Rep. **11**, 15576 (2021)

Information Gain Sampling for Active Learning in Medical Image Classification

Raghav Mehta[1,2(✉)], Changjian Shui[1,2], Brennan Nichyporuk[1,2], and Tal Arbel[1,2]

[1] Centre for Intelligent Machines, McGill University, Montreal, Canada
raghav@cim.mcgill.ca
[2] MILA Quebec AI Institute, Montreal, Canada

Abstract. Large, annotated datasets are not widely available in medical image analysis due to the prohibitive time, costs, and challenges associated with labelling large datasets. Unlabelled datasets are easier to obtain, and in many contexts, it would be feasible for an expert to provide labels for a small subset of images. This work presents an information-theoretic active learning framework that guides the optimal selection of images from the unlabelled pool to be labeled based on maximizing the expected information gain (EIG) on an evaluation dataset. Experiments are performed on two different medical image classification datasets: multi-class diabetic retinopathy disease scale classification and multi-class skin lesion classification. Results indicate that by adapting EIG to account for class-imbalances, our proposed Adapted Expected Information Gain (AEIG) outperforms several popular baselines including the diversity based CoreSet and uncertainty based maximum entropy sampling. Specifically, AEIG achieves ∼95% of overall performance with only 19% of the training data, while other active learning approaches require around 25%. We show that, by careful design choices, our model can be integrated into existing deep learning classifiers.

Keywords: Deep learning · Active learning · Information theory · Classification · Skin lesions · Diabetic retinopathy

1 Introduction

The performance of deep learning methods is largely dependent on the availability of large, labelled datasets for model training [28]. However, large, annotated datasets are not widely available in medical image analysis due to the prohibitive time, costs, and challenges associated with labelling large datasets. The labeling task is particularly challenging in patient images with pathological structures (e.g., lesions, tumours) and requires significant clinical and domain expertise.

Supplementary Information The online version contains supplementary material available at https://doi.org/10.1007/978-3-031-16749-2_13.

Various approaches have been proposed for optimally leveraging a small subset of annotated data that has been (passively) provided along with an otherwise unlabelled medical imaging dataset. These approaches range from transfer learning [2,13], weakly supervised [14,18], semi-supervised [9,17] to synthetic data generation [7,16].

Active learning (AL) frameworks [23,34], on the other hand, have been successfully developed for "human-in-loop" computer vision [25] and medical imaging classification contexts [34]. A comprehensive survey of active learning methods in medical image analysis can be found in [1]. These AL approaches work by training a model on a small, available, labeled subset, running inference on the larger unlabeled dataset, and then identifying an optimal set of samples to be labelled and added to the training pool in an iterative fashion. Sampling is optimized to attain the highest performance with the smallest number of samples. Sampling strategies can be broadly categorized as: (i) *uncertainty based*, which includes selecting samples with the least confidence in its estimated most probable class [4], the smallest margin between the first and second most probable classes [21], the maximum predicted entropy [24], the minimum expected generalization loss [19], as well as deep Bayesian active learning approaches [8] (MCD-Entr and MCD-BALD [12]) and (ii) *representative based*, which focuses on selecting the most representative and diverse images from the unlabeled set (e.g. CoreSet [22], variational adversarial [26,27], reinforcement learning [30]). Combinations of multiple strategies [15,32,33] have also been proposed.

Generally, uncertainty-based active learning approaches, particularly entropy-based methods, have been popular in medical imaging contexts where they have shown some effectiveness in addressing the issue of high-class imbalance. However, while entropy based methods select the samples which are the hardest for the current model to classify, entropy alone does not convey the particular source of the uncertainty (e.g., which classes are the source of confusion in a multi-class classification task). In addition, it does not provide information about how the addition of the sample's labels will influence downstream performance.

This paper proposes an information-theoretic active learning framework that drives the selection of new image samples to label based on maximal information gain. An active learning framework which selects samples based on Expected Information Gain (EIG) has been previously used [19] for structure prediction tasks using Support Vector Machines (SVM). As the first contribution of this paper, we first adapt an efficient EIG computation to deep networks with careful design choices. In order to alleviate the high class-imbalance issue in medical imaging, we further improve the original EIG by proposing a novel Adapted Expected Information Gain (AEIG) method. In AEIG, the predicted softmax probability of the trained model is adjusted with the class frequencies of the validation distribution. The hypothesis is that AEIG based sampling strategy will lead to higher performance with a lower number of labeled samples, as different labelled samples provide different information about inter-class ambiguity.

Experiments are performed on two different challenging medical image classification tasks: (1) multi-class diabetic retinopathy (DR) classification into disease scales from colour fundus images, (2) multi-class skin lesion classification

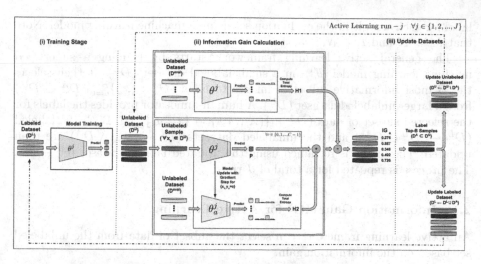

Fig. 1. Active Learning via Information Gain framework. Each active learning run consists of three different phases: **(i) Training Stage** - Model $(\theta^{j-1} \rightarrow \theta^j)$ is trained using the labeled set D^L, **(ii) Information Gain Calculation** - AEIG$_a$ (Equation (2)), EIG$_a$ (Equation (1)), or its variants are calculated for each image in the unlabeled dataset $(\forall x_a \in D^U)$. The entropy H1 of the evaluation set (D^{eval}) is calculated using the trained model (θ^j). For each image x_a, The conditional entropy (H2) of the evaluation set is calculated after updating the trained model (θ^j) using a single gradient step $(\theta^j \rightarrow \theta^j_a)$ for all possible labels $y_a = c$, $\forall c \in \{0, 1, ..., C-1\}$. **(iii) Update Datasets** - Finally, the top-B images (D^A) from the unlabeled set is selected and both the labeled $(D^L \leftarrow D^L \cup D^A)$ and unlabeled datasets $(D^U \leftarrow D^U \setminus D^A)$ are updated. The framework is executed for a total of J runs.

from dermoscopic images. Our experiments indicate that for the DR dataset AEIG achieves 95% of overall performance with only 19% of the training data. In comparison, other active learning methods require around 25% (random: 27%, maximum entropy: 21%, CoreSet: 27%, MCD-Entropy: 24%, MCD-BALD: 21%). AEIG achieves higher performance than competing methods due to its ability to sample more images from the minority classes compared to other methods on highly imbalanced datasets.

2   Active Learning Framework with Information Gain Sampling

Consider a labeled training dataset $D^L : \{(X_L, Y_L)\}$. Here, $(X_L, Y_L) = \{(x_i, y_i = c)\}_{i=1}^M$, represents that there are a total of M samples (x_i) in the dataset; and $y_i = c$ represents its corresponding classification label, where there are a total of C classes $(c \in \{0, 1, ..., C-1\})$. Now, consider an unlabeled dataset $D^U : \{(X_U)\}$, with N samples. Similarly, an evaluation dataset $D^{\mathrm{eval}} : \{(X_{\mathrm{eval}}, Y_{\mathrm{eval}})\}$ with K samples. Here, X^{eval} represents the set of all samples in the evaluation set, and Y^{eval} its corresponding labels. $\hat{Y}^{\mathrm{eval}}$ would represent the predicted classification label for each sample in the evaluation set using a machine learning model. Note that $M \ll N$ and $K < N$.

The general active learning framework starts by training a supervised machine learning model (θ^0) on a small labeled dataset (D^L). It then selects the B most informative subset of images to label ($D^A : \{x_a\}_{a=0}^{B}$, $D^A \subset D^U$) from a larger unlabeled dataset (D^U). A human-annotator provides the labels for the selected subset of data ($D^{A*} : \{(X_A, Y_A\} = \{x_a, y_a\}_{a=0}^{B})$. Both the labeled ($D^L \leftarrow D^L \cup D^{A*}$) and the unlabeled datasets ($D^U \leftarrow D^U \setminus D^A$) are then updated. The model is retrained using the updated labeled dataset ($\theta^0 \rightarrow \theta^1$). The process is repeated for a total of J runs.

2.1 Information Gain (IG) for Active Learning

An active learning framework can select the subset of data from the unlabeled set based on the information gain.

Expected Information Gain (EIG): Let us consider the case of Expected Information Gain (EIG). In active learning context, EIG($\hat{Y}^{\text{eval}}; y_a$) measure the reduction in the entropy of the predicted labels $\hat{Y}^{\text{eval}}$ of the evaluation set, if we have access to the true state (label - y_a) of an image (x_a) in the unlabeled set. In short, EIG($\hat{Y}^{\text{eval}}; y_a$) measures difference in the entropy of $\hat{Y}^{\text{eval}}$ for two models. (i) **H1**: the entropy of the $\hat{Y}^{\text{eval}}$ for a model trained on D^L. (ii) **H2**: the conditional entropy of the $\hat{Y}^{\text{eval}}$ for a model trained on $\{D^L \cup (x_a, y_a)\}$.

$$\text{EIG}(\hat{Y}^{\text{eval}}; y_a) = \text{EIG}(\hat{Y}^{\text{eval}}; y_a | X^{\text{eval}}, x_a, D^L)$$

$$= \mathbf{H}[\hat{Y}^{\text{eval}} | X^{\text{eval}}, D^L] - \mathbf{H}[\hat{Y}^{\text{eval}} | X^{\text{eval}}, y_a, x_a, D^L]$$

$$= \underbrace{\mathbf{H}[\hat{Y}^{\text{eval}} | X^{\text{eval}}, D^L]}_{\mathbf{H1}} - \sum_{c=0}^{C-1} \underbrace{p(y_a = c | x_a, D^L)}_{\mathbf{P}} \underbrace{\mathbf{H}[\hat{Y}^{\text{eval}} | X^{\text{eval}}, y_a = c, x_a, D^L]}_{\mathbf{H2}}$$

$$(1)$$

$\mathbf{P} = p(y_a = c | x_a, D^L)$ denotes the predicted softmax probability of output having class label $y_a = c$ for an image x_a using a model trained on D^L.

Adapted Expected Information Gain (AEIG): The predicted softmax probability $\mathbf{P}$ can be quite erroneous, due to the limited observations and poor calibration [10]. Thus, other alternatives can be considered to improve the reliability of $\mathbf{P}$ such as injecting prior information about the class distribution. In the natural image classification literature, several methods [20,29,31] have been proposed that adadpt the softmax probabilities in the context of highly imbalanced datasets. As such, a variant of the EIG method is considered here, where the predicted softmax probability ($\mathbf{P}$) of the training model is adjusted with the class frequencies of the validation distribution. The adapted version of EIG, denoted Adapted Expected Information Gain (AEIG), provides a modification for $\mathbf{P}$ to become $p(y_a = c | x_a, D^L) * \frac{|y_{\text{eval}} = c|}{\sum_{j=0}^{C-1} |y_{\text{eval}} = j|}$, where $|y_{\text{eval}} = c|$ denotes the total number of samples with class-label c in the evaluation dataset:

$$\mathrm{AEIG}(\hat{Y}^{\mathrm{eval}}; y_a) = \mathbf{H1} - \underbrace{p(y_a = c | x_a, D^L) \frac{|y_{\mathrm{eval}} = c|}{\sum_{j=0}^{C-1} |y_{\mathrm{eval}} = j|}}_{P} \mathbf{H2}. \qquad (2)$$

2.2   Efficient IG Computation in Deep Networks

As we saw in the previous section, computing both EIG (1) and AEIG (2) involes estimating the conditional entropy (**H2**) by retraining the models for each possible label for an image (i.e., a total of C classes) in the unlabeled set. In the active learning framework, this calculation is repeated for each image in the unlabeled set (i.e., total N images). Although this process might be feasible in the context of SVMs [19], it would be very computationally expensive (almost infeasible) in the context of a deep learning model (i.e., a total N*C model retraining). In this paper, design simplifications are made to reduce the associated computation load.

Choice of Evaluation Set: In the first design simplification, we consider the validation set as our evaluation dataset ($D^{\mathrm{eval}} = D^{\mathrm{valid}}$).

Model Parameters: The second design simplification is based on the observation [5] that any machine learning model, including deep learning, consists of two components: representation and classification. In the context of modern convolutional neural network architectures, initial convoltional layers can be considered as a feature representation learning layers, while the last MLP layers can be considered as a classification layer. While updating the model parameters during the IG calculation, only the classification layer parameters are updated. The convolutional layer's parameters are not updated. Given that most of the computation cost comes from the convolutional layers, this design permits computing IG scores (EIG or AEIG) with minimal computational overhead.

Model Updates: In the third design simplification, instead of retraining the whole model with the labeled dataset and each sample in the unlabeled dataset, the already trained model on labeled set is only updated once through a single gradient step for one sample in the unlabeled set. This design simplification is based on the assumption that the size of labeled dataset is greater than a single sample, and inclusion of just one sample would not lead to a drastic change in the model parameters.

3   Multi-class Medical Image Disease Classification

The active learning framework is applied to two different medical imaging contexts. The first context involves multi-class disease classification of Diabetic Retinopathy (DR) patients from colour fundus images. Fundus images are classified into five disease scales representing disease severity: No DR, Mild DR, Moderate DR, Severe DR, Proliferative DR. A publicly available DR disease scale classification dataset is used for this task. This paper uses a subset of

8408 retinal fundus images provided by the kaggle challenge organizers. A label with one of the five disease scales is provided with each retinal fundus image. For each of the five disease scales there are 6150/588/1283/221/166 images, respectively. The differences in the total number of images per class highlight a high-class imbalance for the task. We randomly divide the whole dataset into 5000/1000/2408 images for training/validation/testing sets.

The second context involves multi-class classification of skin lesions from dermoscopic images. We use publicly available International Skin Imaging Collaboration (ISIC) 2018 dataset [3]. In this dataset, dermoscopic images are classified into 7 different classes: Melanoma, Melanocytic nevus, Basal cell carcinoma, Actinic keratosis, Benign keratosis, Dermatofibroma, and Vascular lesion. The challenge organizers provide a subset of 10015 dermoscopic images. A label with one of the seven disease scales is provided with each dermoscopic image. For each of the seven classes there are 1113/6705/514/327/1099/115/142 images, respectively. The differences in the total number of images per class highlight a high-class imbalance for the task. We randomly divide the whole dataset into 6000/1500/2515 images for training/validation/testing sets.

4   Experiments and Results

4.1   Implementation Details

Network Architectures: For both tasks, the DR and the ISIC multi-class disease scale classification, an imagenet pre-trained ResNet-18 architecture [11] was deployed. A Dropout layer with p = 0.2 was introduced before the MLP layer. The networks were trained for a total of 100 epochs, using the Adam optimizer with a learning rate of 0.0001/0.0005 for ISIC/DR datasets[1][2]. The 'macro' Area Under the Receiver Operating Characteristic Curve (ROC AUC) was used as a metric for both classification tasks. For both tasks, a macro average (unweighted) of one-vs-rest (ovr) classifier ROC AUC [6] was performed.

AL Framework: The active learning framework was initialized by randomly selecting 10% of the training dataset (i.e., 500 for DR, 600 for ISIC) as the labeled dataset and the rest as the unlabeled dataset. It was deployed for a total of $J = 6$ active learning runs in both cases. Based on previous studies [15,30], in each run, we select a total of $\approx 6\%$ of the dataset ($B = 300$ for the DR, and $B = 350$ for the ISIC) from the unlabeled dataset (D^U). We acquire an oracle label, and then, once labelled, these are used to update the labeled dataset ($D^L \leftarrow D^L \cup D^{A*}$) and the unlabeled dataset ($D^U \leftarrow D^U \setminus D^A$). Active learning experiments were repeated five times with different initial randomly selected images. The means and variances of the evaluation metrics were then recorded across the five repetitions.

---

[1] The exact architecture and training details are provided in the appendix.
[2] Code: https://github.com/RagMeh11/IGAL.

4.2   Information Gain Performance

In this section, we compare the proposed AEIG and EIG based active learning sample selection against two different baseline alternatives for IG computation. Equation (1) describes the estimation of EIG, which includes weighing H2 with the predicted softmax probability $\mathbf{P}$. Instead of relying on the predicted probabilities, we can compute two different baseline alternatives based on the prior information of the class distributions: (i) Uniform Information Gain (UIG) assumes a uniform distribution such that $\mathbf{P} = \frac{1}{C}$, $\forall c \in \{0, 1, ..., C - 1\}$. (ii) Class-Frequency Information Gain (CFIG) assumes a distribution based on the class frequency such that $\mathbf{P} = \frac{|y_{\text{eval}}=c|}{\sum_{j=0}^{C-1} |y_{\text{eval}}=j|}$, where $|y_{\text{eval}} = c|$ denotes the total number of samples with class-label c in the evaluation dataset.

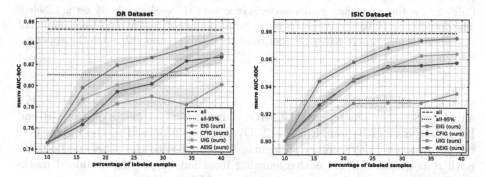

Fig. 2. Comparison of the EIG, AEIG, UIG, and CFIG based active learning sampling methods for both the DR dataset (left) and the ISIC dataset (right). The horizontal solid dashed line ('all') at the top represents model performance with the entire training set is labeled. The doted line ('all-95%') represents 95% of that performance. We report mean and std of evaluation metric across five different runs. (See Table-1 and Table-2 in the appendix for exact values.)

In Fig. 2, we compare EIG, UIG, CFIG, and AEIG by experimenting on both datasets. Experiments indicate that the AEIG achieves 95% of the overall performance ('all-95%') with only 19% (for DR) and 14% (for ISIC) of the training dataset. CFIG, UIG, and EIG requires 29%, 30% and >40% of the training dataset for DR; and 17%, 17.5%, and 35% of the training dataset for ISIC. We hypothesize that better performance of AEIG is due to its ability of sampling more images from minority classes[3].

4.3   Comparisons Against Active Learning Baselines

In this section, the proposed AEIG based sampling active learning framework was compared against five different baseline methods: Random, Entropy-based

---

[3] See Fig:2 and Fig:3 in the appendix.

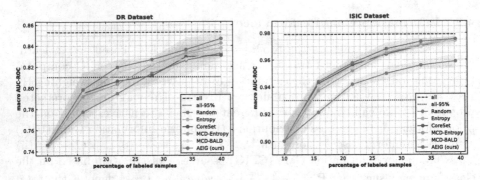

Fig. 3. Comparison of the AEIG based active learning sampling method with Random, Entropy, MCD-Entropy, MCD-BALD, and CoreSet based sampling methods for both the DR dataset (left) and the ISIC dataset (right). The horizontal solid dashed line ('all') at the top represents model performance with the entire training set is labeled. The doted line ('all-95%') represents 95% of that performance. We report mean and std of evaluation metric across five different runs. (See Table-3 and Table-3 in the appendix for exact values.)

sampling [24], MC-Dropout with Entropy [8], MC-Dropout with BALD [12], and CoreSet [22]. The macro AUC ROC curve for experiments on the DR and ISIC datasets can be found in Fig. 3. Overall, the proposed method gives better (or in some cases similar) performance compared to the other methods for both datasets and all six active learning iterations. Applying standard methods for comparison, the proposed method (AEIG) achieves 95% of the overall performance ('all-95%') with only 19% of the labeled training dataset for the DR dataset. MCD-Entropy, MCD-BALD, Entropy, CoreSet, and Random require approximately 24%, 21%, 21%, 27%, and 27% of the labeled training dataset to achieve similar performances. For the ISIC dataset, the proposed method (AEIG) achieves 95% of the overall performance ('all-95%') with only 14% of the labeled training dataset for the DR dataset. MCD-Entropy, MCD-BALD, Entropy, CoreSet, and Random require approximately 14.8%, 14.2%, 14.7%, 14.1%, and 18.2% of the labeled training dataset to achieve similar performances. It is worth pointing out although all methods are giving somewhat similar performance at 'all-95%' cutoff, the trend is consistant for all 6 AL acquisitions. The total active learning score computational time for each image in the unlabeled set was around 1 ms, 6 ms, 10 ms, 10 ms, 16 ms, and 28 ms for Random, Entropy, MCD-Entropy, MCD-BALD, CoreSet, and AEIG based methods. The computation times highlight that although the proposed method can achieve better performance in comparison to other methods, it is a bit slower. Compared to the time taken by a human annotator for additional labelling, this difference in computational time will not be significant.

Figure 4 illustrates the different number of acquired images per class on the DR dataset at each of the active learning acquisition steps for all six acquisition methods (Random, Entropy, CoreSet, MCD-Entropy, MCD-BALD, and

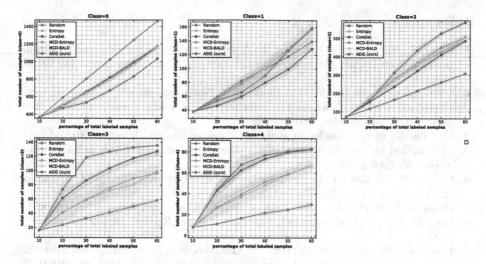

Fig. 4. Plots depicting the total number of samples labelled per class against the percentage of labeled samples for the DR dataset for the competing active learning sampling methods. Classes 1,3, and 4 are the minority classes.

AEIG). The results indicate that the AEIG based active learning sampling policy results in sampling and labelling of a higher number of images from the minority classes (e.g., classes 1, 3, and 4) compared to other sampling methods. This, in turn, leads to better overall performance for contexts with highly class-imbalance datasets, as is the case with the DR dataset[4].

5   Conclusions

In this paper, we proposed an active learning framework that drives the selection of new image samples to label based on maximal Adapted expected information gain on an unseen evaluation dataset. Experiments were performed on two different medical image classification datasets, and results showed that the AEIG method achieves better performance than Random, maximum Entropy, MCD-Entropy. MCD-BALD, and CoreSet based sampling strategies. The AEIG samples minority classes at a greater rate than competing strategies, improving performance on highly imbalanced datasets, although with a small computational overhead.

Acknowledgement. This investigation was supported by the Natural Sciences and Engineering Research Council of Canada, the Canada Institute for Advanced Research (CIFAR) Artificial Intelligence Chairs program, and a technology transfer grant from Mila - Quebec AI Institute.

---

[4] Similar curves for the ISIC dataset are included in the appendix.

References

1. Budd, S., Robinson, E.C., Kainz, B.: A survey on active learning and human-in-the-loop deep learning for medical image analysis. Med. Image Anal. **71**, 102062 (2021)
2. Cheplygina, V., de Bruijne, M., Pluim, J.P.: Not-so-supervised: a survey of semi-supervised, multi-instance, and transfer learning in medical image analysis. Med. Image Anal. **54**, 280–296 (2019)
3. Codella, N., et al.: Skin lesion analysis toward melanoma detection 2018: A challenge hosted by the international skin imaging collaboration (ISIC). arXiv preprint arXiv:1902.03368 (2019)
4. Culotta, A., McCallum, A.: Reducing labeling effort for structured prediction tasks. In: AAAI. vol. 5, pp. 746–751 (2005)
5. Duda, R.O., Hart, P.E., et al.: Pattern classification. John Wiley & Sons (2006)
6. Fawcett, T.: An introduction to roc analysis. Pattern Recogn. Lett. **27**(8), 861–874 (2006)
7. Frid-Adar, M., Klang, E., Amitai, M., Goldberger, J., Greenspan, H.: Synthetic data augmentation using gan for improved liver lesion classification. In: 2018 IEEE 15th International Symposium on Biomedical Imaging (ISBI 2018), pp. 289–293, IEEE (2018)
8. Gal, Y., Islam, R., Ghahramani, Z.: Deep bayesian active learning with image data. In: International Conference on Machine Learning, pp. 1183–1192, PMLR (2017)
9. Ganaye, P.-A., Sdika, M., Benoit-Cattin, H.: Semi-supervised learning for segmentation under semantic constraint. In: Frangi, A.F., Schnabel, J.A., Davatzikos, C., Alberola-López, C., Fichtinger, G. (eds.) MICCAI 2018. LNCS, vol. 11072, pp. 595–602. Springer, Cham (2018). https://doi.org/10.1007/978-3-030-00931-1_68
10. Guo, C., Pleiss, G., Sun, Y., Weinberger, K.Q.: On calibration of modern neural networks. In: International conference on machine learning, pp. 1321–1330, PMLR (2017)
11. He, K., Zhang, X., Ren, S., Sun, J.: Deep residual learning for image recognition. In: Proceedings of the IEEE Conference on Computer Vision and Pattern Recognition, pp. 770–778 (2016)
12. Houlsby, N., Huszár, F., Ghahramani, Z., Lengyel, M.: Bayesian active learning for classification and preference learning. arXiv preprint arXiv:1112.5745 (2011)
13. Huh, M., Agrawal, P., Efros, A.A.: What makes imagenet good for transfer learning? arXiv preprint arXiv:1608.08614 (2016)
14. Kervadec, H., Dolz, J., Tang, M., Granger, E., Boykov, Y., Ayed, I.B.: Constrained-cnn losses for weakly supervised segmentation. Med. Image Anal. **54**, 88–99 (2019)
15. Kim, S.T., Mushtaq, F., Navab, N.: Confident coreset for active learning in medical image analysis. arXiv preprint arXiv:2004.02200 (2020)
16. Movshovitz-Attias, Yair, Kanade, Takeo, Sheikh, Yaser: How useful is photo-realistic rendering for visual learning? In: Hua, Gang, Jégou, Hervé (eds.) ECCV 2016. LNCS, vol. 9915, pp. 202–217. Springer, Cham (2016). https://doi.org/10.1007/978-3-319-49409-8_18
17. Papandreou, G., Chen, L.C., Murphy, K.P., Yuille, A.L.: Weakly-and semi-supervised learning of a deep convolutional network for semantic image segmentation. In: Proceedings of the IEEE International Conference on Computer Vision, pp. 1742–1750 (2015)
18. Pathak, D., Krahenbuhl, P., Darrell, T.: Constrained convolutional neural networks for weakly supervised segmentation. In: Proceedings of the IEEE International Conference on Computer Vision, pp. 1796–1804 (2015)

19. Roy, N., McCallum, A.: Toward optimal active learning through monte carlo estimation of error reduction. ICML, Williamstown **2**, 441–448 (2001)
20. Saerens, M., Latinne, P., Decaestecker, C.: Adjusting the outputs of a classifier to new a priori probabilities: a simple procedure. Neural Comput. **14**(1), 21–41 (2002)
21. Scheffer, T., Wrobel, S.: Active learning of partially hidden markov models. In: In Proceedings of the ECML/PKDD Workshop on Instance Selection. Citeseer (2001)
22. Sener, O., Savarese, S.: Active learning for convolutional neural networks: A coreset approach. arXiv preprint arXiv:1708.00489 (2017)
23. Settles, B.: Active Learning Literature Survey. University of Wisconsin-Madison Department of Computer Sciences, Tech. rep. (2009)
24. Shannon, C.E.: A mathematical theory of communication. The Bell Syst. Tech. J. **27**(3), 379–423 (1948)
25. Shi, X., Dou, Q., Xue, C., Qin, J., Chen, H., Heng, P.-A.: An active learning approach for reducing annotation cost in skin lesion analysis. In: Suk, H.-I., Liu, M., Yan, P., Lian, C. (eds.) MLMI 2019. LNCS, vol. 11861, pp. 628–636. Springer, Cham (2019). https://doi.org/10.1007/978-3-030-32692-0_72
26. Shui, C., Zhou, F., Gagné, C., Wang, B.: Deep active learning: Unified and principled method for query and training. In: International Conference on Artificial Intelligence and Statistics, pp. 1308–1318. PMLR (2020)
27. Sinha, S., Ebrahimi, S., Darrell, T.: Variational adversarial active learning. In: Proceedings of the IEEE/CVF International Conference on Computer Vision. pp. 5972–5981 (2019)
28. Sun, C., Shrivastava, A., Singh, S., Gupta, A.: Revisiting unreasonable effectiveness of data in deep learning era. In: Proceedings of the IEEE International Conference on Computer Vision. pp. 843–852 (2017)
29. Tian, J., Liu, Y.C., Glaser, N., Hsu, Y.C., Kira, Z.: Posterior re-calibration for imbalanced datasets. Adv. Neural. Inf. Process. Syst. **33**, 8101–8113 (2020)
30. Wang, J., Yan, Y., Zhang, Y., Cao, G., Yang, M., Ng, M.K.: Deep reinforcement active learning for medical image classification. In: Martel, A.L. (ed.) MICCAI 2020. LNCS, vol. 12261, pp. 33–42. Springer, Cham (2020). https://doi.org/10.1007/978-3-030-59710-8_4
31. Weiss, G.M., Provost, F.: Learning when training data are costly: the effect of class distribution on tree induction. J. Artif. Intell. Res. **19**, 315–354 (2003)
32. Yang, L., Zhang, Y., Chen, J., Zhang, S., Chen, D.Z.: Suggestive annotation: a deep active learning framework for biomedical image segmentation. In: Descoteaux, M., Maier-Hein, L., Franz, A., Jannin, P., Collins, D.L., Duchesne, S. (eds.) MICCAI 2017. LNCS, vol. 10435, pp. 399–407. Springer, Cham (2017). https://doi.org/10.1007/978-3-319-66179-7_46
33. Yoo, D., Kweon, I.S.: Learning loss for active learning. In: Proceedings of the IEEE/CVF Conference on Computer Vision and Pattern Recognition, pp. 93–102 (2019)
34. Zhang, J., Xie, Y., Wu, Q., Xia, Y.: Skin lesion classification in dermoscopy images using synergic deep learning. In: Frangi, A.F., Schnabel, J.A., Davatzikos, C., Alberola-López, C., Fichtinger, G. (eds.) MICCAI 2018. LNCS, vol. 11071, pp. 12–20. Springer, Cham (2018). https://doi.org/10.1007/978-3-030-00934-2_2

Author Index

Agrawal, Utkarsh   80
Ahn, Joshua   125
Alvarez Olmo, Andres   89
Anand, Deepa   80
Anstruther, Meagan   125
Arbel, Tal   135
Ayache, Nicholas   3

Bai, Wenjia   59
Battié, Michele C.   125
Baugh, Matthew   103
Bhat, Ishaan   113

Carse, Jacob   89
Chaves-de-Plaza, Nicolas F.   70
Chen, Chen   59

Delingette, Hervé   3
Dolz, Jose   36

Fortin, Maryse   125

Hamzaoui, Dimitri   3
Hildebrandt, Klaus   70
Hong, Chunsan   47

Jenkinson, Mark   26

Kainz, Bernhard   59, 103
Kim, Bohyung   47
Kim, Won Hwa   47
Konukoglu, Ender   14
Kuijf, Hugo J.   113

Ladický, Ľubor   14
Li, Zeju   59
Lodygensky, Gregory   36

McKenna, Stephen   89
Mehta, Raghav   135
Mirza, Hamza   125
Mody, Prerak   70
Montagne, Sarah   3
Müller, Johanna P.   103

Naghdi, Neda   125
Nichyporuk, Brennan   135

Ouyang, Cheng   59

Park, Gangin   47
Patil, Rohan   80
Pluim, Josien P. W.   113
Pollefeys, Marc   14

Ravishankar, Hariharan   80
Renard-Penna, Raphaële   3
Rivaz, Hassan   125
Roshanzamir, Parinaz   125
Rueckert, Daniel   59

Shui, Changjian   135
Singhal, Vanika   80
Staring, Marius   70
Sudhakar, Prasad   80

Tan, Jeremy   103
Thul, Daniel   14
Tóthová, Katarína   14

Van Waerebeke, Martin   36
Venkataramani, Rahul   80
Vlontzos, Athanasios   103

Wang, Shuo   59
Whitbread, Luke   26

Xiao, Yiming   125

Printed in the United States
by Baker & Taylor Publisher Services

Printed in the United States
by Baker & Taylor Publisher Services